# THE
# AMERICAN
# LIGHTHOUSE
# COOKBOOK

CUMBERLAND HOUSE™

AN IMPRINT OF SOURCEBOOKS, INC.®

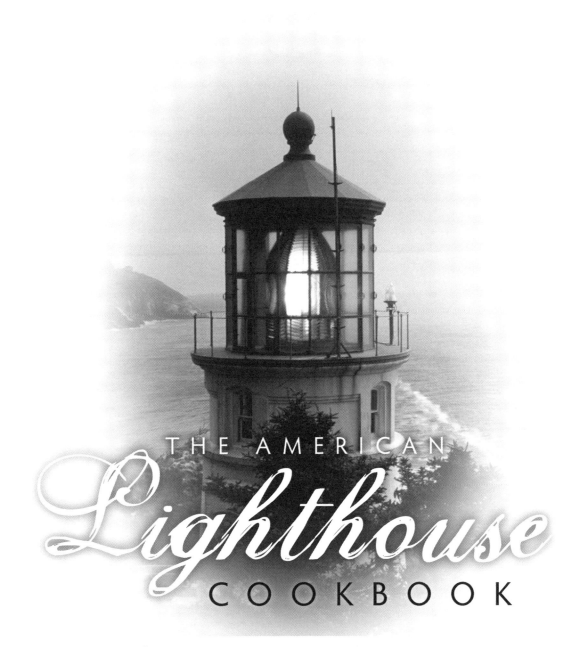

# THE AMERICAN

# *Lighthouse*

# COOKBOOK

*The Best Recipes and Stories from
America's Shorelines*

## BECKY SUE EPSTEIN AND ED JACKSON

Published by Cumberland House, an imprint of Sourcebooks, Inc.
P.O. Box 4410, Naperville, Illinois 60567-4410
(630) 961-3900
Fax: (630) 961-2168
www.sourcebooks.com

Library of Congress Cataloging-in-Publication Data

Epstein, Becky Sue
  The American lighthouse cookbook : the best recipes and stories from America's shorelines / by Becky Sue Epstein and Ed Jackson.
    p. cm.
  Includes bibliographical references and index.
  1. Cookery, American. 2. Lighthouses. I. Jackson, Ed. II. Title.

TX715.E652 2009
641.5973—dc22

2009016524

Printed and bound in the United States of America.
IN 10 9 8 7 6 5 4 3 2 1

*This book is dedicated to everyone who has helped
and encouraged us, especially:*

All American Gator
Liz Bedell
BarBara Bools
Michelle Korgan Bursey
Captain Marden's Seafoods
Marissa Colon-Margolies
(Abita) Lucía Osorio Cruz
Sue Curtin
Barbara DeGroot
Hope Denekamp
Marissa D'Vari
David Epstein
Doris Epstein
Karen Epstein
Katharine Esty
Laura Justice Evans
Lauren Franzblau
Rachel Franzblau
Sari Friedman
Sally Frye
Jeff Gales

Betty Gau
Branko Gerovac
Nada Gerovac
Fran Grigsby
Balika Haakanson
Sven Haakanson
Cicely Hall
Marta Chavez Handey
Corrie Hopley
Mayme Jackson
Mary Jacobs
Benita Kane Jaro
Fred Johnson
Karin Jones
Chad Kaiser
Charles Kirkwood
Patrick Landewe
Lexington, MA
  Farmers' Market
Alexis Lloyd
Rachel Lloyd

Chris Lyons
Laurie Margolies
Mary Mathews
Shawn O'Leary
Fernando Colon Osorio
Terry Pepper
Pat Rabby
Ann Redman
Joyce Rudolph
Cathy Schmitz
Larry Schmitz
Hope White Scott
Sendik's on Downer
Paul Sennott
Katy Stewart
Lydia Swan
Don Terras
Elizabeth Townsend
Anne-Marie Trapani
Bob Trapani
Ike Williams

# Contents

# Introduction

*Passion and idealism underscored by loneliness. Bravery at sea, on a daily basis. Danger, defeated by the warmth of a meal at home.*

THE AMERICAN LIGHTHOUSE COOKBOOK couples food with the romance of the seacoast, adding a dash of history and wrapping it in the very current "eat local" movement. We have chosen some of the most fascinating lighthouses in the country and built menus of local foods around them. Lighthouse keepers were the ultimate locavores, or "local eaters." After all, how far could you go when you had to be at work 24/7, and your only transportation was a rowboat or a horse? Keepers and their families dined on foods that were in season and found at their doorstep: from the sea, from their gardens, and from nearby farms and forests.

Surrounded by extremes of weather and ocean, the lighthouses themselves witnessed heroic rescues as well as tragedies during their decades of history. Some lights are haunted. Some have disappeared. Others stand proud and alone, uninhabited for decades. But they are not lost to us. We can visit many lighthouses on every coast, lighthouses that have been saved from the elements and turned into inns, cottages for rent, and museums. The stories of their local dishes are the tales of the people of America's coastlines, lighthouse keepers, and their neighbors—both in the past and today.

## COASTAL FOOD

*A packet of seeds, a bundle of herbs, and a memory of happy faces around a festive table.*

People of all nations have brought their cultures, customs, and foods to our coasts as they settled along the shores of the sea and moved inland along lakes and

*Some lighthouses were periodically visited by a lighthouse service tender, which would drop off necessary lamp oil and provisions. In 1881, the annual allowance per man at one lighthouse was:*

*pork, 200 pounds; beef, 100 pounds; flour, 2 barrels; rice, 50 pounds; brown sugar, 50 pounds; coffee, 24 pounds; beans and peas, 10 gallons; vinegar, 4 gallons; and potatoes, 2 barrels.*

*Presumably, they were on their own for fresh foods, such as fish and vegetables.*

rivers. These are reflected in the coastal menus we've created in this book.

In the northeastern Atlantic, in the area near the Bass River on Cape Cod, we found residents who believe that the best clam pie is made the day after the full moon—a legend born, perhaps, because people could go clamming (digging for clams) on the sand flats under the light of the full moon in any season. In nearby Rhode Island, we found a Native American recipe taught to the Pilgrims that is still a cherished regional dish: a vegetable stew called succotash, with ingredients interplanted in Pilgrim and Native American gardens. Native American food also surfaces in the Pacific Northwest, with a delectable recipe for planked salmon. When we tried it, we found out how incredibly flavorful the fish becomes when grilled on a plank of local alder or cedar wood.

In San Francisco, we discovered that Italian immigrants originally brought the traditional recipe for a tomato-based fish and shellfish stew called cioppino, which is still a specialty of this part of California. In the Midwest, we found fruits uniquely developed for cold climates by the University of Minnesota; one is used here in a local orchard's recipe for apple cake. The Gulf Coast, Caribbean, and Pacific are home to more unusual recipes that use fun-to-explore, locally available foods like alligator, goat, and exotic tropical fruits.

## LIGHTHOUSE KEEPERS

*The strong, brave lighthouse keeper pulls his boat up on the rocky shore, hurrying home to his wife with a string of glistening fresh fish or a basket of cool, briny seafood.*

That's our romantic image of the past. In real life, some keepers spent weeks or months on their own, or in the sole company of an assistant keeper. Some lighthouse keepers were women—most often because they had taken over the job when their husbands or fathers died.

Married keepers with families often lived right alongside their assigned lighthouses. Everyone helped with the duties of the lighthouse, and even the children had to hunt, farm, and gather food for the family.

In summer, they reveled in the freedom of the outdoors; in winter, the wives and children were sometimes sent back to town to be closer to school and protected from the terrible winds and waves.

Lighthouses were often situated on cliffs, islands, or rocky spits of land. Keeping chickens took very little room, and many families built coops to have a steady supply of eggs and the occasional chicken to eat. Where possible, the keepers and their families also planted gardens and kept goats, or occasionally a cow. Otherwise, the lighthouse keepers would have to make weekly—sometimes monthly—trips into town in a small boat and return with grain, flour, butter, cheese, meat, and any other provisions they could afford on their meager salaries.

In one sense, lighthouse keepers were luckier than many townspeople of (equally) modest means, because they had a ready source of food in the surrounding sea. Fishing, however, could be dangerous—especially in harsh weather. Keepers were forced to learn to work with the ocean, whether foraging for food or setting out to save a ship. Even so, a certain number died on their way to and from lighthouses in stormy seas in all seasons of the year.

## LIGHTHOUSES IN AMERICA

*An oil lantern, hung on a stick in the sand, was lit every night at dusk. A thick, pitch-soaked branch was set afire and thrust between rocks at the edge of a causeway when ships were expected.*

These were the first "lights" of America, even before the United States became a country. Later, many types of towers were built under varying theories of construction and support—and with varying results—in order to lift a light high enough that sailors in danger could spy them from afar. Winds and waves wore down these early attempts at lighthouses. Sometimes fire consumed them by accident—or, during wartime, by design.

After the War of 1812, maritime trade boomed along the eastern and southern coasts. The completion of the Erie Canal in 1825 encouraged inland trade through New York and into the Great Lakes. Soon, river and oceangoing steamships took shipping to a new level. Dozens of lighthouses were built along the East Coast, and then the Gulf of Mexico. The Great Lakes had hundreds of lighthouses. In the late 1800s and early 1900s, still more beacons arose on the rocky cliffs of the Pacific.

While shipping continued to be a fast, cost-effective method of moving freight and passengers, lighthouse construction blossomed through the nineteenth century.

Supported by the United States government, lighthouse engineers learned from earlier mistakes and built ever better and stronger lighthouses.

Their next innovation was electricity, which spread very slowly to outlying points on the coasts. Very shortly afterward, automation was on its way. By the mid-twentieth century, nearly all manned lighthouses were obsolete. The U.S. Coast Guard, which had taken over lighthouse management just prior to World War II, began a program to automate and decommission the hundreds of lighthouses along our coasts. The romantic era of the brave and noble lighthouse keeper had run its course. Or had it?

## LIGHTHOUSE PRESERVATION

*The lights—and sometimes the foghorns—were still there, but people were no longer needed to turn them on and off. Yet rather than lighthouses disappearing, they became a cause célèbre for local communities, and a whole new era of lighthouse enthusiasts was born.*

Many of us find ourselves unaccountably drawn to these tapered towers that have witnessed so many stories of tragedy and heroism. Recognizing lighthouses' allure for Americans, some enterprising families in the twentieth century began turning lighthouses into inns and cottages for coastal vacationers.

In 2001, the Coast Guard began a program of actively decommissioning lighthouses a few at a time. The buildings were handed over to associations, private and public, that agreed to restore and maintain them. Surprisingly, the Coast Guard retains ownership of the automated beacons within the buildings. So the lights themselves still illuminate our coasts to keep boats, ships, and their passengers safe.

We celebrate the heritage of those brave lighthouse keepers and their families who spent decades of their lives in enduring service. In every state with lighthouses, preservation societies sprang up at the end of the twentieth century. Their members multiplied into tens of thousands in every region. With festivals, grants, donations, dedication, and perseverance, local groups are taking possession of these historic buildings to renovate and preserve them. The lighthouses of the United States are being saved to continue illuminating our coastlines and inspiring our menus.

## HOW TO USE THIS BOOK

We have identified eight regions of America, moving clockwise on a map and roughly following the settlement of the United States: Northeastern Atlantic, Mid-Atlantic,

Southeastern Atlantic, Puerto Rico and the U.S. Virgin Islands, the Gulf Coast, California and Hawaii, the Pacific Northwest, and the Great Lakes.

Arranged geographically, this book merges lighthouses along oceans, seas, and lakes with recipes of regional coastal cuisine.

Though each area has many lighthouses, we have chosen those with the most interesting backgrounds and stories—and maybe even ghosts—and we have created a menu for a modern-day lighthouse meal for each of them. These recipes capture the essence of the local foods available to lighthouse keepers and coastal dwellers both historically and today.

For the 47 lighthouses in this book, we have compiled nearly 300 recipes, all with locally available foods and definitive regional styles. Most have been developed by Chef Ed Jackson; a few were contributed by lighthouse bed-and-breakfasts, in keeping with the local theme of *The American Lighthouse Cookbook*.

Some of the dishes are traditional, some are ethnically derived, and some have fusion elements appropriate to their location. In each chapter, we have a range of menus from breakfast to simple luncheon items to dinners and parties. Many menus are seasonal. Whether you're cooking for hearty winter appetites, embracing the bounty of summer, or transitioning through spring or fall, you'll find a perfect match of a meal.

# NORTHEAST ATLANTIC REGION

*The Northeast was home to the first lighthouses in America. These first lights were nothing more than lanterns hung on tall sticks at the mouths of harbors in the evenings. But by the beginning of the 1700s, sailors and sea captains were petitioning for permanent lighthouses, and from 1749 on, the government (initially the British empire) began designing and building them at critical points on the seacoast.*

*When the Revolutionary War began in 1775, construction ceased. In some cases, British soldiers retreated to the lighthouses and held them as bastions of the empire against the colonists. In others, Crown soldiers left as early as 1776—taking the lighting equipment with them and burning the lighthouses as they fled.*

*When peace came, shipping routes that were made safe by lighthouses also provided keepers and their families with imported spices, such as pepper, ginger, sugar, and molasses. But foods shipped in were often costlier than locally farmed produce, and they were used sparingly by thrifty Yankees.*

*While some seasonal vegetables and greens tended to be eaten as they ripened, the settlers had to pickle or can surplus vegetables like green beans, cauliflower, beets, and cabbage. In every household, summer fruits were preserved for the long winter. Often, fall fruits and root vegetables—most commonly apples, blueberries, carrots, onions, parsnips, potatoes, and turnips—were stored safely for months in dark, naturally cooled earthen cellars.*

*New England's climate, which is similar to that of England and Holland, provides a short growing season that was familiar to the early settlers and colonists. Native American foods, such as corn and beans, became staples of the New England diet. From the cool ocean waters, there was plenty of cod, haddock, and lobster, along with delicate oysters, shrimp, crab, and scallops.*

Two to three hundred years later, immigrants from more southern climates brought a wealth of new foods, recipes, and cooking techniques to standard New England fare. Notably, the Portuguese and Italians introduced their Mediterranean flavors, with herbs and tomatoes added to seafood dishes. From plain, boiled foods, New Englanders' menus slowly evolved to include rich chowders, kale and sausage soup, pizza and pasta, herbed and grilled seafood and game, and even desserts with a touch of lemon or lavender.

# Matinicus Rock Lighthouse
MATINICUS, MAINE

First constructed in 1827, the twin lighthouse towers sit on a rock island six miles out to sea from Matinicus Island, which is itself twenty miles from Rockland, Maine. During the severe winter storms of 1856, lighthouse keeper Captain Samuel Burgess left one morning for Matinicus Island to obtain supplies for his large family, expecting to return that evening. Storms trapped him onshore for more than a month, during which time his fourteen-year-old daughter, Abbie Burgess, heroically kept the lights in both towers burning. The young girl's bravery was immortalized in the poem "Keep the Lights Burning, Abbie," which is studied by schoolchildren to this day.

Abbie also kept the rest of her family fed by rescuing their chickens moments before the coop was swept into the sea under the forty-foot waves that ravaged the tiny island. After moving out of the keepers' cottage and into the relative safety of the lighthouse tower, Abbie and her family subsisted on daily rations of an egg and a cup of cornmeal until her father returned with more supplies.

Currently, the island is headquarters for the National Audubon Society's Project Puffin, which studies this jaunty-looking (and formerly endangered) bird. Matinicus Island, with a population of fifty-one hardy souls, is located some twenty miles off the coast of Rockland, Maine. The island is serviced by private boats or planes and the occasional public ferry. If you are a birder, or seek solitude, there are also two vacation cottages for rent on the island in the summer season. Boats occasionally take sightseers to Matinicus Rock Light, which can be visited seasonally.

Project Puffin (www. projectpuffin.org)

# EARLY SPRING DINNER

This is a modernized menu for a spring meal that takes advantage of the first greens to appear. The menu is influenced by the Italians who immigrated to various East Coast cities and then moved north to settle in the Portland area. Seafood is plentiful year-round, and when the earth warms and is nourished by melted snow, new greens, such as ramps and spring onions, start to appear in the forests and fields. Rhubarb and asparagus, two of the first vegetables of the season, are celebrated in this menu.

SALT COD FRITTERS AND HOMEMADE KETCHUP
BOILED LOBSTER WITH MELTED BUTTER
BAKED POTATOES WITH SMOKED SALMON, SPRING
    ONIONS, CAPERS, AND HAND-PACKED RICOTTA
    CHEESE
SAUTÉED FIDDLEHEAD FERNS AND ASPARAGUS
RHUBARB PIE

## SALT COD FRITTERS AND HOMEMADE KETCHUP
*Salt cod has been the staple of every seafaring people for centuries. This is a different spin on a classic.*

2 MEDIUM RUSSET POTATOES, PEELED AND CUBED (ABOUT 1 POUND)
2 TEASPOONS SALT, DIVIDED
2 SLICES BACON, DICED
1 TABLESPOON VEGETABLE OIL
¼ CUP DICED ONION
¼ CUP DICED CELERY
8 OUNCES PREPARED SALT COD (RECIPE FOLLOWS)
4 EGGS, BEATEN, DIVIDED
¼ CUP CHOPPED FRESH PARSLEY
1 CUP ALL-PURPOSE FLOUR
1 CUP PANKO BREAD CRUMBS
½ TEASPOON FRESHLY GROUND BLACK PEPPER, DIVIDED
VEGETABLE SHORTENING, FOR FRYING
HOMEMADE KETCHUP, FOR DIPPING (SEE RECIPE ON PAGE 6)

1. Put the potatoes in a pot with 1 teaspoon salt and cover with cold water. Boil until they can be easily pierced with a fork. When finished, strain and put through a ricer or food mill.

2.  While potatoes are cooking, heat oil in a heavy large pot over medium heat. Sauté bacon for 3 to 4 minutes. Add the onions and celery to the bacon and sauté for 10 minutes, or until tender.
3.  Combine the potatoes, cod, bacon, 2 eggs, parsley, ½ teaspoon salt, and ¼ teaspoon pepper into a bowl and stir with a spoon. Form cod mixture into 1-inch balls for fritters.
4.  Put the flour, remaining 2 eggs, and bread crumbs into 3 separate shallow dishes. Season each with remaining salt and pepper.
5.  Pick up each fritter, dust it in the flour, dip it in the egg mixture, and finally dredge it in the bread crumbs, shaking off the excess after each step. Place fritters on a rack, cover and refrigerate for 15 to 20 minutes before frying.
6.  Preheat the oven to 200°F. Fritters may need to be fried in batches, and they should be kept warm.
7.  Heat ½ inch vegetable shortening in a heavy pot over medium-high heat to 360°F.
8.  Place fritters into hot oil. Do not overcrowd. Fry for 2 to 3 minutes, turning over once, until golden brown on both sides.
9.  Drain on a rack. Place in a warm oven while the balance of the fritters are being fried. Serve hot with Homemade Ketchup.

YIELD: 20–25 fritters
PREPARATION TIME: 15–20 minutes
COOKING TIME: 25–30 minutes for the potatoes, 10–12 minutes for the bacon and vegetables, and
2–3 minutes per batch for the fritters

*Salt Cod*

**Note:** This dish requires the cod to be soaked for 3 days.

6 OUNCES SALT COD
2 CUPS MILK
1 BAY LEAF
2 SPRIGS FRESH PARSLEY
4 WHOLE CLOVES

1.  Put the cod into a bowl and cover with water. Cover dish with plastic wrap. Refrigerate for 3 days, changing the water each day. This will remove most of the salt.
2.  Pour the milk, bay leaf, parsley, and cloves into a pot along with the cod. Simmer for 20 to 25 minutes, until the cod is tender. Remove the cod from pot, and discard milk, bay leaf, parsley, and cloves.. Allow cod to cool. Pick through the cod, removing any skin and bones. Break the cod into small pieces.

YIELD: About 8 ounces prepared cod
PREPARATION TIME: Less than 5 minutes
SOAKING TIME: 3 days
COOKING TIME: 20–25 minutes

**Note:** Ketchup will keep for up to 10 days in refrigerator.

1 (15-OUNCE) CAN DICED TOMATOES
¼ CUP APPLE CIDER VINEGAR
¼ CUP MOLASSES
¼ TEASPOON GARLIC POWDER
¼ TEASPOON CELERY SEED
1 TEASPOON SALT
PINCH GROUND ALLSPICE
PINCH FRESHLY GROUND BLACK PEPPER

1. Combine all the ingredients in a saucepan and simmer for 40 minutes.
2. Remove from heat and purée in a blender.
3. Return to pot and simmer until reduced and very thick. Stir frequently to avoid burning.
4. Cool. Tightly cover and refrigerate.

YIELD: ¾–1 cup
PREPARATION TIME: 10 minutes
COOKING TIME: 2 hours total

## BOILED LOBSTER WITH MELTED BUTTER

*With a delicacy like lobster, keep things simple—use just enough melted butter to enrich the experience. Nutcrackers and cocktail forks are a must.*

4 LIVE MAINE LOBSTERS (ABOUT 1¼–1½ POUNDS EACH)
SEA SALT
1 POUND MELTED BUTTER

1. You will need a pot large enough to easily hold all the lobsters. A pot used for canning is great. If a pot that large is not available, use 2 smaller pots.
2. Fill pot or pots two-thirds full with water, and add ¼ cup sea salt for each gallon of water. Cover and bring to a rolling boil.
3. Grasp each lobster by hand or with tongs, and plunge head first into water. Repeat for all.
4. Cover and start timing when water returns to a boil. Boil for 15 minutes. The lobsters will be bright red.
5. Remove from water and place in a colander to drain for several minutes.
6. Serve with melted butter.

YIELD: 4 servings
COOKING TIME: 15 minutes

## BAKED POTATOES WITH SMOKED SALMON, SPRING ONIONS, CAPERS, AND HAND-PACKED RICOTTA CHEESE

*Use hand-packed ricotta if you can find it. It is smooth and creamy.*

4 RUSSET POTATOES
2 TABLESPOONS VEGETABLE OIL
8 OUNCES SMOKED SALMON, CHOPPED
4 TABLESPOONS DICED SPRING ONIONS (USE SCALLIONS IF SPRING ONIONS
   ARE NOT AVAILABLE)
4 TEASPOONS CAPERS, RINSED
1 CUP HAND-PACKED RICOTTA CHEESE

1. Preheat the oven to 400°F.
2. Rub the potatoes with the oil. Bake until easily pierced with a fork, about 60 to 70 minutes.
3. While potatoes are baking, fold together the salmon, onions, capers, and ricotta. Place in refrigerator until ready to use or up to two hours.
4. Remove the potatoes from oven and split down the middle. Pinch the sides to open them up. Divide the ricotta mixture equally among each, and serve.

YIELD: 4 servings
PREPARATION TIME: 10 minutes
BAKING TIME: 60–70 minutes

## SAUTÉED FIDDLEHEAD FERNS AND ASPARAGUS

*Two of spring's earliest vegetables, these are at their best when they are very new and freshly picked. The butter will give you a wonderful sauce.*

1 POUND FIDDLEHEAD FERNS
1 POUND ASPARAGUS
3 TABLESPOONS VEGETABLE OIL
2 SHALLOTS, DICED (ABOUT ¼
   CUP)

½ CUP CHICKEN STOCK
2 TABLESPOONS BUTTER
ZEST OF 1 LEMON
1 ½ TEASPOONS SALT
½ TEASPOON FRESHLY GROUND
   BLACK PEPPER

1. Wash the fiddlehead ferns by placing them in a bowl, covering them with water, and gently agitating them. Remove the ferns from the water and trim any discolored ends.
2. Trim the tough ends of the asparagus and cut them into 1-inch pieces.
3. Heat pan over medium heat and add oil.
4. Sauté the shallots for 5 minutes, or until tender. Toss in the asparagus and ferns and cook for 10 minutes, stirring occasionally. (If the asparagus is thick, add it first and cook for 5 minutes, and then add the fiddleheads and continue to cook for 10 minutes.)
5. Pour in the stock and simmer for 5 minutes, until the asparagus gives a little when pinched. Stir in the butter, zest, salt, and pepper.

YIELD: 6–8 servings
PREPARATION TIME: 10 minutes
COOKING TIME: 15–20 minutes

## RHUBARB PIE

*Rhubarb is the first fruit (a vegetable, really) of the spring that you can sink your teeth into. Turn it into crisps, pandowdies, or pies. The flavors in this pie will make you wish it was bottomless.*

6 CUPS CUBED RHUBARB

2 CUPS SUGAR

1 TABLESPOON VERY FINELY CHOPPED FRESH, OR 1 TEASPOON DRIED, ROSEMARY

½ TEASPOON GROUND CARDAMOM

½ TEASPOON GROUND NUTMEG

½ CUP QUICK-COOKING TAPIOCA

¼ CUP WATER

1 (9-INCH) PIE CRUST (RECIPE FOLLOWS), PREBAKED

2 TABLESPOONS BUTTER, CUT INTO 8 PIECES

2 CUPS CRISP TOPPING (RECIPE FOLLOWS)

1. Preheat the oven to 350°F.
2. Mix together the rhubarb, sugar, rosemary, cardamom, nutmeg, and tapioca in a pot. Add water and simmer for 20 minutes, until the sugar has melted.
3. Pour the rhubarb mixture into the pie crust. Dot with butter. Cover with Crisp Topping.
4. Place pie on a foil-covered baking sheet and bake for 50 to 60 minutes. Cover with foil during the last 30 minutes.

YIELD: 6–8 servings
PREPARATION TIME: 10–15 minutes
COOKING TIME: 20–25 minutes on the stovetop, and 50–60 minutes in the oven

*Pie Crust*

1½ CUPS ALL-PURPOSE FLOUR

⅛ TEASPOON SALT

¾ CUP SHORTENING, COLD

⅓ CUP COLD WATER

1. Mix the flour and salt in a bowl and cut the shortening into the flour with 2 knives or a pastry blender, until the mixture is in clumps the size of peas. Gradually add the water and blend together.
2. Form the pie dough into a ball, cover with plastic wrap, and refrigerate for at least 30 minutes.
3. Lightly flour work surface. Roll out the pie dough to be 1 inch larger than the pie plate. Fold the dough over rolling pin and place in the pie plate. Unfold to cover the entire plate. Fold the extra dough under, and crimp the edges.
4. With a fork, poke holes in the bottom of the crust, and place in the refrigerator for at least 10 minutes.
5. Preheat the oven to 450°F. Take the pie crust from the refrigerator, line the bottom with foil, and fill it with dried beans or rice. Bake for 15 to 20 minutes, or until lightly browned. Remove the pie crust from the oven, remove the foil and beans, and let cool on a rack.

YIELD: 1 (9-inch) pie crust
PREPARATION TIME: 15–20 minutes
REFRIGERATION TIME: 40 minutes
BAKING TIME: 20 minutes

*Crisp Topping*

1 CUP ROLLED OATS
½ CUP BROWN SUGAR
½ CUP ALL-PURPOSE FLOUR
4 TABLESPOONS BUTTER, MELTED

1.  Combine all the ingredients.

YIELD: 2 cups
PREPARATION TIME: 5 minutes

# Portsmouth Harbor Lighthouse

NEW CASTLE, NEW HAMPSHIRE

IN THE 1600S, THIS AREA WAS KNOWN AS STRAWBERRY BANK BECAUSE THE hillside was thick with wild strawberries. Although the berries are not still part of the landscape, a restored Colonial village in this location is now called Strawberry Banke.

The first lighthouse here was established in 1771, before the colonies had separated from Britain. The current lighthouse was built in 1878. It was automated in 1960, and several of the original buildings have since been restored.

Early keepers who lived here relied on what they called "Indian corn" as a staple, but they could get into town for fresh meat, as this is the only lighthouse in New Hampshire built on the mainland. Perhaps that's why it was visited by many early political heroes, including General Lafayette, George Washington, and Daniel Webster. Today, the site is accessible only on rare open-house days, but you can see it from the water on tour boats that depart from Portsmouth.

# FALL SUPPER

Fall has just begun. The last of the corn is made into chowder. Turnips, apples, and squash are still fresh from the farms. As it has been for centuries, striped bass is just offshore. It's time for supper.

CORN CHOWDER

MASHED TURNIPS

BAKED BUTTERNUT SQUASH WITH CRANBERRIES AND MAPLE SYRUP

ROAST STRIPED BASS WITH ONION AND FENNEL

UPSIDE-DOWN APPLE PANDOWDY

## CORN CHOWDER

*To ensure that this soup is at its fullest flavor, buy fresh corn and use it the same day. Corn begins to lose flavor and sweetness as soon as it is picked.*

2 TABLESPOONS VEGETABLE OIL
4 SLICES BACON, DICED
1 CLOVE GARLIC, DICED
1 ONION, DICED
1 CUP CHOPPED CHANTERELLE
    MUSHROOMS
3 CUPS CHICKEN STOCK
¾ POUND YUKON GOLD POTATOES,
    DICED

2½ CUPS CORN KERNELS (ABOUT
    5 EARS)
1 CUP HEAVY CREAM
2 CUPS WHOLE MILK
1 TEASPOON SALT
¼ TEASPOON FRESHLY GROUND
    BLACK PEPPER
¼ CUP CHOPPED BASIL
½ CUP GRATED PARMESAN CHEESE
    (ABOUT 2 OUNCES)

1. Heat oil in a heavy large pot over medium heat. Sauté bacon for 3–5 minutes.
2. Add the garlic, onion, and mushrooms, and sauté for 10 minutes, stirring occasionally.
3. Mix in the stock and potatoes. Bring stock to a boil and reduce to a simmer. Cook until the potatoes are easily pierced with a fork, about 10 minutes.
4. Stir in the corn and cook for 5 minutes.
5. Reduce heat and add the cream, milk, salt, and pepper. Heat gently, making sure that the stock does not boil.
6. Serve in warm bowls. Garnish with basil and Parmesan cheese.

**Note:** If you wish to avoid using any dairy products, the soup can be thickened by puréeing an additional 1 cup of corn and adding it back in to the soup.

YIELD: 8–10 servings
PREPARATION TIME: 20–25 minutes
COOKING TIME: 30–35 minutes

## MASHED TURNIPS

*The potatoes give this dish a creamier texture, and it's a wonderful way introduce turnips to the younger members of your family.*

2 POUNDS PURPLE-TOP TURNIPS
3 TEASPOONS SALT, DIVIDED
1 POUND RUSSET POTATOES
¼ CUP WHOLE MILK

2 TABLESPOONS BUTTER
¼ TEASPOON FRESHLY GROUND
   BLACK PEPPER

1. Peel the turnips and cut into quarters. Place in a pot, cover with water, and add 1 teaspoon salt. Bring to a boil, reduce to a simmer, and cook until easily pierced with a fork.
2. Peel the potatoes and cut into quarters. Place in a separate pot, cover with water, and add 1 teaspoon salt. Bring to a boil, reduce to a simmer, and cook until easily pierced with a fork.
3. Preheat the oven to 350°F.
4. Combine the turnips and potatoes, and place in the oven for 5 minutes. The heat in the oven will dry out the potatoes and turnips so they will easily incorporate the milk and butter.
5. In a saucepan, heat the milk and butter. Remove the turnips from the oven, put in a bowl, and mash with a hand masher. Fold the milk–butter mixture into the turnips. Season with remaining salt and pepper.

YIELD: 6 servings
PREPARATION TIME: 10 minutes
COOKING TIME: 25–30 minutes

## BAKED BUTTERNUT SQUASH WITH CRANBERRIES AND MAPLE SYRUP

*The sweetness of the maple syrup is balanced by the tartness of the cranberries. A great side dish for Thanksgiving.*

4 CUPS CUBED BUTTERNUT SQUASH (ABOUT 2 POUNDS)
2 TEASPOONS SALT, DIVIDED
1 CUP DRIED CRANBERRIES
4 TABLESPOONS BUTTER, MELTED
¼ CUP MAPLE SYRUP
¼ TEASPOON FRESHLY GROUND BLACK PEPPER

1. Peel, seed, and cut the squash into 1-inch cubes. Place in a pot, cover with water, and add 1 teaspoon salt. Bring to a boil, reduce to a simmer, and cook until easily pierced with a fork, about 20 minutes.
2. Preheat the oven to 400°F.
3. Carefully remove the squash from water with a slotted spoon and put in a bowl. Fold in the cranberries, butter, maple syrup, remaining salt, and pepper. Mix gently so as not to break the squash.
4. Put squash mixture in an ovenproof dish and bake for 20 minutes.

YIELD: 6 servings
PREPARATION TIME: 10 minutes
BAKING TIME: 40 minutes

## ROAST STRIPED BASS WITH ONION AND FENNEL

*The fennel is a wonderful flavor note with the fish.*

4 STRIPED BASS FILLETS (ABOUT 6 OUNCES EACH, 1 INCH THICK)
2 TABLESPOONS VEGETABLE OIL
1 VIDALIA, OR OTHER SWEET, ONION, SLICED
1 FENNEL BULB, SLICED
2 CLOVES GARLIC, SLICED
1 TEASPOON SALT, DIVIDED
¼ TEASPOON FRESHLY GROUND BLACK PEPPER
¼ CUP WHITE WINE
4 TABLESPOONS EXTRA VIRGIN OLIVE OIL

1. Preheat the oven to 375°F.
2. Rinse the fillets under cold water and pat dry with paper towel. Cut crosswise slits into the skin. (This will keep the fillet from curling.)
3. Heat vegetable oil in a skillet, then add onion, fennel, and garlic, and sautée over medium heat for 10 minutes. Season with ½ teaspoon salt and ⅛ teaspoon pepper.
4. Add the white wine.
5. Season the fillets on both sides with remaining salt and pepper. Place fillets in pan, skin side up, and put in oven. Roast for 25 to 30 minutes.
6. Set broiler to high and broil fillets for 5 minutes to crisp the skin.
7. Spoon 1 tablespoon of olive oil over each fillet, and serve.

YIELD: 4 servings
PREPARATION TIME: 10–15 minutes
COOKING TIME: 10 minutes to sauté the vegetables, and 30–35 minutes in the oven

## UPSIDE-DOWN APPLE PANDOWDY

*Here, we took an old favorite, a simple New England dessert, and literally turned it upside down. It's great with whipped cream.*

6 GRANNY SMITH APPLES, PEELED, CORED, AND SLICED THIN
ZEST AND JUICE OF 1 LEMON
½ CUP MOLASSES
1 TEASPOON CINNAMON, DIVIDED
½ TEASPOON GINGER, DIVIDED
½ TEASPOON NUTMEG, DIVIDED
9 TABLESPOONS BUTTER SOFTENED, DIVIDED
½ CUP SUGAR
2 EGGS
1¼ CUPS ALL-PURPOSE FLOUR
1½ TEASPOONS BAKING POWDER
¼ TEASPOON SALT

½ CUP SOUR CREAM
½ CUP MILK
WHIPPED CREAM, FOR SERVING

1. Preheat the oven to 375°F.
2. Mix together the apples, lemon zest and juice, molasses, and half each of the cinnamon, ginger, and nutmeg.
3. Butter a shallow baking dish with 1 tablespoon butter. Spoon the apples into the dish, cover, and bake for 35–40 minutes, or until apples are tender.
4. In a separate mixing bowl, cream together remaining butter and sugar using an electric mixer. Add the eggs, one at a time. Blend thoroughly. In a separate mixing bowl, mix the flour, baking powder, salt, and remaining cinnamon, ginger, and nutmeg. Add the flour mixture, sour cream, and milk to the butter mixture in thirds. Repeat until all is used. Scrape down sides of bowl periodically.
5. Spread this batter over the apples and bake for 30 to 35 minutes, or until golden brown. Insert cake tester into the center; if it comes out clean, it's done. If top begins to brown before the topping is done, tent with aluminum foil.
6. Remove from oven and allow to cool for 20 to 30 minutes. Run a knife around the edge. Place a platter on top of pandowdy. Put one hand on top of the platter and the other under the pandowdy dish, and invert.
7. Serve with whipped cream.

YIELD: 6–8 servings
PREPARATION TIME: 20 minutes
BAKING TIME: 30–35 minutes

# Boston Harbor Lighthouse

LITTLE BREWSTER ISLAND, MASSACHUSETTS

A DRAMATIC SITE, THIS 1716 LIGHTHOUSE WAS THE FIRST ON THE AMERICAN continent, and the last to be automated (in 1998). Unfortunately, it was also the site of an early tragedy, when its first lighthouse keeper and most of his family drowned one day in 1718 when returning to the island.

Benjamin Franklin, who was only 12 at the time, wrote a poem called "The Lighthouse Tragedy" about this event, and sold his work on the streets of Boston. The poem itself was thought to be lost for 200 years—until the son of a lighthouse keeper found a copy in an old jacket in the ruins of a house on a nearby island in 1940.

In 1776, the British, who had control of the lighthouse, blew up the original building when they retreated from Boston Harbor. A new lighthouse was not built until after the end of the Revolutionary War, in June 1783.

In the early twentieth century, Georgia Norwood related that when she went into town for supplies with her father, the grocer would sometimes slip in an additional humble donation, such as a cabbage, which would be very welcome at home. According to accounts, children at the lighthouse also gathered abundant crabs, periwinkles, and mussels for the family's dinners, and found plenty of lobsters in their traps, too.

# WINTER SUPPER

The dishes in this menu are made with staples like corn and dried beans that any local person would have on hand, as well as vegetables that could be held in a root cellar over the winter. Native American legend has it that people could walk across Cape Cod Bay on the backs of cod fish, they were so plentiful. And fresh clams could be gathered any morning—even on a cold winter day.

CLAM CHOWDER

BOSTON BROWN BREAD

BAKED BEANS

BAKED PEARL ONIONS AND RAISINS WITH NUTMEG AND SHERRY

BAKED COD TOPPED WITH A MIXTURE OF SMASHED POTATOES AND PROSCIUTTO HAM, GARNISHED WITH LEMON MAYONNAISE

DRIED CRANBERRY WALNUT PIE

## CLAM CHOWDER
*One of the most famous dishes of this region, white clam chowder is actually a very thrifty New England preparation, because all the ingredients are staples in a household, with clams to be had with a little digging on the nearby sand flats at low tide.*

2 TABLESPOONS VEGETABLE OIL

4 SLICES BACON, DICED

1 ONION, DICED

1 CELERY STALK, DICED

½ CUP DICED CARROTS

3 CUPS CLAM JUICE

1 POUND BAKING POTATOES, PEELED AND CUT INTO ½-INCH PIECES

1 QUART SHUCKED CLAMS

1 CUP HALF-AND-HALF OR LIGHT CREAM

1 CUP WHOLE MILK

1 TEASPOON SALT

½ TEASPOON FRESHLY GROUND BLACK PEPPER

2 TABLESPOONS CHOPPED FRESH CHIVES

2 TABLESPOONS CHOPPED FRESH PARSLEY

1. Heat the oil in a heavy large pot over medium heat. Sauté the bacon until it begins to brown. Remove half the bacon, and reserve for garnish.
2. In the same pot, sauté the onions, celery, and carrots for 10 to 15 minutes, stirring occasionally.
3. Add the clam juice and potatoes. Bring to boil and reduce to simmer. Cook until the potatoes are tender and can be pierced with a fork.
4. Reduce heat; add the clams, half-and-half, and milk. Cook for 10 minutes. Do not boil.
5. Season with the salt and pepper.
6. Serve in warm bowls. Garnish with reserved bacon, chives, and parsley.

**Note:** Substitute skim milk for the half-and-half and milk to reduce the fat. To keep that creamy texture, purée 1 cup of the cooked potatoes and return the purée to the soup. The puréed potatoes will provide creaminess and help thicken the soup.

YIELD: 6–8 servings
PREPARATION TIME: 20 minutes
COOKING TIME: 1 hour

## BOSTON BROWN BREAD

*On the Puritan Sabbath, no work was to be done, so the bread was steamed the day before and served with baked beans.*

**Note:** This is a great way to recycle large cans.

1 CUP BUTTERMILK

⅓ CUP MOLASSES

½ CUP ALL-PURPOSE FLOUR

½ CUP RYE FLOUR

½ CUP CORNMEAL

½ TEASPOON BAKING SODA

½ TEASPOON BAKING POWDER

½ TEASPOON SALT
¼ CUP RAISINS
1 TABLESPOON BUTTER, SOFTENED

1. Mix the buttermilk and molasses together in a bowl. In a separate bowl, combine the flours, cornmeal, baking soda, baking powder, salt, and raisins. Mix the buttermilk mixture with the flour mixture.
2. Remove the top from a 28-ounce can. Remove and save contents. Wash and dry can. Coat the inside with butter. Pour batter into can and cover loosely first with wax paper, and then aluminum foil. Secure by tying twine around the can.
3. Place can in a large pot and fill with boiling water halfway up the side of can. Bring water to a simmer and cover pot. Simmer for 2½ hours. Add water as needed.
4. Remove from water. Remove bottom of the can and push out the bread. Slice and serve with Baked Beans.

YIELD: 8 servings
PREPARATION TIME: 15 minutes
COOKING TIME: 2½ hours

## BAKED BEANS

*Serve this with the Boston brown bread for a traditional New England meal.*

8 SLICES BACON, DICED
1 ONION, DICED
1 CELERY STALK, DICED
1 POUND DRIED NAVY BEANS, SOAKED OVERNIGHT IN WATER UNDER REFRIGERATION
2 CUPS CHICKEN STOCK
1 CUP KETCHUP
¼ CUP MOLASSES
¼ CUP MAPLE SYRUP
2 TABLESPOONS DIJON-STYLE MUSTARD
1 TABLESPOON CARAWAY SEEDS
2 TEASPOONS SALT
½ TEASPOON FRESHLY GROUND BLACK PEPPER

1. Preheat the oven to 300°F.
2. Sauté the bacon, onion, and celery in a large pot over medium heat for 10 minutes, or until the vegetables are tender.
3. Add the beans, stock, ketchup, molasses, maple syrup, mustard, caraway seeds, salt, and pepper. Bring to a boil.
4. Transfer to a large casserole dish, and bake, covered, for 4–4½ hours. Add more water or stock if beans begin to look dry. Remove the cover for the last 15 minutes to achieve a beautiful rich brown color.

YIELD: 8–10 servings
PREPARATION TIME: 20 minutes
SOAKING TIME: Overnight
BAKING TIME: 4–4½ hours

## BAKED PEARL ONIONS AND RAISINS WITH NUTMEG AND SHERRY

*Three types of sweetness, with a hint of spice.*

2 POUNDS PEARL ONIONS
½ CUP GOLDEN RAISINS
2 TABLESPOONS DRY SHERRY
¼ CUP CHICKEN STOCK
2 TABLESPOONS BUTTER
¼ TEASPOON GRATED NUTMEG
1 TEASPOON SALT
¼ TEASPOON FRESHLY GROUND BLACK PEPPER

1. Preheat the oven to 350°F.
2. Bring a pot of water to a boil. Blanch the onions for 1 to 2 minutes. Cut blossom ends and squeeze. The onions will pop out, leaving the outer skin behind.
3. Place the onions and raisins in a baking dish. Pour sherry and stock over onions. Dot with butter, and sprinkle on nutmeg, salt, and pepper, and mix. Cover and bake for 50 to 60 minutes. Remove cover during the last 15 minutes to reduce liquid.

YIELD: 4 servings
PREPARATION TIME: 15 minutes, including blanching onions
BAKING TIME: 50–60 minutes

## BAKED COD TOPPED WITH A MIXTURE OF SMASHED POTATOES AND PROSCIUTTO HAM, GARNISHED WITH LEMON MAYONNAISE

*Creamy, mild fish and potatoes, livened up with herbs, piquant ham, and a touch of lemon in the sauce.*

1 POUND BAKING POTATOES, PEELED AND QUARTERED
2 OUNCES PROSCIUTTO HAM
1 TABLESPOON FINELY CHOPPED FRESH PARSLEY
2 TABLESPOONS BUTTER, MELTED
2 TEASPOONS SALT, DIVIDED
¼ TEASPOON FRESHLY GROUND BLACK PEPPER, DIVIDED
6 COD FILLETS (ABOUT 6 OUNCES EACH)
LEMON MAYONNAISE (RECIPE FOLLOWS), FOR SERVING

1. Preheat the oven to 425°F, and position the rack to highest level.
2. Put the potatoes in a pot with 1 teaspoon salt and cover with cold water. Boil until they can be easily pierced with a fork. Remove from water, and place in a bowl with the prosciutto, parsley, butter, ½ teaspoon salt and ⅛ teaspoon pepper. Smash together until roughly mixed.
3. Rinse the fillets under cold water and pat dry with paper towels. Place fillets on a work surface, season on both sides with remaining salt and pepper, and press the potato mixture on top of each fillet. Place on a cooking sheet, potato side up, and bake for 10 to 15 minutes.

4. To brown even more, place under a broiler for the last minute or so of cooking. Watch carefully, so as not to burn. Serve hot, with Lemon Mayonnaise.

YIELD: 6 servings
PREPARATION TIME: 10–15 minutes
COOKING TIME: 20–25 minutes for the potatoes, and 10–15 minutes for the cod

**Note:** The potato mixture can be prepared ahead and refrigerated overnight.

*Lemon Mayonnaise*

½ CUP MAYONNAISE
1 TABLESPOON LEMON ZEST
1 TABLESPOON LEMON JUICE
½ TEASPOON SALT
⅛ TEASPOON FRESHLY GROUND BLACK PEPPER

1. Combine all the ingredients in a bowl, and mix.

YIELD: ½ cup
PREPARATION TIME: 5 minutes

## DRIED CRANBERRY WALNUT PIE

*Imagine it's the middle of winter, all you have is dried fruit, and the children need dessert. This recipe turns out much better than you could ever imagine.*

2 CUPS DRIED CRANBERRIES
1½ CUPS CHOPPED DRIED APPLES
½ CUP MAPLE SYRUP
2 TEASPOONS CINNAMON
1 CUP WATER
2 CUPS APPLE JUICE, DIVIDED
3 TABLESPOONS CORN STARCH
1 CUP WALNUT PIECES
1 9-INCH RICH PIE CRUST (RECIPE FOLLOWS), PREBAKED
3 TABLESPOONS BUTTER, CUT INTO PIECES

1. Preheat the oven to 350°F.
2. Combine the cranberries, apples, maple syrup, and cinnamon in a pot. Pour in the water and 1 cup apple juice. Bring to a boil, reduce to a simmer, and cook for 10 minutes. Mix the corn starch with remaining apple juice, and stir into the cranberry mixture. Cook until thickened. Stir in walnuts.
3. Pour cranberries into prebaked pie crust, and dot with butter.
4. Bake for 30 minutes.
5. Remove from oven and let cool.

YIELD: 6–8 servings
PREPARATION TIME: 5–10 minutes
COOKING TIME: 10–12 minutes on the stovetop, and 30 minutes in the oven

*Rich Pie Crust*

1½ CUPS ALL-PURPOSE FLOUR
⅛ TEASPOON SALT
¾ CUP SHORTENING, COLD
⅓ CUP COLD WATER
2 EGG YOLKS, LIGHTLY BEATEN

1. Mix the flour and salt in a bowl and cut the shortening into flour with 2 knives or a pastry blender, until the mixture is in clumps the size of peas. Gradually add in the water and yolks, and blend together.
2. Form the pie dough into a ball, cover with plastic wrap, and refrigerate for at least 30 minutes.
3. Lightly flour work surface. Roll out the pie dough to be 1 inch larger than the pie plate. Fold the dough in half, and place in pie plate. Unfold to cover the entire plate. Fold the extra dough under, and crimp the edges.
4. Take a fork, poke holes in the bottom of the crust, and place in the refrigerator for at least 10 minutes.
5. Preheat the oven to 450°F.
6. Remove pie crust from the refrigerator, line the bottom with foil, and fill it with dried beans or rice. Bake for 15 to 20 minutes, or until lightly browned.
7. Remove crust from oven, remove foil and beans, and let cool on a rack.

YIELD: 1 (9-inch) pie crust
PREPARATION TIME: 5–10 minutes
REFRIGERATION TIME: 40 minutes
BAKING TIME: 15 minutes

## Bass River Lighthouse
WEST DENNIS, MASSACHUSETTS

BASS RIVER LIGHTHOUSE WAS BUILT—AND SURVIVES TO THIS DAY—BY POPULAR demand. According to the current owners, for years early American sea captains contributed to the upkeep of a lantern near this location. This practice continued until 1850, when the government finally decided to appropriate funds for a lighthouse. It wasn't built until 1854, and it was lit for the first time on May 1, 1855. The Bass River Lighthouse was sold at auction and the light discontinued in 1880, after Stage Harbor Lighthouse was built in Chatham, Massachusetts, right at the "elbow" of Cape Cod. Following months of complaints, the government repurchased and relit the lighthouse in 1881.

When the Cape Cod Canal was cut through the land at the base of the Cape Cod peninsula, ships no longer had to round the ninety-mile-long cape, and it was thought the lighthouse was no longer needed. However, in 1989, on the two-hundredth anniversary of the U.S. Lighthouse Service (now the U.S. Coast Guard), the beacon was relit as a privately maintained aid to navigation for summer boaters. It is now called West Dennis Light.

# The Lighthouse Inn

*Bass River Lighthouse remained in service until after the Cape Cod Canal was opened in 1914, when ships did not have to round Cape Cod with their cargoes. The property was sold to Harry Noyes, who improved it with landscaping and additional buildings. After he died in 1933, the property languished on the market until it was purchased by Everett and Gladys Stone, who planned to develop and sell it off to summer tourists. But the Stones's purchase was finalized so late in the 1938 season that Gladys Stone decided to take in overnight guests to help pay the mortgage that summer. Many of these guests asked to return, so the Stones changed their minds about developing the land, and thus began The Lighthouse Inn.*

*Since there were very few restaurants nearby, in 1939, the Stones decided their son Bob would run a dining room for the Lighthouse. When a young woman named Mary came to the inn to work as a waitress, romance blossomed; she married Bob, and they continued to run the inn after Everett Stone died. They had five children— Betty Anne, Deborah, Barbara, Jonathan, and Gregory—all of whom worked at the inn. Today, Gregory's wife manages The Lighthouse Inn.*

*http://www.lighthouseinn.com/*

## BREAKFAST—LUNCH, 1930S STYLE

Bass River Lighthouse became an inn in the 1930s, and shortly thereafter, it began to serve meals for its guests. Brunch is a fairly recent concept; at that time, people were more likely to call this meal either breakfast or luncheon. The menu would have depended exclusively on local foods accented by New England thrift but presented in hearty portions—cod, oysters, hash, corn fritters, sausages, and other regional favorites.

CRANBERRY NUT BREAD
CORNMEAL GRIDDLE CAKES WITH MAPLE SYRUP
POPOVERS WITH A SELECTION OF LOCAL JAMS
OYSTER FRITTERS
SHIRRED EGGS
SAGE AND DRIED APPLE PORK SAUSAGES
CHICKEN LIVERS AND BACON

### CRANBERRY NUT BREAD
*Some people like this sliced plain with tea or coffee, while others spread slices with very good butter before eating.*

2 EGGS, SLIGHTLY BEATEN
1 CUP SUGAR
2 TABLESPOONS BUTTER, MELTED
2 CUPS ALL-PURPOSE FLOUR
¾ TEASPOON SALT
2 TEASPOONS BAKING POWDER
¼ TEASPOON BAKING SODA
½ CUP MILK
1 CUP WALNUT PIECES, TOASTED
½ CUP DRIED CRANBERRIES

1. Preheat the oven to 350°F. Grease a standard-size loaf pan. (8½ x 4½ x 2½-inch)
2. In a mixing bowl, beat together the eggs and sugar. Mix in the butter.
3. In a separate bowl, blend together the flour, salt, baking powder, and baking soda.

4. Alternately add the flour mixture and the milk to the egg mixture. Fold in walnuts and cranberries.
5. Pour batter into greased loaf pan. Bake for 50 to 60 minutes. Insert a cake tester; if it comes out clean, the bread is done.

YIELD: 1 loaf
PREPARATION TIME: 10–15 minutes
BAKING TIME: 50–60 minutes

## CORNMEAL GRIDDLE CAKES WITH MAPLE SYRUP

*Heartier than pancakes, these are a tradition in the region.*

2 TABLESPOONS VEGETABLE OIL, FOR GRIDDLE
1 CUP ALL-PURPOSE FLOUR
½ CUP YELLOW CORNMEAL
2¼ TEASPOONS BAKING POWDER
2 TABLESPOONS SUGAR
¼ TEASPOON SALT
1 CUP BUTTERMILK
1 EGG
2 TABLESPOONS BUTTER, MELTED
MAPLE SYRUP OR JAM, FOR SERVING

1. Preheat a cast-iron griddle. If you are using an electric griddle, preheat to 325°F. Brush with vegetable oil
2. Sift together the dry ingredients into a large bowl. Mix together the wet ingredients and pour into the dry mixture. Do not overmix. The batter will be light and fluffy.
3. Test the griddle by putting a drop of water on it. When the drop dances, the temperature is right.
4. Spoon about ¼ cup of batter onto the griddle. Spread the batter out to 3 to 4 inches in diameter using an oiled rubber spatula. Smooth the batter as much as possible.
5. Turn after 2 to 3 minutes, when the top will begin to look dry, and the bubbles begin to break.
6. Cook for an additional 2 minutes. Remove griddle cakes to a warm platter and cover with a towel while the balance of the batter is being cooked.
7. Serve with maple syrup or jam.

YIELD: 12 griddle cakes
PREPARATION TIME: 5–10 minutes
COOKING TIME: 4–5 minutes per batch

## POPOVERS WITH A SELECTION OF LOCAL JAMS

*It's amazing how impressive you can be with a very simple batter.*

1 TABLESPOON VEGETABLE OIL
1 CUP ALL-PURPOSE FLOUR
¼ TEASPOON SALT
1 CUP MILK
2 EGGS

1. Preheat the oven to 450°F. Position the oven rack to its lowest setting. Prepare a popover pan, muffin pan, or six ½-cup custard cups by brushing with oil. Place on a baking sheet and put in hot oven.
2. Combine the flour and salt. In a separate bowl, whisk together the milk and eggs. Pour the wet mixture into the dry mixture, and beat for 2 minutes (you can use an electric mixer), until mixture is completely smooth. Pour the batter into a measuring cup. This will make it faster to pour into the prepared pan or cups.
3. Quickly pour the batter into the prepared pan, filling no more than halfway full. Bake for 20 minutes at 450°F, and then reduce temperature to 350°F and continue to bake for an additional 10 minutes. Turn off oven and allow to rest in the oven with the door closed, for an additional 10 minutes.
4. Remove from the oven, unmold, and serve immediately.

YIELD: 6 popovers
PREPARATION TIME: 5 minutes
BAKING TIME: 30 minutes
RESTING TIME: 10 minutes


## OYSTER FRITTERS

*Wellfleet, another town on Cape Cod, is known worldwide for its oysters.*

2½ CUPS ALL-PURPOSE FLOUR
2½ TEASPOONS BAKING POWDER
1 TEASPOON SALT
½ TEASPOON FRESHLY GROUND BLACK PEPPER
1 TABLESPOON OLD BAY SEASONING MIX
2 TABLESPOONS CHOPPED FRESH PARSLEY
3 EGGS, BEATEN
1 SMALL RED ONION, FINELY CHOPPED (ABOUT ½ CUP)
½ CUP CORN KERNELS (ABOUT 1 EAR)
¾ CUP MILK
1 PINT WELLFLEET SELECT OYSTERS, CHOPPED FINE
VEGETABLE SHORTENING, FOR FRYING

1. Combine the flour, baking powder, salt, pepper, Old Bay, and parsley in a medium bowl. In a separate bowl, combine the eggs, onion, corn, milk, and oysters.
2. Add the wet ingredients to the dry ingredients, and mix. Do not overmix.
3. Refrigerate for at least 10 minutes.

4. Heat ½ inch vegetable shortening in a heavy pot over medium-high heat, to 360°F.
5. Preheat the oven to 200°F to keep cooked fritters warm while frying in batches.
6. Gently drop walnut-sized portions of batter into the hot oil, being careful not to over-crowd the pot. Cook for 2 minutes per side, turning over once, until browned.
7. Drain on a rack. Place in a warmed oven while the balance of the batter is being cooked. Serve hot.

YIELD: 6 servings
PREPARATION TIME: 15–20 minutes
REFRIGERATION TIME: 10 minutes
COOKING TIME: 4 minutes per batch

## SHIRRED EGGS

*An incredibly simple and elegant way to prepare eggs for a group of friends.*

6 CUSTARD CUPS OR RAMEKINS (6 OUNCES EACH)
1 TABLESPOON BUTTER, SOFTENED, FOR CUSTARD CUPS
½ TEASPOON SALT
⅛ TEASPOON FRESHLY GROUND BLACK PEPPER
1 DOZEN EGGS
6 TABLESPOONS HEAVY CREAM OR HALF-AND-HALF
3 TABLESPOONS PARMESAN CHEESE (1½ TEASPOONS PER CUSTARD CUP)
3 TABLESPOONS CHOPPED CHIVES (1½ TEASPOONS PER CUSTARD CUP)

1. Preheat the oven to 325°F.
2. Butter custard cups. Season each with salt and pepper.
3. Crack 2 eggs into each custard cup and top with equal amounts cream, Parmesan cheese, and chives.
4. Bake for 12 to 15 minutes, depending on desired doneness.

YIELD: 6 servings
PREPARATION TIME: 5–10 minutes
BAKING TIME: 12–15 minutes

## SAGE AND DRIED APPLE PORK SAUSAGES

*In some ways, this is a small piece of heaven. We love any and all types of sausage.*

2 POUNDS FINELY GROUND PORK SHOULDER
¼ POUND FINELY GROUND FATBACK (OPTIONAL)
2 TABLESPOONS FINELY CHOPPED FRESH SAGE
4 TABLESPOONS DICED DRIED APPLES
1½ TEASPOONS SALT
½ TEASPOON ONION POWDER
½ TEASPOON GROUND NUTMEG
¼ TEASPOON FRESHLY GROUND BLACK PEPPER
¼ TEASPOON CAYENNE PEPPER

1. Mix all the ingredients together in a large bowl. The fatback can be omitted, but be careful when cooking, because the sausage can become dry.
2. Preheat the oven to 350°F.
3. Form the mixture into 3-ounce patties. (At this point, they can be frozen.)
4. Place the patties on a foil-lined baking sheet. Bake for 10 to 15 minutes.

YIELD: 12-15 patties (3 ounces each)
PREPARATION TIME: 5–10 minutes
COOKING TIME: 10–15 minutes


## CHICKEN LIVERS AND BACON

*A welcome dish at brunch that combines two favorites of the 1930s.*

2 POUNDS CHICKEN LIVERS
6 TABLESPOONS VEGETABLE OIL, DIVIDED
4 SLICES BACON, DICED
½ CUP SLICED SHALLOTS
1 TEASPOON SALT
¼ TEASPOON FRESHLY GROUND BLACK PEPPER
1 CUP ALL-PURPOSE FLOUR
¼ CUP CHOPPED FRESH PARSLEY
¼ CUP DRY SHERRY OR BRANDY
¼ CUP CHICKEN STOCK
¼ CUP HEAVY CREAM

1. Clean the livers, removing any membranes and fat. Rinse under cold water and pat dry.
2. Heat 2 tablespoons of oil in a heavy large pot over medium heat. Sauté the bacon for 5 minutes. Mix in the shallots and cook for an additional 5 to 7 minutes, or until the bacon is crispy and the shallots are tender. Remove and set aside.
3. While the bacon and shallots are cooking, season livers with salt and pepper, and dredge with flour.
4. Add 4 more tablespoons of oil to the pan, and increase heat to high. When the oil begins to smoke, carefully add the livers. The oil will splatter, so be careful.
5. Sauté the livers for 2-3 minutes on each side, until browned. Add bacon–shallot mixture and parsley. Carefully stir in sherry, stock, and cream.

YIELD: 4–6 servings
PREPARATION TIME: 10–15 minutes
COOKING TIME: 20–25 minutes

*the Gully*

# Beavertail Lighthouse

CONANICUT ISLAND, RHODE ISLAND

ONE OF CAPTAIN KIDD'S LAST FEASTS LIKELY TOOK PLACE HERE IN 1696, before he was invited to Boston by his (alleged) friend, Governor Bellomont. Kidd was then captured, deported to Britain, and hanged.

In 1696, this shoreline would have been a dark and dangerous place. Bonfires were lit on the point of Conanicut Island as a navigational aid until 1749, when the third lighthouse in the Colonies was built. Fires from lamps were a constant threat; in 1753, the tower did catch fire and was destroyed. A newer lighthouse tower was burned in 1779 by retreating British soldiers. This area remained dark until 1783, when the old tower was repaired and a new light was installed. A new tower was built in 1856, and the site is now part of Beavertail National Park, open seasonally for tours.

Beavertail Light is situated at the entrance to Narragansett Bay. This bay is named after the Narragansett Indians who showed early colonists how to make succotash, a vegetable stew which kept them alive in lean times. Much later, other immigrant fishermen settled along Cape Cod and the Rhode Island coasts, especially people from Portugal, the Cape Verde Islands, and the Azores.

# PORTUGUESE INSPIRED DINNER

In addition to the Native American contribution, this menu is also based on the traditions of the Portuguese fishermen who immigrated to this part of the New England coast. Here, they continued to fish familiar Atlantic waters, and commingled their own cooking traditions with locally available foods.

PEI MUSSELS WITH TOMATOES AND HERBS SERVED
   WITH JOHNNY CAKES
JOHNNY CAKES
STUFFIES (STUFFED QUAHOGS WITH LINGUICA SAUSAGE)
KALE SOUP
SUCCOTASH WITH BASIL BUTTER
GRILLED BLUEFISH TOPPED WITH SALSA DIABLO
PORTUGUESE LEMON CUSTARD
BLUEBERRY SLUMP

*PEI stands for Prince Edward Island, an island province of Canada located in the Gulf of St. Lawrence. It is famous along the East Coast for its large, succulent mussels with shiny blue–black shells.*

## PEI MUSSELS WITH TOMATOES AND HERBS SERVED WITH JOHNNY CAKES

*Shelling the mussels allows for a natural break in eating that can be filled with good conversation.*

48 MUSSELS (ABOUT 3 POUNDS)
3 TABLESPOONS VEGETABLE OIL
1 TABLESPOON CHOPPED GARLIC
1 CUP TOMATOES, SEEDED AND CHOPPED
½ CUP DRY WHITE WINE
½ CUP CHICKEN STOCK
¼ CUP CHOPPED FRESH PARSLEY
¼ CUP CHOPPED FRESH OREGANO
1 TEASPOON SALT, OPTIONAL
¼ TEASPOON FRESHLY GROUND BLACK PEPPER
JOHNNY CAKES (RECIPE FOLLOWS)

1. Rinse the mussels under cold water and remove beards.
2. Heat a large saucepan over high heat. Add the oil to the pan, and after 1 minute, add the garlic and cook until aromatic. Stir in the mussels, tomatoes, wine, stock, and herbs. Cover and let mussels steam for 5 minutes. Discard unopened mussels.
3. Add salt and pepper to taste.
4. Transfer the contents of the pan to a large serving bowl. Serve with Johnny Cakes.

YIELD: 4–6 servings
PREPARATION TIME: 15–20 minutes
COOKING TIME: 5–7 minutes

## JOHNNY CAKES

*This recipe is from Ed's friend Josh's mother. She told us, "My late mother-in-law, a native of South County in Rhode Island, was a real 'Swamp Yankee.' This recipe is as authentic as you could ever find."*

1 CUP WATER
1 CUP WHITE CORNMEAL
1 TEASPOON SALT
SCANT ½ CUP OF MILK
4 TABLESPOONS BUTTER

1. Bring water to a boil.
2. Heat a cast-iron griddle on high heat.
3. Stir the cornmeal and salt quickly into the boiling water. It will be lumpy like mashed potatoes. Thin the mixture with the scant ½ cup of milk.
4. Put 2 tablespoons butter on griddle. As soon as it melts, place the batter by tablespoons on the hot griddle.
5. Cook over medium heat until golden brown on each side.
6. Add remaining butter as needed for cooking.

**Note**: A true Yankee tops Johnny Cakes with real butter, but the newer residents like to use real maple syrup when eating them for breakfast (without mussels).

YIELD: 10–12
PREPARATION TIME: 5 minutes
COOKING TIME: 1–2 minutes per side

## STUFFIES (STUFFED QUAHOGS WITH LINGUICA SAUSAGE)

*If you're by the sea and looking for something tasty to eat, go out and get some local clams (quahogs) and make an herbed crumb filling with a little linguica for authenticity.*

12 CLAMS (QUAHOGS)
2 TABLESPOONS VEGETABLE OIL
¼ CUP DICED SHALLOTS
1 CLOVE GARLIC, DICED
1 TEASPOON DRIED OREGANO
2 TABLESPOONS CHOPPED FRESH PARSLEY
½ TEASPOON GROUND FENNEL SEED
½ TEASPOON SALT

⅛ TEASPOON FRESHLY GROUND BLACK PEPPER
½ POUND LINGUICA SAUSAGE, DICED (CASING REMOVED)
¼ CUP BREAD CRUMBS
4 TABLESPOONS EXTRA VIRGIN OLIVE OIL

1. Place the clams in a steamer and cook until they begin to open. Remove from steamer, open clams, remove the clam meat, and reserve shells. Dice the clams and place in a bowl,.
2. Heat a pan over medium heat and add the vegetable oil. Cook the shallots and garlic for 5 to 10 minutes, or until vegetables are tender.
3. Preheat the oven to 350°F.
4. Mix together the shallot mixture, clams, oregano, parsley, ground fennel, salt, pepper, linguica sausage, and bread crumbs.
5. Spoon mixture into reserved clam shells, smooth tops, and bake for 15 minutes.
6. Drizzle each clam with 1 teaspoon of olive oil.

YIELD: 4–6 servings
PREPARATION TIME: 15–20 minutes
COOKING TIME: 10 minutes for steaming, and 15 minutes in the oven

## KALE SOUP

*This soup is a meal in itself. The chorizo can be spicy, so substitute sweet Italian sausage if you like a milder taste.*

1 POUND KALE
3 TABLESPOONS VEGETABLE OIL
½ POUND CHORIZO (CHOURICO), SLICED
1 ONION, DICED
2 CLOVES GARLIC, SLICED
2 TEASPOONS SALT, DIVIDED
½ TEASPOON FRESHLY GROUND BLACK PEPPER, DIVIDED
1 (15-OUNCE) CAN DICED TOMATOES
6 CUPS CHICKEN STOCK
12 LITTLENECK CLAMS

1. Wash the kale, trim away thick stems and ribs, and cut into 1-inch pieces.
2. Heat a pot over medium heat and add vegetable oil. Sauté the chorizo, onions, and garlic, season with half the salt and pepper, and cook for 10 minutes, or until onions are tender. Stir in kale and cook for another 4 minutes.
3. Mix in the tomatoes and chicken stock. Simmer for 40 minutes. Add clams and cook for another 5 minutes, or until clams open. Taste and season with remaining salt and pepper. After 10 minutes, discard unopened clams.

YIELD: 8 servings
PREPARATION TIME: 15 minutes
COOKING TIME: 40 minutes

## SUCCOTASH WITH BASIL BUTTER

*This dish was a traditional dish of the Narragansett Indians. They did not have the Basil Butter, but they probably would have enjoyed it.*

2 TEASPOONS SALT, DIVIDED
2 CUPS LIMA BEANS, FRESH OR FROZEN
2 TABLESPOONS VEGETABLE OIL
2 SHALLOTS, DICED
½ RED BELL PEPPER, DICED
2 CUPS CORN KERNELS (ABOUT 4 EARS)
½ TEASPOON FRESHLY GROUND BLACK PEPPER
BASIL BUTTER (RECIPE FOLLOWS)

1. Bring a large pot of water to a boil. Stir in 1 teaspoon salt. Drop in the lima beans and cook for 10 minutes. Drain and reserve.
2. Heat the oil in a large saucepan over medium heat. Sauté the shallots and bell pepper for 10 minutes, or until vegetables are tender, stirring occasionally.
3. Blend in the corn, reserved lima beans, remaining salt, and pepper to the shallots. Mix together and continue to cook for 10 minutes, stirring occasionally.
4. Finish by adding the Basil Butter.

YIELD: 6 servings
PREPARATION TIME: 10 minutes
COOKING TIME: 20 minutes

*Basil Butter*

1 ¼ TEASPOONS SALT, DIVIDED
½ CUP BASIL LEAVES
2 TABLESPOONS BUTTER, SOFTENED
⅛ TEASPOON FRESHLY GROUND BLACK PEPPER

1. Bring a pot of water to a boil. Stir in 1 teaspoon salt.
2. Drop the basil leaves into boiling water and blanch for 10 seconds. Remove and put immediately into ice water.
3. Drain and squeeze excess water from the basil leaves, and finely chop.
4. Mix together basil leaves, butter, remaining salt, and pepper.

YIELD: 3 tablespoons
PREPARATION TIME: 10 minutes

# GRILLED BLUEFISH TOPPED WITH SALSA DIABLO

*This salsa cuts the richness of the fish with wonderfully complementary flavors.*

VEGETABLE OIL, TO COAT GRILL RACK
2¼ POUNDS BLUEFISH FILLETS (ABOUT 6 OUNCES EACH)
½ TEASPOON SALT
¼ TEASPOON FRESHLY GROUND BLACK PEPPER
SALSA DIABLO (RECIPE FOLLOWS), FOR SERVING

1. Start the grill.
2. When the coals are red hot, clean and oil the grill rack, and position the rack 4 inches from heat. The coals are the right temperature if you can only hold your hand above the rack for a count of 2.
3. Season the fillets on both sides with salt and pepper. Place the fillets, skin side down, on the hot grill and cover. Turn over after 3 minutes. When turning, lift gently with tongs and a metal spatula. If the grill is clean, fillets should turn easily. Grill for another 3 to 4 minutes, depending on thickness and desired doneness.
4. Serve with Salsa Diablo.

YIELD: 6 servings
PREPARATION TIME: 5 minutes for fish
COOKING TIME: 6–8 minutes

*Salsa Diablo*

3 TABLESPOONS VEGETABLE OIL
2 CLOVES GARLIC, CHOPPED
½ TEASPOON CHILE FLAKES
2 TABLESPOONS DICED CHERRY PEPPERS
2 ANCHOVY FILLETS, CHOPPED
1 (15-OUNCE) CAN DICED TOMATOES
2 HARD-BOILED EGGS, CHOPPED
¼ CUP CHOPPED FRESH PARSLEY
½ TEASPOON SALT
¼ TEASPOON FRESHLY GROUND BLACK PEPPER

1. Heat pan over medium heat and add oil. In oil, sauté garlic, chile flakes, peppers, and anchovy fillets for 3 to 5 minutes, stirring occasionally. Be careful not to burn garlic. Pour in tomatoes and cook for 20 minutes, or until most of the liquid has evaporated, stirring occasionally.
2. Remove from heat and allow to cool.
3. Stir in eggs and parsley. Season with the salt and pepper.

YIELD: 2 cups
PREPARATION TIME: 10 minutes
COOKING TIME: 25 minutes

## PORTUGUESE LEMON CUSTARD

*Delicate, lemony, and easy to make.*

2 WHOLE EGGS PLUS 2 EGG YOLKS
6 TABLESPOONS SUGAR
3 CUPS MILK
¼ TEASPOON SALT
ZEST OF 1 LEMON
1 TABLESPOON BUTTER

1. Preheat the oven to 325°F. Position rack in the center of the oven.
2. Whisk together the whole eggs, yolks, and sugar until the mixture is thick and lemon-colored. Blend in the milk, salt, and lemon zest.
3. Butter the insides of eight ½-cup custard cups or ramekins. Pour the mixture into the prepared cups and place cups in a shallow pan. Pull out oven rack and place pan on it. Fill pan with boiling water ¾ of the way up the sides of the cups. Bake for 35 minutes. Cool.
4. Cover with plastic wrap and refrigerate for at least 1 hour.

YIELD: 8 servings
PREPARATION TIME: 5 minutes
BAKING TIME: 35 minutes

## BLUEBERRY SLUMP

*Whether it's called a slump or a grunt, this dish tastes great. It's made with seasonal berries and local honey.*

4 CUPS FRESH BLUEBERRIES
¾ CUP WATER
3 TABLESPOONS HONEY
½ TEASPOON CINNAMON
2 TABLESPOONS LEMON JUICE
DUMPLING BATTER (RECIPE FOLLOWS)

1. Combine berries, water, honey, cinnamon, and lemon juice in a pot and simmer until the berries begin to collapse.
2. Spoon Dumpling Batter on top of blueberries. The batter will sink, but do not worry; dumplings will rise to the surface in time. Cover and simmer on low for 20 minutes. The dumplings are done when a cake tester comes out clean.

YIELD: 6 servings
PREPARATION TIME: 5 minutes
COOKING TIME: 30 minutes

*Dumpling Batter*

1½ CUPS ALL-PURPOSE FLOUR
3 TABLESPOONS SUGAR
2 TEASPOONS BAKING POWDER
¼ TEASPOON SALT
1 TABLESPOON LEMON ZEST
4 TABLESPOONS BUTTER, COLD
1 CUP BUTTERMILK

1. Mix together the flour, sugar, baking powder, salt, and lemon zest. Cut in the butter until the mixture is in clumps the size of peas.
2. Pour in the buttermilk and stir, until all the flour is incorporated. Do not overmix or the dumplings will be tough.

YIELD: 3 cups (6 large dumplings)
PREPARATION TIME: 5–10 minutes

# Sheffield Island Lighthouse

SHEFFIELD ISLAND, CONNECTICUT

THE SHEFFIELD ISLAND LIGHTHOUSE WAS ORIGINALLY BUILT MUCH CLOSER to the mouth of Norwalk Harbor than it is today. The shore of Sheffield Island eroded over the course of forty years, so in the mid-1800s, the lighthouse was moved back, to its present position.

The first lighthouse keeper here was Gershom Smith, who sold the United States government three acres of the land he owned on Sheffield Island in 1826. He lived with his family in the keeper's house, and also built a barn for animals and a building to store his corn. In addition to his keeper's work, Smith and his family were able to farm, collect oysters, and raise a herd of cows. But the cows would wander off toward small surrounding islands at low tide and sometimes they got stranded when the tide came in. When that happened, Smith had to row around to each of the little islands to milk his cows.

# Summer on Sheffield Island

The keeper's farm is the inspiration for this menu. Recipes featuring garden vegetables and local seafood, dairy, and herbs have been modernized for a fine-dining experience.

Cold Tomato Soup

Radish Salad with Lemon Honey Thyme Vinaigrette

Stewed Bell Peppers, Onions, and Fennel

Scallops Dusted with Wild Mushroom Powder

Grilled Swordfish Kabobs

Poached Peaches with Puff Pastry Biscuits and Lavender
    Cream

## COLD TOMATO SOUP

*Fresh tomatoes in August are one of the joys of summer. Here's a new way to highlight your garden's yield. This is a Northern version of gazpacho that can also be made year-round with canned tomatoes.*

5 RIPE TOMATOES, PEELED AND SEEDED, OR 1 (28-OUNCE) CAN PLUM
    TOMATOES, SEEDED
1 SMALL RED ONION, CHOPPED (ABOUT ½ CUP)
1 CLOVE GARLIC, CHOPPED
½ RED PEPPER, CHOPPED
1 CELERY STALK, PEELED (LONG FIBERS REMOVED) AND CHOPPED, PLUS 2
    TABLESPOONS CHOPPED CELERY LEAVES, FOR GARNISH
¼ CUP EXTRA VIRGIN OLIVE OIL
1 TABLESPOON SHERRY VINEGAR
½ TEASPOON SALT
¼ TEASPOON FRESHLY GROUND BLACK PEPPER

1. Put all the ingredients in a blender and purée for 20 seconds.
2. Ladle soup into bowls. Garnish with celery leaves and croutons (recipe follows).

YIELD: 4 servings
PREPARATION TIME: 10-15 minutes

*Croutons*

3 TABLESPOONS VEGETABLE OIL
1 CLOVE GARLIC, SLICED
1 CUP CUBED BREAD

1. Preheat the oven to 400°F.

2. Heat oil in a sauté pan over medium heat. Add garlic and cook until fragrant. Do not let it burn. Remove garlic and discard. Reserve oil.
3. Put bread cubes in a bowl and toss in reserved oil. Put on a baking sheet in a single layer and bake for 10 minutes, turning over occasionally until all sides are golden brown.

YIELD: 1 cup croutons
PREPARATION TIME: 5 minutes
COOKING TIME: 10–12 minutes

## RADISH SALAD WITH LEMON HONEY THYME VINAIGRETTE

*With this salad, we use the entire radish, including its bulbs and leaves. The lemon, honey, and the spice of the radish all work together splendidly. If you cannot get radish tops, use 4 cups of arugula.*

2 BUNCHES OF RADISHES, WITH TOPS (ABOUT 2 POUNDS)
ZEST AND JUICE OF 1 LEMON
1 TABLESPOON HONEY
½ TEASPOON DIJON-STYLE MUSTARD
1 TABLESPOON FRESH, OR 1 TEASPOON DRIED, THYME
½ CUP EXTRA VIRGIN OLIVE OIL
1 TEASPOON SALT
¼ TEASPOON FRESHLY GROUND BLACK PEPPER

1. Remove the radish tops. Wash the tops twice, spin them dry, and cut them into bite-size pieces. Wash the radishes, remove ends, and slice bulbs into discs.
2. Zest and juice lemon into a bowl. Stir in the honey, mustard, and thyme. Whisk in the olive oil, salt, and pepper.
3. Toss radish slices and tops together. Dress with the vinaigrette.

YIELD: 6 servings
PREPARATION TIME: 15 minutes

## STEWED BELL PEPPERS, ONIONS, AND FENNEL

*A beautiful summer trinity of vegetables forms a colorful mélange of hues.*

2 RED BELL PEPPERS (ABOUT 1¼ POUNDS)
2 YELLOW BELL PEPPERS (ABOUT 1¼ POUNDS)
2 ONIONS
1 FENNEL BULB
¼ CUP EXTRA VIRGIN OLIVE OIL
1 TEASPOON SALT
¼ TEASPOON FRESHLY GROUND BLACK PEPPER

1. Cut the peppers in half, through the stem. Remove the seeds and any thick ribs, and slice. Peel and slice the onions. Slice the fennel.
2. Heat the olive oil in a pot over medium heat. Add the vegetables, salt, and pepper.
3. Cook for 1 hour and 15 minutes, stirring occasionally.

YIELD: 6 servings
PREPARATION TIME: 15 minutes
COOKING TIME: 1 hour 15 minutes

## SCALLOPS DUSTED WITH WILD MUSHROOM POWDER

*This combination of ingredients goes together beautifully. You cannot go wrong with this dish.*

2 POUNDS SEA SCALLOPS, PREFERABLY U-10 (THIS MEANS 10 OR FEWER
    SCALLOPS PER POUND)
2 TEASPOONS SALT
½ TEASPOON FRESHLY GROUND BLACK PEPPER
¼ CUP MUSHROOM POWDER (RECIPE FOLLOWS)
2 TABLESPOONS VEGETABLE OIL
4 TABLESPOONS BUTTER, DIVIDED
1 TABLESPOON MINCED SHALLOTS
2 TABLESPOONS WHITE WINE
¼ CUP CHICKEN STOCK

1. Season the scallops with salt and pepper. Dip both ends into the Mushroom Powder. Reserve remaining powder for sauce.
2. Heat a large sauté pan over medium heat. Add the oil, allow to heat up, and then add 2 tablespoons butter.
3. When the butter has melted and stopped foaming, put the scallops in pan and increase heat to medium-high. Do not overcrowd.
4. Sauté for 3 to 4 minutes per side. Remove the scallops from the pan, place on a plate, and cover to keep warm.
5. Drain and discard all but 2 tablespoons of oil from the pan. Turn heat to medium. Sauté the shallots for 2 to 3 minutes. Stir in remaining Mushroom Powder, white wine, and stock. Reduce by half. Stir in remaining butter, 1 teaspoon at a time.
6. Return scallops and any juices to the pan. Serve scallops and sauce immediately.

YIELD: 4–6 servings
PREPARATION TIME: 5 minutes
COOKING TIME: 8 minutes

1½ OUNCES DRIED MUSHROOMS (SHIITAKES, MORELS, OR CEPES)

1. Preheat the oven to 200°F.
2. Break the mushrooms into small pieces and place on a baking sheet. Place in oven.
3. Bake for 45 to 60 minutes, checking every 15 minutes. Remove any pieces that may burn.
4. Remove and allow to cool. Place the mushrooms in spice grinder and grind to powder.
5. Pass powder through a sieve to remove large particles. The larger pieces can be saved to flavor soups and sauces.

YIELD: ½ cup
PREPARATION TIME: 2 minutes
COOKING TIME: 45–60 minutes

## GRILLED SWORDFISH KABOBS

*A few herbs and a short marinade add a lot of flavor to this fish.*

20 WOODEN SKEWERS (6 INCHES LONG)
2 POUNDS SWORDFISH (1-INCH-THICK STEAKS)
2 TABLESPOONS MINCED GARLIC
2 TABLESPOONS FINELY CHOPPED ROSEMARY
¼ CUP EXTRA VIRGIN OLIVE OIL
1 TEASPOON SALT
¼ TEASPOON FRESHLY GROUND BLACK PEPPER
VEGETABLE OIL, TO COAT GRILL RACK

1. Start the grill. Soak skewers in water for at least 20 minutes.
2. Cut the swordfish into 1-inch cubes. Run 2 skewers through each cube, making the kabobs easier to rotate on the grill. Continue to skewer fish until all cubes are used and there are 10 equal-sized kabobs.
3. Place the kabobs in a shallow glass dish and rub them with garlic, rosemary, and olive oil. Refrigerate for 15 to 20 minutes.
4. When the coals are red-hot, clean and oil the grill rack, and position the rack 4 inches from heat. The coals are the right temperature if you can only hold your hand above the rack for a count of 2.
5. Season the kabobs with salt and pepper on all sides. Place kabobs on hot grill and cover. Turn over after 3 minutes. When turning, lift gently with tongs and a metal spatula. If grill is clean, kabobs should turn easily. Grill for another 3 minutes.

YIELD: 4–6 servings
PREPARATION TIME: 30 minutes, including marinating time
REFRIGERATION TIME: 15–20
GRILLING TIME: 6 minutes

# POACHED PEACHES WITH PUFF PASTRY BISCUITS AND LAVENDER CREAM

*Use just a touch of Lavender Cream—it's very intense, but necessary to tie all the flavors together.*

6 PEACHES, RIPE BUT FIRM
3 QUARTS WATER, DIVIDED
2 CUPS SUGAR
2 TEASPOONS VANILLA EXTRACT
PUFF PASTRY BISCUITS, FOR SERVING (RECIPE FOLLOWS)
LAVENDER CREAM, FOR SERVING (RECIPE FOLLOWS)

1. Bring 2 quarts of water to a boil. Submerge the peaches in water. Boil for 1 to 2 minutes. Remove the peaches and put into cold water. Peel the peaches, cut in halves, and remove pits.
2. Combine the sugar and remaining water in a pot over medium heat. Stir until the sugar is dissolved and the liquid is clear. Add the vanilla and peach halves. Poach peaches until easily pierced with a skewer. Remove from poaching liquid.
3. Separate Puff Pastry Biscuits into 2 pieces each. Lay half of each biscuit on a plate and top with 2 peach halves and remaining biscuit half. Top with a small amount of Lavender Cream.

YIELD: 6 servings
PREPARATION TIME: 5–10 minutes
COOKING TIME: Check after 10 minutes

*Puff Pastry Biscuits*

1 (9×9-INCH) SHEET FROZEN PUFF PASTRY

1. Preheat the oven to 400°F.
2. Thaw pastry. Unfold and lay flat. Using a knife, cut out 12 square biscuits to ensure no waste. Place biscuits on a parchment-lined baking sheet, and bake for 10–13 minutes.

PREPARATION TIME: 10 minutes
COOKING TIME: 10–13 minutes

*Lavender Cream*

1 PINT HEAVY CREAM
2 TABLESPOONS LAVENDER BLOSSOMS
1½ TEASPOONS HONEY

1. Place all the ingredients in a small pot and bring to a simmer. Simmer until reduced by half. Cream has a tendency to boil over, so watch carefully if you don't want a big mess to clean up.

YIELD: 1 cup
COOKING TIME: 10 minutes

# MID-ATLANTIC REGION

*From indigenous fish, seafood, and waterfowl to hearty Dutch fare, the first settlers here combined Native American and European traditions when they began to create their own regional favorites in this area, which stretches from New York's coast through the mid-Atlantic states of New Jersey, Delaware, Maryland, and Virginia.*

*With the spread of farming, early immigrants were able to add Northern European recipes that included potatoes, sausages, and meats. Various ethnic and Mediterranean-influenced dishes arrived with later waves of Italians and Greeks, who brought along cuisines rich with fresh cheeses, garden-grown tomatoes, and green herbs liberally sprinkled with extra virgin olive oil.*

*Cooking here feels more expansive than further north—and somehow self-confident and relaxed at the same time. There are sophisticated creations, such as Waldorf salad and Manhattan clam chowder from cosmopolitan New York City. New Jersey, the Garden State, contributes fresh tomatoes, blueberries, and other distinctively seasonal fruits and vegetables from its generous growing season. And down the coast, hints of the South are incorporated into dishes like plump crabcakes, thrifty braised greens, and succulent peach desserts—with decadent multi-layered cakes to top off a meal.*

# Saugerties Lighthouse Inn

SAUGERTIES, NEW YORK

ONE OF THE VERY FEW—YET CRITICALLY IMPORTANT—LIGHTHOUSES ON A river, Saugerties was built in 1869, when Hudson River traffic was booming. Replacing an earlier wooden light that had lasted about thirty years, the current stone building was in use for less than one hundred years. Throughout the mid-twentieth century, it languished in disrepair until the building was purchased by the Saugerties Lighthouse Conservancy in 1986. Remarkably, many local artisans and craftsman were mobilized to the cause, and they spent the next five years renovating the light and restoring the building to the way it would have looked in its heyday, during the early 1900s.

Saugerties is now a bed-and-breakfast. Built out on the water, this lighthouse attracts guests who enjoy hiking in on the half-mile trail for their overnight stays. Today, the favorite activities around this peaceful islet are the same as they were one hundred years ago—picnics, bird-watching, and swimming.

# HUDSON RIVER HEARTY BREAKFAST

## In May 2008, current keeper Patrick Landewe told us:

*In keeping with lighthouse tradition, I use whole-bean coffee, which I grind each morning using a hand mill. I also serve buckwheat pancakes with real maple syrup from the nearby Catskill Mountains.*

*My predecessor as keeper, Allen, developed a reputation for cooking delicious pancakes for breakfast. Lucky for me, Allen shared his pancake recipe with me. With practice, my pancakes earned praise as well. The recipe for lighthouse pancakes gradually changed from the original over the years as I made modifications. For instance, I leave sugar out of the recipe because people put syrup on their pancakes anyway, which is sweet enough. My most recent changes were to incorporate locally grown, freshly milled flours from Wild Hive Farm. Combined with Hudson Valley Fresh milk and eggs from the nearby Sauer family farm, the main ingredients for the pancakes originate within a 50-mile radius.*

*What's the secret to great pancakes? Recipes may vary, but a proper pancake flipper is essential. I am fortunate that a clever keeper made a terrific pancake spatula out of an old, worn-out pull-saw. He filed the serrated teeth off the saw blade and trimmed the handle. The saw blade was thin spring steel, which slides smoothly under pancakes.*

SAUGERTIES LIGHTHOUSE PANCAKES

NEW YORK CHERRIES WITH GRANOLA AND YOGURT

OVEN-ROASTED BACON

SCRAMBLED EGGS

FRIED POTATOES WITH CHEDDAR CHEESE AND SCALLIONS

### SAUGERTIES LIGHTHOUSE PANCAKES

*Patrick, the lighthouse keeper, says to serve these with real maple syrup and seasonal fruit.*

DRY INGREDIENTS:
1 CUP ALL-PURPOSE UNBLEACHED FLOUR
½ CUP BUCKWHEAT FLOUR
1 TABLESPOON BAKING POWDER
1 TEASPOON SALT
⅛ TEASPOON CINNAMON
⅛ TEASPOON NUTMEG

WET INGREDIENTS:
1½ CUPS MILK
2 EGGS, BEATEN
2 TABLESPOONS VEGETABLE OIL

1. Preheat a cast-iron griddle or skillet on medium-low heat. If the cast iron is well seasoned, the pancakes won't stick.
2. Sift together the dry ingredients. Stir in the milk, then the eggs, and finally the oil. I find that stirring in the wet ingredients separately helps prevent clumps in the batter.
3. Scoop ¼ cup of batter for each pancake onto the hot griddle. Flip with a spatula, browning evenly on each side. Cook for 2 to 3 minutes per side.

YIELD: 4 servings
PREPARATION TIME: 10 minutes
COOKING TIME: 4–6 minutes per batch

## NEW YORK CHERRIES WITH GRANOLA AND YOGURT

*If you've got fresh cherries and artisanal yogurt, you're in heaven.*

1½ POUNDS FRESH MONTMORENCY TART
    RED CHERRIES, PITTED
6-8 TABLESPOONS HONEY
3 CUPS GRANOLA
1½ PINTS PLAIN YOGURT

1. Mix the cherries and 6 tablespoons honey together and allow to rest for 15 to 30 minutes. Taste and add additional honey, if still too tart.
2. Pick out 6 tall glasses that can hold 2 cups of liquid each. Into each, spoon ½ cup of granola, then a ½ cup yogurt, and then top with the cherries and honey mixture.

YIELD: 6 servings
PREPARATION TIME: 15 minutes to pit cherries,
    plus 15 to 30 minutes resting time
ASSEMBLY TIME: 5 minutes

## OVEN-ROASTED BACON

*You can make bacon for the masses without dirtying your stove!*

1 POUND BACON

1. Preheat the oven to 400°F.
2. Place a rack in a shallow baking pan lined with aluminum foil. Arrange the bacon strips in a single layer on the rack. Two pans may be needed. Bake for 10 to 15 minutes.

YIELD: 4 servings
PREPARATION TIME: 5 minutes
COOKING TIME: 10–15 minutes

## SCRAMBLED EGGS

*Chefs know how to do this. Now you do, too—the perfect scrambled eggs.*

1 DOZEN LARGE EGGS
½ CUP WATER
1 TEASPOON SALT
¼ TEASPOON FRESHLY GROUND BLACK PEPPER
2 TABLESPOONS VEGETABLE OIL
4 TABLESPOONS BUTTER

1. Crack the eggs into a bowl. Whisk together eggs, water, salt, and pepper.
2. Heat a large sauté pan. Add the oil and butter. When the butter has melted, reduce heat to low, give the eggs another stir, and pour into the pan.
3. After they begin to set, scrape the eggs to one side of the pan, and allow the uncooked eggs to flow into the scraped area.
4. Continue until eggs are still soft and fluffy, remove pan from heat, and serve immediately.

YIELD: 6 servings
PREPARATION TIME: Less than 5 minutes
COOKING TIME: 5–10 minutes

## FRIED POTATOES WITH CHEDDAR CHEESE AND SCALLIONS

*Always a great combination. The best part is the crust left in the pan after you've served your family.*

6 TABLESPOONS VEGETABLE OIL, DIVIDED
2½–3 POUNDS RUSSET POTATOES, COOKED AND SLICED
1 TEASPOON SALT
¼ TEASPOON FRESHLY GROUND BLACK PEPPER
¼ POUND CHEDDAR CHEESE, GRATED
6 SCALLIONS, DICED

1. Heat 4 tablespoons of oil in a large pan over high heat until oil begins to smoke.
2. Carefully layer the potatoes in the pan. Season with the salt and pepper.
3. Cook until the potatoes begin to brown, about 6 minutes.
4. Turn potatoes over, add remaining 2 tablespoons oil, and cook for 4 minutes. Turn again and cook for 2 minutes.
5. Fold in the cheese and scallions.
6. Transfer to a large, warmed platter.

YIELD: 4–6 servings
PREPARATION TIME: 5 minutes
COOKING TIME: 10–15 minutes

# Fire Island Lighthouse

FIRE ISLAND, NEW YORK

BUILT IN 1858, THIS LIGHTHOUSE WAS THE FIRST SIGHT OF AMERICA FOR many immigrants on their way into New York Harbor by ship. Actually, this was the second lighthouse built on this site; the first, constructed in 1826, was nearly one hundred feet shorter. With larger ships and increased traffic, longer visibility was necessary; the light in the current building is visible for over twenty miles at sea.

Fire Island Lighthouse, now also one of the most visited lighthouses in America, is located on the Fire Island National Seashore. In addition to tower tours, volunteers at the lighthouse have created many educational programs for adults and children. With its dramatic background, the terrace of the keepers' quarters is also a popular site for wedding ceremonies.

# Big Apple Weekend Lunch

We have created a menu that includes local foods, like Long Island's homegrown potatoes and duckling and nearby New York City's famous Waldorf Salad. The Empire State's Empire apples baked sweetly into a pie—and served with a slice of sharp Herkheimer cheese—finish the meal delightfully.

WALDORF SALAD

ROASTED FINGERLING POTATOES, GARLIC, AND SAGE

LONG ISLAND DUCK BREAST WITH BRAISED CABBAGE, CHESTNUTS, AND APPLES

BIG APPLE PIE AND HERKHIMER CHEESE

## WALDORF SALAD
*This takes 15 minutes from start to finish, even for someone who is pokey.*

3 APPLES (2 GRANNY SMITH AND 1 EMPIRE)
2 TABLESPOONS LEMON JUICE
3 CELERY STALKS
1 CUP CHOPPED WALNUTS, TOASTED
1 CUP SEEDLESS RED GRAPES, HALVED
¾ CUP MAYONNAISE
½ TEASPOON SALT
6 ICEBERG LETTUCE LEAVES

1. Core the apples and cut into ½-inch cubes. Put in a bowl and toss with the lemon juice.
2. Cut the celery into ½-inch pieces. Add to the apples, along with the walnuts and grapes.
3. Toss with the mayonnaise and salt.
4. Serve on a bed of iceberg lettuce.

YIELD: 4–6 servings
PREPARATION TIME: 10–15 minutes

## ROASTED FINGERLING POTATOES, GARLIC, AND SAGE
*When you serve the potatoes, make sure you get all the goodness in the bottom of the dish.*

2 POUNDS FINGERLING POTATOES
4 CLOVES GARLIC, SLICED
2 TABLESPOONS CHOPPED FRESH SAGE
2 TEASPOONS SALT
¼ TEASPOON FRESHLY GROUND BLACK PEPPER
3 TABLESPOONS VEGETABLE OIL

1. Preheat the oven to 400°F.
2. Cut the potatoes in half lengthwise.
3. Toss the potatoes with the garlic, sage, salt, pepper, and oil. Put into a baking dish and cover with foil.
4. Roast the potatoes for 50 to 60 minutes. Check for doneness by piercing a potato with a fork.

YIELD: 4 servings
PREPARATION TIME: 15 minutes
COOKING TIME: 50–60 minutes

## LONG ISLAND DUCK BREAST WITH BRAISED CABBAGE, CHESTNUTS, AND APPLES

*The succulent duck amplifies all the flavors. Don't be afraid to try this.*

6 LONG ISLAND DUCK BREAST HALVES
2 TEASPOONS SALT
½ TEASPOON FRESHLY GROUND BLACK
    PEPPER
VEGETABLE OIL, TO COAT PAN
BRAISED CABBAGE, CHESTNUTS, AND
    APPLES (RECIPE FOLLOWS), FOR SERV-
    ING

1. Score the skin of the breast by drawing a sharp knife over the skin. Do not cut so deeply that you cut the flesh. Make 4 slits in the skin one way, and then turn the breast 90° and repeat. You will get a diamond pattern. This helps when rendering the fat from the skin.
2. Heat a large sauté pan on medium-high heat. Season both sides of the breast with salt and pepper. Add enough oil to the pan to coat the bottom. Put the breast in pan, skin side down, and cook for 5 to 7 minutes. Turn over and cook for 5 to 7 minutes more. Remove from the pan and tent with foil. The duck breasts should be rare to medium-rare.
3. Slice and arrange on top of Braised Cabbage, Chestnuts, and Apples.

YIELD: 6 servings
PREPARATION TIME: 5–10 minutes
COOKING TIME: 10–14 minutes

*Braised Cabbage, Chestnuts, and Apples*

3 OUNCES SALT PORK, DICED
1 SMALL SAVOY CABBAGE (ABOUT 1½ POUNDS)
2 TABLESPOONS VEGETABLE OIL
1 ONION, SLICED

2 Granny Smith apples, peeled, cored and sliced
1 cup chicken stock
½ cup white wine
2 teaspoons salt
¼ teaspoon freshly ground black pepper
10 ounces chestnuts, canned or frozen

1. Bring a pot of water to a boil. Put the salt pork in water and cook for 4 minutes to remove extra salt. Remove the salt pork from water.
2. Cut the cabbage into quarters. Remove the stems and thick ribs, and slice into ¼-inch strips.
3. Heat a large pot over medium heat. Sauté the salt pork in oil for 4 minutes. Stir in the onions and sauté for 10 minutes, or until tender. Mix in the cabbage, apples, stock, wine, salt, and pepper.
4. Cook on medium-low heat for 30 minutes, stirring frequently. Stir in the chestnuts, being careful not to break them up while stirring. Cook for 10 more minutes. The liquid should be almost evaporated.

YIELD: 6 servings
PREPARATION TIME: 15 minutes
COOKING TIME: 55 minutes

## BIG APPLE PIE AND HERKHIMER CHEESE

*This is what Ed's friend Cicely makes for her kids—it's the only apple pie in the world they'll eat.*

3 tablespoons all-purpose flour
⅓ cup sugar
1 teaspoon cinnamon
⅛ teaspoon salt
6–7 Empire apples, peeled, cored, and sliced
1 Double (9-inch) Pie Crust (recipe follows), unbaked
1 tablespoon butter, cut into pieces
1 egg
1 tablespoon water
12 ounces Herkhimer cheese, cut into 6–8 slices, for serving

1. Preheat the oven to 425°F.
2. Mix the flour, sugar, cinnamon and salt. Pour over the apples and toss until apples are evenly coated.
3. Line a pie plate with half of the unbaked pie crust dough. Pour apples into pie crust and dot with butter. Lay remaining half of pie crust on top. Fold the extra dough under, and crimp the edges. Use your fingers or a fork to seal the edges. Cut four slashes in top crust to vent.
4. Stir together the egg and water, and brush top of pie.

5.  Bake at 425°F for 10 minutes, reduce temperature to 350°F, and continue baking for 35–40 minutes. Serve with slices of Herkhimer cheese on top.

YIELD: 6–8 servings
PREPARATION TIME: 15–20 minutes
COOKING TIME: 50 minutes

*Double Pie Crust*

3 CUPS ALL-PURPOSE FLOUR
¼ TEASPOON SALT
1½ CUPS SHORTENING, COLD
⅔ CUP COLD WATER

1.  Mix the flour and salt in a bowl and cut the shortening into the flour with 2 knives or a pastry blender, until the mixture is in clumps the size of peas. Gradually add the water and blend together.
2.  Form the dough into a ball, cover with plastic wrap, and refrigerate for at least 30 minutes.
3.  Lightly flour work surface, divide the dough in half, and roll out pie dough to be 1 inch larger than the pie plate. Fold the dough over rolling pin and place in pie plate. Unfold to cover the entire plate.
4.  Repeat the rolling process with the other half of the pie dough. Use this half to top the pie.

YIELD: 2 (9-inch) pie crusts
PREPARATION TIME: 20–25 minutes
REFRIGERATION TIME: 30 minutes

# Sandy Hook Lighthouse
SANDY HOOK, NEW JERSEY

NEW YORK MERCHANTS PETITIONED FOR SANDY HOOK LIGHT TO BE BUILT in 1764 to attract more business to New York Harbor. An octagonal tower built of stone and fragments, it stands to this day—but not in the same state, and this was disputed for some time. New York and New Jersey's fight over the lighthouse ended when the young United States government took over administration of lighthouses for the new nation in 1789.

Now part of the Gateway National Park Recreation Area in Sandy Hook, New Jersey, this lighthouse is considered the oldest original lighthouse tower in the United States. It's only about ten miles from Manhattan, making it a great day trip for many New Yorkers.

Many former New Yorkers have moved to North Jersey where they enjoy having more space to grow everything from wine grapes, figs, and blueberries to tomatoes, peppers, and herbs. After all, New Jersey *is* the Garden State.

# Grilled Summer Menu

This casual summer menu is also a tribute to the many Italian families who have made New Jersey their home. They brought not only their cuisine but also their insistence on fresh, local ingredients, such as garden vegetables, fish just out of the sea, and blueberries farmed nearby.

Grilled Pizza with Basil, Tomatoes, and Mozzarella

Grilled Summer Vegetables Dressed with Herbs and Extra
   Virgin Olive Oil

Grilled Striped Bass with Salsa Verde

Lemon Granita with Fresh Raspberries

## GRILLED PIZZA WITH BASIL, TOMATOES, AND MOZZARELLA

*This is a minimalist pizza, almost a glorified cheese-and-cracker appetizer—something for you and your guests to nibble on while you finish the rest of the meal on the grill.*

PIZZA DOUGH (RECIPE FOLLOWS)
VEGETABLE OIL, TO COAT GRILL RACK
¼ CUP EXTRA VIRGIN OLIVE OIL, DIVIDED
20 BASIL LEAVES
2 RIPE TOMATOES, SLICED
½ POUND FRESH MOZZARELLA CHEESE, SLICED
1 TEASPOON SALT
6 GRINDS CRACKED BLACK PEPPER

1. Start the grill.
2. Divide Pizza Dough into 2 pieces. Cut the dough; do not tear, as tearing will disrupt the gluten. Roll each dough ball into a disk about 8 to 10 inches in diameter. Cover with a damp towel or plastic wrap.
3. When the coals are red-hot, clean and oil the grill rack, and position the rack 4 inches from heat. The coals are the right temperature if you can only hold your hand above the rack for a count of 3.
4. Brush one side of the dough with 1 tablespoon olive oil. Lift the dough gently and place it on the grill rack, oiled side down. Cover the grill and allow the dough to cook for 2 minutes. Be mindful of the heat, and check the bottom of dough after 1 minute.
5. Remove cover of grill. Brush top of dough with 1 tablespoon olive oil and flip dough using a metal spatula and tongs.
6. Put an equal amount of the basil, tomatoes, and mozzarella cheese on each pizza. Cover grill and cook for an additional 1 to 2 minutes.
7. Remove pizza from grill and top with remaining olive oil, salt, and fresh cracked pepper.

YIELD: 2 pizzas
PREPARATION TIME: 15–20 minutes
COOKING TIME: 4 minutes per pizza

*Pizza Dough*

1 PACKET DRY YEAST
⅔ CUP WARM WATER (105°F TO 115°F, APPROXIMATELY)
¼ CUP EXTRA VIRGIN OLIVE OIL
2 CUPS ALL-PURPOSE FLOUR
½ TEASPOON SALT

1. Dissolve the yeast in water, and wait for the yeast to start bubbling.
2. Add to the yeast-water mixture the olive oil, flour, and salt. Knead for 5 minutes and form into a ball.
3. Put the dough in an oiled bowl, cover with a damp towel, and allow to rise for 1–1½ hours, or until it doubles in size. Punch down, cover and allow to rise for another 30 minutes.

YIELD: 2 pizza crusts, 8–10 inches in diameter
PREPARATION TIME: 1½–2 hours

## GRILLED SUMMER VEGETABLES DRESSED WITH HERBS AND EXTRA VIRGIN OLIVE OIL

*From garden to grill to table in as little time as possible.*
*Vegetable oil, to coat grill rack*

VEGETABLE OIL, TO COAT GRILL RACK
2 RED BELL PEPPERS
1 ZUCCHINI
1 YELLOW SQUASH
8 LARGE SHALLOTS
1 QUART WATER
4 PLUM TOMATOES
¼ CUP VEGETABLE OIL
3 TEASPOONS SALT, DIVIDED
½ TEASPOON FRESHLY GROUND BLACK PEPPER
2 TABLESPOONS CHOPPED FRESH BASIL
2 TABLESPOONS CHOPPED FRESH PARSLEY
2 TABLESPOONS CHOPPED FRESH MINT
⅓ CUP EXTRA VIRGIN OLIVE OIL

1. Start the grill.
2. When the coals are red hot, clean and oil the grill rack, and position the rack 4 inches from heat. The coals are the right temperature if you can only hold your hand above the rack for a count of 3.
3. Cut the peppers through the stems, remove stems and seeds, and cut into 1-inch strips. Cut the zucchini and yellow squash lengthwise, ¼ inch thick.
4. Peel the shallots. Bring water to a boil and add 1 teaspoon salt. Add the shallots and poach for 4 to 5 minutes.
5. Shallots and tomatoes are grilled whole. Place the peppers, squash, shallots, and tomatoes in a bowl. Toss with vegetable oil and remaining salt and pepper.

6.  Put vegetables on the grill. The squash will cook the quickest, followed by the peppers, tomatoes, and shallots.
7.  In a separate bowl, mix the basil, parsley, and mint with the olive oil. When the vegetables are done, place immediately on a platter and toss with the herb–olive oil mixture. The heat from the vegetables will help release the flavor of the herbs.

YIELD: 6 servings
PREPARATION TIME: 20 minutes
COOKING TIME: 5–7 minutes

## GRILLED STRIPED BASS WITH SALSA VERDE

*This is a favorite East Coast fish. The Salsa Verde is a brightly flavored herb sauce that complements anything grilled.*

VEGETABLE OIL FOR GRILL RACK
6 STRIPED BASS FILLETS (ABOUT 6 OUNCES EACH, 1 INCH THICK)
2 TEASPOONS SALT
½ TEASPOON FRESHLY GROUND BLACK PEPPER
SALSA VERDE (RECIPE FOLLOWS), FOR SERVING

1.  Start the grill.
2.  When the coals are red hot, clean and oil the grill rack, and position the rack 4 inches from heat. The coals are the right temperature if you can only hold your hand above the rack for a count of 2.
3.  Cut several slices through the skin of the fish to prevent it from curling. Season both sides of the fish with salt and pepper. Place fillets, skin side down, on the hot grill and cover. Turn over after 3 minutes. When turning, lift gently with tongs and a metal spatula. If grill is clean, fillets should turn easily. Grill for another 3 minutes. (This is a good grilling time for fillets that are 1 inch thick.)
4.  Serve with Salsa Verde.

YIELD: 6 servings
PREPARATION TIME: 5 minutes
COOKING TIME: 6–8 minutes

*Salsa Verde*

¼ CUP CHOPPED FRESH PARSLEY
2 TABLESPOONS CHOPPED FRESH
    CHIVES
10 FRESH BASIL LEAVES
5 FRESH MINT LEAVES

2 TEASPOONS CAPERS
1 GARLIC CLOVE
2 TEASPOONS LEMON ZEST
1 ANCHOVY FILLET
¼ CUP EXTRA VIRGIN OLIVE OIL
¼ TEASPOON FRESHLY GROUND
    BLACK PEPPER

1.  Put all the ingredients into a food processor and blend until smooth.
2.  You may need to add salt, but taste the mixture first. The capers and anchovy fillet might impart enough salt by themselves.

YIELD: ½ cup
PREPARATION TIME: 15 minutes

## LEMON GRANITA WITH FRESH RASPBERRIES

*You can use this as a dessert or as a palate refresher.*

6 LEMONS
3 CUPS OF WATER
1 CUP SUGAR
1 CUP FRESH RASPBERRIES

1. Peel all 6 lemons using a vegetable peeler, peeling off only the yellow skin and not the white pith underneath. Put skins into a pot with the water and sugar, bring to a boil, and simmer for 5 minutes. Remove peels from pot and discard peels.
2. Squeeze the juice from the 6 lemons into the liquid.
3. Pour the liquid into a 13×9-inch pan and place in freezer. Ice crystals will begin to form after 30 to 45 minutes. Stir with a fork, breaking up the ice crystals. Continue to stir every 15 minutes, for 2½ to 3 hours.
4. Spoon into chilled bowls. Top with raspberries.

YIELD: 4–6 servings
PREPARATION TIME: 5 minutes
COOKING TIME: 5–10 minutes
FREEZER TIME: 2½–3 hours

*A less involved way is to freeze the mixture in ice cube trays and crush in a blender after it has frozen.*

# Fenwick Island Lighthouse
FENWICK ISLAND, DELAWARE

SINCE 1856 THIS LIGHTHOUSE HAS BEEN POINTING THE WAY INTO DELAWARE Harbor. It stands on Fenwick Island, which is the eastern-most end of a formerly disputed border between Delaware and Maryland. The boundary became famous as the Mason–Dixon Line; the lighthouse is located on the northern side. The light's white tower was restored and then rededicated in 1998, thanks to a movement spear-headed by Paul Pepper, an elderly man who was the great-grandson of one of its keepers and lived near the light for his entire life.

Since 1940, this state has been famous for its locally developed "Delawares," which are plump broiler chickens. As far as fish are concerned, once a year the shad come in from the ocean to spawn in the freshwater rivers. Shad roe is a rare, prized delicacy only available for a few weeks in the early spring, just when the greens are starting to appear in the fields. At the same time, fruits and vegetables preserved from the previous summer had to be used up, so the jars would be ready for the next season's bounty.

# SPRING ON FENWICK ISLAND

This menu is pure spring: young roasted chicken, fresh seasonal shad roe, new greens, and the flavor of peaches as a harbinger of summer.

DELAWARE CRAB PUFFS

WATERCRESS WALNUTS AND PEAR SALAD

SHAD ROE PICATTA

ROASTED CHICKEN WITH VEGETABLES

PEACH CRISP

## DELAWARE CRAB PUFFS
*An old-style classic, very nice and light.*

1 CUP ALL-PURPOSE FLOUR
1 CUP CRUSHED RITZ CRACKERS
3 TEASPOONS BAKING POWDER
½ TEASPOON SALT
½ TEASPOON POWDERED MUSTARD
⅛ TEASPOON CAYENNE PEPPER
1 TEASPOON ONION POWDER
¼ TEASPOON GARLIC POWDER
½ CUP MAYONNAISE
¾ CUP MILK
1 EGG, SLIGHTLY BEATEN
1 POUND CRABMEAT
VEGETABLE SHORTENING, FOR FRYING
LEMON MAYONNAISE, FOR SERVING (SEE RECIPE ON PAGE 22)

1. Mix together the flour, crackers, baking powder, salt, mustard, cayenne, onion powder, and garlic powder in a bowl. Using a different bowl, mix together the mayonnaise, milk, egg, and crabmeat.
2. Blend the wet ingredients into the dry ingredients; do not overmix. Allow the batter to rest for 5 minutes.
3. Preheat the oven to 200°F. Puffs may need to be cooked in batches, and they can be kept warm in the oven.
4. Heat ½ inch of vegetable shortening in a heavy pot over medium-high heat to 360°F.
5. Spoon walnut-sized portions of batter into the hot oil, being careful not to overcrowd the pan. Cook for 2 to 3 minutes per side, turning over once, until golden brown.
6. Drain on a rack. Keep finished puffs warm in the oven while the rest are cooking. Serve hot, with Lemon Mayonnaise on the side.

YIELD: 30 puffs
PREPARATION TIME: 10–15 minutes
COOKING TIME: 2–3 minutes per batch

## WATERCRESS WALNUT AND PEAR SALAD

*Peppery, salty, and sweet, all on one plate.*

1 ½ POUNDS WATERCRESS
½ CUP WALNUTS, TOASTED
1 BARTLETT PEAR, CORED AND
   SLICED
1 TABLESPOON CIDER VINEGAR

1 TEASPOON BROWN MUSTARD
¼ CUP EXTRA VIRGIN OLIVE OIL
½ TEASPOON SALT
¼ TEASPOON FRESHLY GROUND
   BLACK PEPPER

1. Wash and dry the watercress. Remove thick stems. Chop watercress into bite-sized pieces. Combine the watercress, walnuts, and pear slices in a bowl.
2. In a separate bowl, mix the vinegar and mustard together. Whisk in the olive oil to make a vinaigrette.
3. Toss the salad with the vinaigrette, salt, and pepper.

YIELD: 6 servings
PREPARATION TIME: 5–10 minutes

## SHAD ROE PICATTA

*This has a really interesting, briny taste; it's a delicacy that only comes along for a few weeks a year each spring.*

3 CUPS WATER
2 PAIRS SHAD ROE
1 TEASPOON SALT
¼ TEASPOON FRESHLY GROUND BLACK
   PEPPER
½ CUP SEMOLINA FLOUR
4 TABLESPOONS BUTTER
¼ CUP CHICKEN STOCK
¼ CUP WHITE WINE
8 CAPER BERRIES, HALVED
2 TABLESPOONS CHOPPED FRESH PARSLEY
4 THIN LEMON SLICES

1. Bring the water to a boil.
2. Place the roe in heatproof bowl. Pour boiling water down the sides of the bowl until the roe are covered. Avoid pouring water directly on to the roe. Let sit for 1 minute.
3. Gently remove the roe from water with a slotted spoon and dry with paper towels. Carefully separate the roe using a paring knife. Season with the salt and pepper. Dredge in semolina flour.
4. Starting with a cold pan, melt the butter over medium heat. When butter stops foaming, slide the roe into pan and cover with a splatter guard. Sauté for 3 minutes. Turn over and cook for 2 more minutes. Remove roe from the pan and keep warm.
5. Remove pan from heat and pour in the stock, wine, caper berries, parsley, and lemon slices. Return pan to heat and stir, making a sauce.
6. Pour sauce over the top of shad roe and serve immediately.

YIELD: 4 servings
PREPARATION TIME: 10 minutes
COOKING TIME: 7 minutes


## ROASTED CHICKEN WITH VEGETABLES

*Use a larger chicken, and you'll get better flavors in this family favorite.*

1 WHOLE CHICKEN (3½–4 POUNDS)
2 TABLESPOONS SALT, DIVIDED
1 TEASPOON FRESHLY GROUND BLACK PEPPER, DIVIDED
2 POUNDS RED BLISS POTATOES
2 ONIONS
1 FENNEL BULB
4 CELERY STALKS
3 CARROTS
6 CLOVES GARLIC, PEELED
VEGETABLE OIL, TO COAT CASSEROLE
¼ CUP CHICKEN STOCK

1. Preheat the oven to 375°F.
2. Wash chicken and pat dry inside and out. Lay the chicken, breast side down, on a cutting board. Using kitchen shears, cut along each side of the back bone. Remove backbone. Press down on the leg portion of the chicken to flatten it out. Season with half the salt and pepper.
3. Clean the vegetables. Cut the potatoes in halves or quarters, so they are all the same size. Peel the onions, remove the ends, and quarter them, leaving the stem attached. Remove ends of the fennel bulb and cut into quarters. Cut the celery and carrots into 1-inch pieces.
4. Brush the bottom of a large casserole with oil; cover the bottom with the vegetables, including garlic cloves. Pour in the stock and season with the balance of the salt and pepper. Place the chicken skin side up on top of the vegetables.
5. Bake for 1½ hours, or until internal temperature of chicken (at thigh) reaches 165°F. Baste occasionally.

YIELD: 4–6 servings
PREPARATION TIME: 15–20 minutes
ROASTING TIME: 1½ hours


## PEACH CRISP

*This is a great dish because it can be made any time of the year.*

Note: Save the peach cans to make Boston Brown Bread (see recipe on page 19).

2 (28-OUNCE) CANS PEACHES AND JUICE
½ CUP SUGAR
¼ CUP MOLASSES
¼ CUP DRY SHERRY
2 TABLESPOONS CORNSTARCH
½ TEASPOON ALMOND EXTRACT
CINNAMON CRISP TOPPING (RECIPE FOLLOWS)

1. Preheat the oven to 350°F.
2. Drain the peaches, putting the juice into a pot along with the sugar and molasses. In a separate bowl, combine the sherry and cornstarch, and stir into reserved peach-juice mixture. Cook on medium heat until thickened. Stir in almond extract and reserved peaches.
3. Pour into baking dish and top with Cinnamon Crisp Topping. Bake for 30 to 35 minutes.

PREPARATION TIME: Less than 5 minutes
COOKING TIME: 5 minutes on the stovetop, and 30–35 minutes in the oven

*Cinnamon Crisp Topping*

1 CUP BROWN SUGAR
1 CUP ALL-PURPOSE FLOUR
1 TEASPOON CINNAMON
8 TABLESPOONS BUTTER, MELTED
2 CUPS ROLLED OATS

1. Combine all the ingredients.

YIELD: 4 cups
PREPARATION TIME: 5 minutes

# Solomon's Lump Lighthouse
SOLOMON'S LUMP, MARYLAND

THIS 1895 CAISSON LIGHT REPLACED AN EARLIER LIGHTHOUSE TO THE south, which had been destroyed by ice. Originally, the keeper lived in a wooden, two-story house built on one side of the tower. The lighthouse sits in the middle of the bay, marking the entrance to Kedges Strait, and the reefs near Smith Island.

More recently, Smith Island was in the news when the two major local industries—crabbing and oystering—fell on hard times. Fishing restrictions have threatened this idyllic community on an island less than ten miles off the mainland, where residents speak a dialect reminiscent of Elizabethan English.

# FAMILY REUNION MENU

This meal is based on an old-fashioned family reunion dinner, where everyone brings his or her signature dish. Ingredients and dishes that are native to this part of the Atlantic coast include crab, chicken, biscuits, and tall frosted cakes.

MARYLAND CRAB CAKES

BAKED CRAB AND CORN PUDDING

COUNTRY HAM STUFFED WITH GREENS

MARYLAND FRIED CHICKEN WITH MILK GRAVY

SMITH ISLAND SWEET POTATO BISCUITS

SMITH ISLAND CAKE

## MARYLAND CRAB CAKES

*Maryland's signature dish. There's a reason why these are popular all over the country. Eat many—eat often.*

1 EGG
½ CUP MAYONNAISE
¼ CUP BROWN MUSTARD
2 TABLESPOONS CHOPPED FRESH PARSLEY
2 TABLESPOONS CHOPPED FRESH CHIVES
1 TEASPOON DRY MUSTARD
JUICE AND ZEST OF 1 LEMON
1½ POUNDS FRESH CRABMEAT
¾ CUP PANKO BREAD CRUMBS
1 TEASPOON SALT
¼ TEASPOON FRESHLY GROUND BLACK PEPPER
2 TABLESPOONS VEGETABLE OIL

1. Mix together the egg, mayonnaise, mustard, parsley, chives, dry mustard, and lemon juice and zest.
2. Fold together the crabmeat, bread crumbs, salt, and pepper. Combine with the mayonnaise mixture. Do not overmix, because you will shred the crab. Form into 12 patties.
3. Heat a sauté pan on medium-high heat. Pour the oil into pan. Sauté cakes for 2 to 3 minutes, or until golden brown. Turn over and cook for another 2 to 3 minutes.

YIELD: 6 servings as appetizer, 4 servings as entrée
PREPARATION TIME: 10–15 minutes
COOKING TIME: 4-6 minutes per batch

## BAKED CRAB AND CORN PUDDING

*Sweet crab, sweet corn, and a complement of herbs and spices.*

2 TABLESPOONS VEGETABLE OIL
3 SLICES BACON, DICED
1 ONION, DICED
1 CUP DICED TOMATOES
1 CUP CORN KERNELS (ABOUT 2 EARS)
2 EGGS, BEATEN
1 CUP MILK
8 OUNCES FRESH CRABMEAT
¼ CUP CHOPPED FRESH PARSLEY
½ TEASPOON OLD BAY SEASONING MIX
¼ CUP CRUSHED SALTINE CRACKERS
½ TEASPOON SALT
⅛ TEASPOON FRESHLY GROUND BLACK
   PEPPER

1. Preheat the oven to 350°F.
2. Heat the oil in a heavy large pot over medium heat. Sauté bacon for 3 to 4 minutes. Add the onion and sauté for 10 minutes, or until tender. Mix in the tomatoes and corn, and cook for 5 minutes.
3. In a separate bowl, mix together the eggs, milk, crabmeat, parsley, Old Bay seasoning, crackers, salt, and pepper. Fold in the bacon–tomato mixture and pour into a 2-quart casserole dish.
4. Bake for 35 to 40 minutes, or until set.

YIELD: 6 servings
PREPARATION TIME: 15–20 minutes
COOKING TIME: 15–20 minutes on the stovetop, and 35–40 minutes in the oven

## COUNTRY HAM STUFFED WITH GREENS

*When you slice this, the thinner, the better. Paper thin is the best.*

1 CURED HAM, 12–16 POUNDS
   (FULLY COOKED HAMS WORK
   FINE)
1 POUND COLLARD GREENS
1 POUND MUSTARD GREENS
4 TABLESPOONS VEGETABLE OIL
3 ONIONS, 2 DICED AND 1
   CHOPPED
4 CLOVES GARLIC, SLICED

3 TABLESPOONS BUTTER
½ TEASPOON SALT
⅛ TEASPOON FRESHLY GROUND
   BLACK PEPPER
4 PACKAGES CHEESE CLOTH
   (ABOUT 8 YARDS)
1 CARROT, PEELED AND CHOPPED
2 CELERY STALKS, CHOPPED
4 BAY LEAVES

1. Wash greens, remove thick ribs, and chop into pieces.
2. Heat a pan over medium heat and add the oil. Sauté the diced onions and garlic for 10 to 15 minutes. Add the greens, butter, salt, and pepper. Cover and cook for 15 to 20 minutes.
3. Slice 10 to 12 deep 4-inch-long slits into the ham. Stuff the openings with greens.
4. Lay out 4 layers of cheese cloth. Place the ham on top and fold the cloth over the ham. Secure the cheese cloth with butcher twine. It is a good idea to make a handle out of the twine. This will make retrieving the ham easier.
5. Place the ham in a pot large enough that the ham can be completely covered by 1 inch of water. Add water to cover ham. Add remaining chopped onion, carrot, celery, and bay leaves to pot.
6. Bring to a boil and reduce to a simmer. Check the water level from time to time, adding more water when needed. Cover and cook for 3 to 4 hours or about 15 minutes per pound. Fully cooked hams require less cooking time. Cook until the internal temperature reads 140°F.
7. Remove the ham from pot, cool quickly to room temperature and refrigerate for at least 11 to 12 hours.
8. Remove ham from refrigerator, cut away cheese cloth, and slice ham into paper-thin slices, following the bone.

YIELD: 15–20 servings
PREPARATION TIME: 35–40 minutes
COOKING TIME: 20–25 minutes for the greens, and 3–4 hours for the ham
REFRIGERATION TIME: 11–12 hours


## MARYLAND FRIED CHICKEN WITH MILK GRAVY

*Crispiness and smoothness—a great contrast in textures.*

1 WHOLE CHICKEN, CUT INTO 8 PIECES (2½–3 POUNDS)
1 TABLESPOON SALT, DIVIDED
1 TEASPOON FRESHLY GROUND BLACK PEPPER, DIVIDED
2 CUPS ALL-PURPOSE FLOUR

VEGETABLE SHORTENING, FOR FRYING
2 TABLESPOONS RENDERED CHICKEN FAT
1 CUP MILK
1 CUP CHICKEN STOCK

1. Place the chicken in a bowl, season with 2½ teaspoons salt and ¾ teaspoon pepper, and cover with flour.
2. Toss so each piece of chicken is coated. Put in the refrigerator for 1 hour, retossing the chicken every 10 to 15 minutes. Remove the chicken from the refrigerator and shake off excess flour. Reserve 2 tablespoons of flour for the gravy.
3. Heat ½ inch of vegetable shortening in a heavy pot over medium-high heat to 375°F.
4. Preheat the oven to 200°F.
5. Fry the chicken in batches, turning it over often to get an even golden brown. Cook chicken for 12 to 15 minutes for wings, and 25 to 30 minutes for large breasts. Chicken is done when internal temperature reaches 165°F. Or remove a piece and make an incision with a sharp knife. If the juice runs clear, it is done.
6. When the chicken is done, place on a rack and put in oven to keep warm while the other pieces cook.

7. Heat the chicken fat in a pan. Blend in flour. Whisk in the milk and chicken stock, and bring to a boil. Season with remaining salt and pepper.
8. Place the chicken on a platter and spoon gravy over the top.

YIELD: 4–6 servings
PREPARATION TIME: 15 minutes
REFRIGERATION TIME: 1 hour
COOKING TIME: 40 minutes, when cooking chicken in 2 batches

## SMITH ISLAND SWEET POTATO BISCUITS

*This is Laura Justice Evans' recipe, and she says they are perfect with country ham. She had just made some the day we spoke about this menu. She suggests serving the biscuits warm, with butter.*

1 (40-OUNCE) CAN SWEET POTATOES, DRAINED AND MASHED
2 CUPS SUGAR
1¼ CUPS BUTTER, AT ROOM TEMPERATURE
5¼ CUPS ALL-PURPOSE FLOUR
3 TABLESPOONS BAKING POWDER
½ TEASPOON BAKING SODA

1. Mix together the sweet potatoes, sugar, and butter.
2. Mix the dry ingredients separately. Blend together the wet and dry ingredients.
3. Refrigerate for 2 hours or overnight, to allow flavors to blend.
4. Preheat the oven to 350°F.
5. Roll out on floured surface and cut into 2-inch rounds. Place rounds on a greased cookie sheet and bake for 8 to 10 minutes.

YIELD: 36–40 biscuits
PREPARATION TIME: 15–20 minutes
REFRIGERATION TIME: 2 hours
BAKING TIME: 8–10 minutes

## SMITH ISLAND CAKE

*Laura Justice Evans is a member of the Smith Island Cake Co. "I've lived on Smith Island for nearly 21 years. My mother-in-law makes this cake, and she taught me how. She can get 14 layers out of this recipe."*

1 BOX DUNCAN HINES CLASSIC YELLOW CAKE MIX
4 EGGS
1 TEASPOON VANILLA EXTRACT
⅓ CUP VEGETABLE OIL
⅓ CUP WATER
CLASSIC FROSTING (RECIPE FOLLOWS)

1. Mix all ingredients according to directions on box.
2. Preheat the oven to 350°F.
3. Grease 2 (8-inch or 10-inch) nonstick cake pans (beginners should use 8-inch pans).
4. Pour ¼ cup of batter into each, using a soup ladle. Spread very evenly.

5. Bake for 8 minutes. Loosen immediately. Then let cool, leaving cake layers in pans. Remove each layer as you are ready to place it on the cake and frost with Classic Frosting.

YIELD: 8–10 servings
PREPARATION TIME: 30–40 minutes
BAKING TIME: 8 minutes per layer

*Classic Frosting*

8 TABLESPOONS BUTTER
½ CUP MILK CHOCOLATE MORSELS
3 CUPS POWDERED SUGAR
⅓ CUP COCOA POWDER
1 TEASPOON VANILLA EXTRACT
¼ CUP MILK, OR ENOUGH TO ACHIEVE THE RIGHT CONSISTENCY

1. Melt the butter in a saucepan. Add the chocolate morsels and stir until melted.
2. Remove pan from stove and stir in the sugar, cocoa powder, vanilla, and milk.
3. Frost each layer and top with next layer of cake, ending with frosting on top.

YIELD: About 4 cups
PREPARATION TIME: Less than 5 minutes
COOKING TIME: 5 minutes

**Note**: For other occasions, you could drizzle with melted white chocolate or peanut butter.

# Old Cape Henry Lighthouse
FORT STORY, VIRGINIA

OLD CAPE HENRY LIGHT WAS BUILT DURING GEORGE WASHINGTON'S administration, in 1791, and its light shone for nearly a century. After cracks in the tower were observed during an inspection, a new, taller beacon was built in 1881.

But against all odds, the first lighthouse remained standing, and in 1896, it came under the protection of the Association for the Preservation of Virginia Antiquities because it marked the spot where the English colonists first set foot on Virginia soil in 1607. The light was even relit after the tower was restored in 1972.

# Late Summer Sunday Dinner

This menu has a range of recipes from foods of the early settlers who lived off flounder from the sea to later dishes from farmers in the area. Brunswick Stew was originally made with the meat of squirrels trapped in nearby forests, but it now is more commonly prepared with chicken.

Turnip Greens with Boiled Dressing

Fried Green Tomatoes

Stuffed Flounder

Brunswick Stew

Peanut Brittle Pie

## TURNIP GREENS WITH BOILED DRESSING

*The sweet-and-sour dressing meshed with the fresh greens is a classic combination.*

1 POUND TURNIP GREENS, BEET GREENS, OR SWISS CHARD
1 SMALL RED ONION, SLICED
½ RECIPE BOILED DRESSING (RECIPE FOLLOWS), FOR SERVING
½ TEASPOON SALT
⅛ TEASPOON FRESHLY GROUND BLACK PEPPER

1. Wash the greens and remove thick stems and ribs. Cut into ½-inch ribbons and dry completely.
2. Combine the greens and onion in a large bowl. Toss with the Boiled Dressing, and season with the salt and pepper.

YIELD: 4–6 servings
PREPARATION TIME: 10–15 minutes

*Boiled Dressing*

1 TEASPOON POWDERED MUSTARD
¼ TEASPOON CAYENNE PEPPER
1 TEASPOON ALL-PURPOSE FLOUR
1 TEASPOON SUGAR
¼ TEASPOON SALT
½ CUP MILK, DIVIDED
3 EGG YOLKS
¼ CUP CIDER VINEGAR
1 TABLESPOON BUTTER

1. Mix together the mustard, cayenne, flour, sugar, and salt. Slowly add half the milk, and blend until smooth.
2. Blend together the yolks, vinegar, and remaining milk. Cook in a double boiler. Whisk in the mustard–flour mixture. Cook, whisking constantly, for 3 to 4 minutes; then add butter. Cook until the dressing coats the back of a spoon.

YIELD: About 1 cup
PREPARATION TIME: 5 minutes
COOKING TIME: 3–4 minutes

## FRIED GREEN TOMATOES

*A late summer favorite anywhere you find homegrown tomatoes.*

4–5 GREEN TOMATOES
1 CUP BUTTERMILK
1 CUP CORNMEAL
½ CUP ALL-PURPOSE FLOUR
¼ CUP PARMESAN CHEESE
¼ CUP CHOPPED FRESH PARSLEY
1 TEASPOON SALT, DIVIDED
¼ TEASPOON FRESHLY GROUND BLACK
     PEPPER, DIVIDED
¼ CUP VEGETABLE OIL

1. Cut the tomatoes into ½-inch-thick slices. Put into a bowl and add the buttermilk. Soak for 5 minutes.
2. In a mixing bowl, combine the cornmeal, flour, Parmesan cheese, parsley, ½ teaspoon salt, and ⅛ teaspoon pepper.
3. Remove tomato slices, one at a time, from milk. Remove excess milk and dredge tomato slices in the cornmeal mixture. Place on a rack and refrigerate for 20 minutes. Remove from refrigerator and dredge again.
4. Preheat the oven to 200°F. Tomatoes may need to be cooked in batches, and they can be kept warm.
5. In a large pan over medium heat, heat vegetable oil. Allow 2 to 3 minutes for oil to get hot. Fry tomatoes a few at a time for 3 to 4 minutes per side, or until golden brown.
6. Drain on a rack. Place in a warm oven while the balance of the tomatoes are being cooked. Season with remaining salt and pepper, and serve hot.

YIELD: 6 servings
PREPARATION TIME: 10–15 minutes
REFRIGERATION TIME: 20 minutes
COOKING TIME: 6–8 minutes per batch

## STUFFED FLOUNDER

*This is a flavorful but delicate dish, with a shrimp filling for these lovely fillets.*

4 TABLESPOONS VEGETABLE OIL, DIVIDED
½ CUP MINCED SHALLOTS
½ POUND SHRIMP, PEELED AND CLEANED
¼ CUP HEAVY CREAM
1 TABLESPOON DIJON-STYLE MUSTARD
1 TABLESPOON CHOPPED TARRAGON
2 TABLESPOONS CHOPPED CHIVES
1 TEASPOON SALT, DIVIDED
¼ TEASPOON FRESHLY GROUND BLACK PEPPER, DIVIDED
4 MEDIUM FLOUNDER FILLETS (ABOUT 6 OUNCES EACH)
½ CUP CORNMEAL FOR DREDGE

1. Preheat the oven to 400°F.
2. Heat a pan over medium heat. Add 1 tablespoon of the oil and cook the shallots for 5 to 10 minutes, or until tender.
3. Chop the shrimp. Place the shrimp into a food processor and pulse 4 times, for 2 seconds each time.
4. In a mixing bowl, mix thoroughly the shrimp, shallots, heavy cream, mustard, tarragon, chives, ½ teaspoon salt, and ⅛ teaspoon pepper.
5. Lay the flounder fillets out on a cutting board, skinned side up, with the tail end away from you. Place equal amount of shrimp stuffing on each fillet. Place mixture ½ inch from the closest edge. Roll the fillet away from you, toward the tail end. Season with remaining salt and pepper. Dredge in cornmeal. Repeat until each fillet is complete.
6. Heat an oven-proof pan over medium-high heat. Add remaining 3 tablespoons of oil. Put flounder fillets in the pan. Cook for 2 to 3 minutes, turn over and place in oven.
7. Bake for 15 to 20 minutes.

YIELD: 4 servings
PREPARATION TIME: 15 minutes
COOKING TIME: 5–10 minutes for the shallots, and 15–20 minutes for the flounder


## BRUNSWICK STEW

*This could be a meal on its own using everything you have in the larder plus some meat. They used squirrel in the old days, chicken nowadays.*

1 WHOLE CHICKEN, CUT INTO 8 PIECES (2½–3 POUNDS)
2 TEASPOONS SALT
½ TEASPOON FRESHLY GROUND BLACK PEPPER
2 BAY LEAVES
¼ TEASPOON RED PEPPER FLAKES
4 CUPS CHICKEN STOCK
4 SLICES BACON, DICED
2 ONIONS, DICED
4 CELERY STALKS, DICED

1 POUND RED BLISS POTATOES, CUT INTO ½-INCH CUBES
1 (15-OUNCE) CAN WHOLE TOMATOES, SEEDED AND CHOPPED
1 (10-OUNCE) PACKAGE FROZEN LIMA BEANS
1½ CUPS CORN KERNELS, (ABOUT 3 EARS)

1. Place the chicken, salt, pepper, bay leaves, red pepper, and stock into a pot. Cover, bring to a boil, reduce to a simmer, and cook for 1 hour. Skim occasionally.
2. Remove the chicken from the pot and add the bacon, onions, celery, and potatoes. Bring back to a boil and reduce to a simmer. Cook, uncovered, for 30 minutes.
3. When the chicken has cooled, remove the meat from the bone. Reserve in large pieces.
4. Stir in reserved chicken, tomatoes, lima beans, and corn and continue to cook for 30 minutes.

YIELD: 6 servings
PREPARATION TIME: 25 minutes
COOKING TIME: 2 hours

## PEANUT BRITTLE PIE

*This is like eating candy, especially after it's been refrigerated overnight.*

½ CUP MELTED CARAMELS (ABOUT 24 PIECES)
1 CUP LIGHT CORN SYRUP
3 EGGS, BEATEN
6 TABLESPOONS BUTTER, MELTED
½ TEASPOON VANILLA EXTRACT
¼ TEASPOON SALT
½ (4.4-OUNCE) HERSHEY'S MILK CHOCOLATE BAR
1 (9-INCH) PIE CRUST (RECIPE FOLLOWS), PREBAKED
1 CUP PEANUT BRITTLE, BROKEN INTO ½-INCH PIECES

1. Preheat the oven to 375°F.
2. Microwave the caramels for 2½ to 3 minutes at medium-low power, or until they melt. Stir in the corn syrup.
3. Slowly add in the eggs, butter, vanilla, and salt. Mix together until smooth.
4. Arrange the pieces of the chocolate bar on the bottom of the pie crust. Pour mixture into pie crust. If any of the caramel lumps, do not worry, as it will soften while baking.
5. Bake for 30 minutes.
6. Remove the pie from the oven and press the brittle into the pie. Allow to cool on a rack for 1 hour, then refrigerate. Serve chilled.

YIELD: 6–8 servings
PREPARATION TIME: 10 minutes
BAKING TIME: 30 minutes
COOLING AND REFRIGERATION TIME: 2 hours

*Pie Crust*

1 ½ CUPS ALL-PURPOSE FLOUR
⅛ TEASPOON SALT
¾ CUP SHORTENING, COLD
⅓ CUP COLD WATER

1. Mix the flour and salt in a bowl and cut the shortening into the flour with 2 knives or a pastry blender, until the mixture is in clumps the size of peas. Gradually add the water and blend together.
2. Form the pie dough into a ball, cover with plastic wrap, and refrigerate for at least 30 minutes.
3. Lightly flour work surface. Roll out the pie dough to be 1 inch larger than the pie plate. Fold the dough over rolling pin and place in the pie plate. Unfold to cover the entire plate. Fold the extra dough under, and crimp the edges.
4. With a fork, poke holes in the bottom of the crust, and place in the refrigerator for at least 10 minutes.
5. Preheat the oven to 450°F. Take the pie crust from the refrigerator, line the bottom with foil, and fill it with dried beans or rice. Bake for 15 to 20 minutes, or until lightly browned. Remove the pie crust from the oven, remove the foil and beans, and let cool on a rack.

YIELD: 1 (9-inch) pie crust
PREPARATION TIME: 15–20 minutes
REFRIGERATION TIME: 40 minutes
BAKING TIME: 20 minutes

# SOUTHEAST ATLANTIC REGION

*A* long the southeastern coast of the United States—North Carolina, South Carolina, Georgia, and eastern Florida—lighthouses were built from Colonial times through the middle of the twentieth century. Because diverse waves of immigrants landed here, this region now exhibits a wide variety of influences in its cuisine, including English, African, Spanish, Latin American, and modern Mediterranean. With such a rich heritage, the menus here are varied in scope, from simple meals of native-grown foods to country feasts to elaborate historically styled dinners.

Lighthouses along the North Carolina and Georgia coasts guided eighteenth- and nineteenth-century merchants into busy harbors. In the 1860s, several early lighthouses became victims of Civil War conflicts, when both Union and Confederate forces vied for control of the sea in order to bring in supplies for their armies. After they were destroyed, some lighthouses were not rebuilt for decades. Sometimes this had to do with budget, and sometimes it had more to do with malaria and other mysterious diseases that struck crews of construction workers. In the meantime, various legends of hauntings grew up around a few of the lights that had witnessed bloody Civil War battles and personal tragedies. In Florida, one lighthouse even saw German spies land nearby during World War II.

During peacetime, life often proceeds at a slow pace in Southern regions. Traditions that developed here a century or more ago still flourish in these societies, rendering historical customs and foods current. Yet they seem to allow postmodern trends some space, as well. Dumplings and rice often accompany meats with rich gravies and sauces. Roasted, grilled, and fried seafood, such as fresh grouper, clams, oysters, and shrimp, appear often in coastal menus. Local vegetables are available year-round. And a cornucopia of local fruits, from berries to peaches to citrus, creates mouthwatering sweet and tangy desserts.

# Currituck Beach Lighthouse

COROLLA, NORTH CAROLINA

SHINING ITS BEACON OUT OVER THE OCEAN TODAY, CURRITUCK BEACH LIGHT IS ONE OF the very few to do so continuously since it was first lit, back in 1875. It is also constructed with unpainted brick, to set it apart from other lighthouses located to the north and south on this section of the Atlantic Coast. In addition to Currituck lighthouse, the keepers's house and other buildings have been restored. In fact, this light has become so modern, she even has her own MySpace page.

Around the turn of the last century, this part of North Carolina's Outer Banks regularly attracted wealthy hunters, as it is an area rich with wildfowl. Near the lighthouse, the elite Whalehead Club has also been returned to its 1920s hunt-club style grandeur—though now as a museum of indigenous water birds.

Both the lighthouse and the Whalehead Club are now part of Currituck Heritage Park in Corolla, North Carolina. For much of the twentieth century, the city of Corolla existed quietly, bypassed by development. The recent construction of a highway has allowed more people to enjoy the region's charms. Old and new foods combine in traditional and modern dishes nowadays: foods like duck, rice, clams, and shrimp abound, with rich desserts following.

# Wild Horses of the Outer Banks

The people of Corolla have also mobilized to protect the wild Spanish mustangs that have freely roamed North Carolina's Outer Banks for nearly five hundred years. Thought to have escaped from shipwrecks and from Spanish explorers, these small, extremely hardy horses live in self-governing groups on a series of sandy islands many miles long, separated from the mainland by a narrow sound.

Concerned about overdevelopment, with beach houses mushrooming along the coast, local citizens formed the Corolla Wild Horse Fund in 1989. The fund's "sole mission is to protect and preserve the last remaining herd of Spanish Mustangs on the northern Outer Banks. The Colonial Spanish Mustang is on the Threatened Breed list of the American Livestock Conservancy and on the Critical list of the Equus Survival Trust."

Corolla Wild Horse Fund http://www.corollawildhorses.com/

## 1920S HUNT CLUB DINNER

In an area known for elegance as well as abundance, this dinner reflects an earlier golden age. Anchored by several types of game, the menu seems elaborate now, but it would have been considered relatively simple by society men and women of that period—quite appropriate for this Whalehead hunting lodge.

BAKED CLAMS

SHRIMP PASTE WTIH TOAST POINTS

OYSTER STEW

CREAMED SWISS CHARD

MASHED SWEET POTATOES AND ORANGE PURÉE

ROASTED DUCK WITH ORANGE SAUCE

ROASTED VENISON LOIN

FRAN'S MOTHER'S AMBROSIA

CAROLINA TRIFLE

## BAKED CLAMS

*A great dish to serve your guests while dinner is being prepared. It goes very well with a loaf of crusty, white bread.*

30 LITTLENECK OR MAHOGANY CLAMS
1 TABLESPOON VEGETABLE OIL
4 SLICES BACON, DICED
3 TABLESPOONS DICED SHALLOTS (2 LARGE)
2 TEASPOONS DICED GARLIC (2 MEDIUM CLOVES)
¼ CUP FINELY CHOPPED FRESH PARSLEY
12 TABLESPOONS BUTTER, SOFTENED
1 TEASPOON SALT
¼ TEASPOON FRESHLY GROUND BLACK PEPPER

1. Shuck clams over a bowl to catch juice. Reserve 1 half shell from each clam.
2. Heat oil in a heavy large pot over medium heat. Sauté bacon until crispy, about 4 to 5 minutes. Add the shallots and garlic. Cook for 5 minutes. Remove from heat and cool.
3. Mix together the bacon mixture, parsley, butter, salt, and pepper.
4. Preheat the oven to 350°F.
5. Place 1 clam into each shell. Spread butter mixture on top. Place in an ovenproof dish and bake for 10 minutes.

**Note:** If you place clams in the freezer for 20 minutes, they will be easier to shuck. You may also choose to steam them until they begin to open.

YIELD: 30 clam appetizers
PREPARATION TIME: 15–20 minutes
COOKING TIME: 10 minutes on the stovetop, and 10 minutes in the oven

## SHRIMP PASTE WITH TOAST POINTS

*If you're not from the South, don't let the name scare you. It is a great party appetizer.*

3 TABLESPOONS VEGETABLE OIL
2 POUNDS SHRIMP, PEELED AND DEVEINED
1 TEASPOON SALT, DIVIDED
½ TEASPOON FRESHLY GROUND BLACK PEPPER, DIVIDED
1 CUP BUTTER, SOFTENED
3 TABLESPOONS ONION JUICE
3 TEASPOONS PREPARED HORSERADISH
3 TEASPOONS TABASCO SAUCE
2 TEASPOONS CELERY SALT
1 TABLESPOON TOMATO PASTE
TOAST POINTS (RECIPE FOLLOWS), FOR
    SERVING

1. Heat a sauté pan on medium-high heat. Add the oil. Season the shrimp with ½ teaspoon salt and ¼ teaspoon pepper. Cook shrimp for 3 to 4 minutes, or until opaque. Cool in refrigerator for about 1 hour or until cool to the touch.
2. Purée the shrimp in a food processor, pulsing 5 to 6 times.
3. Add the butter, onion juice, horseradish, Tabasco sauce, celery salt, tomato paste, and remaining salt and pepper to the running processor. Stop the processor, remove lid, and scrape the sides as needed to make sure all the ingredients are being well mixed.
4. Line a terrine with plastic wrap, leaving enough extra wrap to fold over the top. Remove shrimp paste from the processor and put into the terrine. Tap terrine on the counter release any air pockets. Refrigerate for at least 4 hours.
5. Unmold and slice. Serve with Toast Points.

YIELD: 8–10 servings
PREPARATION TIME: 15–20 minutes
REFRIGERATION TIME: 5 hours

*Toast Points*

1 PULLMAN LOAF (A FIRM WHITE BREAD)
8 TABLESPOONS BUTTER, MELTED

1. Preheat broiler on high.
2. Cut bread into ½-inch slices.
3. Place on a rack under broiler and broil for 2 to 3 minutes.
4. Turn slices over, brush with butter, and cook until golden brown.
6. Trim crust and cut into triangles.

YIELD: 6–8 servings
PREPARATION TIME: Less than 5 minutes
COOKING TIME: 4–6 minutes


## OYSTER STEW

*Ed's Southern friends always have this as part of their holiday meals. It is served with oyster crackers.*

2 TABLESPOONS VEGETABLE OIL
¼ POUND HAM, DICED
1 ONION, DICED
2 CELERY STALKS, DICED
3 CUPS WHOLE MILK
½ CUP HALF-AND-HALF OR LIGHT CREAM
1 BAY LEAF
1 TEASPOON OLD BAY SEASONING
½ CUP CRUMBLED SALTINE CRACKERS
1 PINT OYSTERS, DRAINED
¾ TEASPOON SALT
¼ TEASPOON FRESHLY GROUND BLACK PEPPER
¼ CUP CHOPPED FRESH PARSLEY

1. Heat the oil in a pot over medium heat and fry the ham for 5 minutes. Stir in the onions and celery and cook for an additional 15 to 20 minutes.
2. Pour in the milk, half-and-half, bay leaf, Old Bay, and saltines. Simmer for 10 to 15 minutes.
3. Stir in oysters, salt, pepper, and parsley. Simmer for 5 minutes.

YIELD: 4–6 servings
PREPARATION TIME: 5–10 minutes
COOKING TIME: 40–45 minutes


## CREAMED SWISS CHARD

*There's an earthiness to Swiss chard that makes this combination of flavors work so well.*

1½ TABLESPOONS PLUS ¾ TEASPOON SALT, DIVIDED
2–2½ POUNDS SWISS CHARD

3 TABLESPOONS BUTTER
4 SHALLOTS, SLICED (ABOUT ½ CUP)
2 TABLESPOONS ALL-PURPOSE FLOUR
1½ CUPS MILK
1 BAY LEAF
¼ TEASPOON GRATED NUTMEG
¼ TEASPOON FRESHLY GROUND BLACK PEPPER
2 TABLESPOONS HEAVY CREAM

1. Bring the water to a boil and add 1½ tablespoons of salt.
2. Remove the stems from the chard leaves. Carefully wash leaves at least twice.
3. Submerge the chard in the boiling water. Cook for 3 to 4 minutes, remove from boiling water, and plunge into cold water. Remove the chard from the water, squeeze out all excess water, and chop.
4. Melt butter in a medium-sized pot on medium heat. Sauté the shallots for 10 minutes, or until tender. Stir to prevent browning.
5. Stir in the flour and cook for 2 minutes. Slowly whisk in the milk, incorporating all the flour, then add bay leaf and nutmeg. Simmer for 10 minutes, stirring occasionally. Remove the bay leaf.
6. Fold in the chard. Season with remaining salt and pepper and simmer until hot, about 10 minutes. The chard will give off liquid, nicely thinning the dish.

YIELD: 4 servings
PREPARATION TIME: 10–15 minutes
COOKING TIME: 30 minutes

## MASHED SWEET POTATOES AND ORANGE PURÉE

*Ed has made sweet potatoes with orange for as long as he can remember. It's a good idea to zest the orange before you squeeze it.*

2 LARGE SWEET POTATOES (ABOUT 1 POUND)
½ CUP FRESH-SQUEEZED ORANGE JUICE (ABOUT 2 ORANGES)
4 TABLESPOONS BUTTER, SOFTENED
1 TEASPOON SALT
¼ TEASPOON FRESHLY GROUND BLACK PEPPER
ZEST OF 1 ORANGE

1. Preheat the oven to 350°F.
2. Place the sweet potatoes in the oven and bake for 60 to 70 minutes, or until they are very soft and moisture begins to leak out.
3. Remove the potatoes from oven, cut them in half, and scoop out the insides with a spoon.
4. Put the potatoes, juice, butter, salt, pepper, and orange zest in a food processor and blend until smooth.

YIELD: 4 servings
PREPARATION TIME: 5–10 minutes
COOKING TIME: 60–70 minutes

## ROASTED DUCK WITH ORANGE SAUCE

*Use a good marmalade. Ed is fortunate to have good friends—Andy and Felicia—who make their own and know how much he loves it.*

1 DUCKLING (5–6 POUNDS)
4 TEASPOONS SALT, DIVIDED
½ TEASPOON FRESHLY GROUND BLACK PEPPER
2 ORANGES, HALVED
1 TABLESPOON CHOPPED FRESH SAGE
1 TABLESPOON CHOPPED FRESH ROSEMARY
1 CUP WATER
2 TABLESPOONS DICED SHALLOTS
PAN JUICES PLUS ORANGE JUICE TO MAKE 2 CUPS
2 TABLESPOONS CORNSTARCH
1 TABLESPOON ORANGE MARMALADE

1. Preheat the oven to 325°F.
2. Remove giblets and neck of the duckling. Wash inside and out with cold water. Pat dry with paper towels.
3. Season cavity with 2 teaspoons salt and pepper. Stuff with the halved oranges, sage, and rosemary.
4. Prick the skin of the duckling, being careful not pierce the meat, 25 to 30 times. Rub remaining salt on the outside.
5. Place the duckling, breast side down, on a rack in a large roasting pan. Add water to the pan. Repeat throughout the roasting. Roast for 2–2½ hours.
6. Drain and reserve duck fat and pan juices. Increase oven temperature to 425°F. Turn duck breast side up and roast for 30 more minutes to crisp the skin.
7. While duck finishes roasting, make the sauce. Heat 1 tablespoon of the reserved duck fat in a small pot; add shallots and sauté 5 minutes, or until tender.
8. Mix the pan juices, orange juice, and cornstarch. Add to the shallots and bring to a boil. Blend in the marmalade.
9. Remove the duck from oven, tent with foil, and allow to rest for 10 minutes. Remove the orange halves from cavity. Using kitchen shears, cut the duck in half along the back and the breastbone. Separate the leg portion from the breast.
10. Serve with the sauce.

YIELD: 4 servings
PREPARATION TIME: 15 minutes
COOKING TIME: 3 hours

## ROASTED VENISON LOIN

*Cook it rare. This dish has a beautiful herbed crust.*

1 VENISON LOIN (3–4 POUNDS)
½ POUND FATBACK, CUBED
2 TABLESPOONS CHOPPED FRESH THYME
1 TABLESPOON CHOPPED FRESH ROSEMARY
1 CLOVE GARLIC, CHOPPED

1 TEASPOON GROUND JUNIPER BERRIES
2 TEASPOONS SALT, DIVIDED
½ TEASPOON FRESHLY GROUND BLACK PEPPER, DIVIDED
½ CUP ALL-PURPOSE FLOUR
2 ONIONS, PEELED AND SLICED INTO DISCS
½ CUP RED WINE
½ CUP CHICKEN STOCK
2 TABLESPOONS BUTTER, SOFTEN

1. Clean loin and remove all silverskin. (Your butcher can do this.)
2. Put the fatback in a food processor and process until smooth. Add the thyme, rosemary, garlic, juniper berries, 1 teaspoon of salt, ¼ teaspoon pepper, and flour. Blend for 1 minute.
3. Preheat the oven to 450°F.
4. Place onion slices on the bottom of a 9×12-inch roasting pan. Season loin with remaining salt and pepper. Rub loin with the fatback mixture and place loin on onions.
5. Roast for 10 minutes at 450°F, reduce oven to 400°F, and continue roasting for 15 to 20 minutes, until loin reaches an internal temperature of 130°F to 135°F.
6. Remove from oven, put on a platter and cover loosely with foil.
7. Put onions and pan drippings into a pan. Turn heat to high. Pour in the wine and stock. Be careful when adding the wine to pan. Reduce the sauce by half, add the butter, and mix in. Check seasoning. Strain before serving.
8. Slice loin into ¼-inch slices and serve with sauce.

YIELD: 6–8 servings
PREPARATION TIME: 10–15 minutes for butchered loin—add 15–20 minutes if loin needs to be cleaned
COOKING TIME: 25–30 minutes


## FRAN'S MOTHER'S AMBROSIA

*Fran, her sisters, and her cousins all collaborated on re-creating this dish from their shared Southern childhood.*

1 (8.4-OUNCE) CAN MANDARIN ORANGE SEGMENTS IN LIGHT SYRUP, DRAINED AND LIQUID RESERVED
1 (20-OUNCE) CAN PINEAPPLE IN SYRUP OR JUICE, CHUNKS OR CRUSHED, DRAINED AND LIQUID RESERVED
1 (16-OUNCE) JAR MARASCHINO CHERRIES, CUT IN HALVES
1 CUP MINI MARSHMALLOWS
1 CUP SWEETENED COCONUT
1 CUP SOUR CREAM

1. Mix together oranges, pineapple, cherries, marshmallows, and coconut. Add sour cream and mix gently.
2. Mix in reserved fruit liquid 1 tablespoon at a time, to taste.

YIELD: 4 servings
PREPARATION TIME: 5–10 minutes

## CAROLINA TRIFLE

*The Colonial version of an English classic.*

1 POUND SPONGE OR POUND CAKE

1 LARGE PACKAGE VANILLA CUSTARD OR PUDDING, FLAVORED WITH ALMOND
EXTRACT OR LIQUEUR (FOLLOW PACKAGE INSTRUCTIONS AND COOL BE-
FORE USING)

2 QUARTS FRESH FRUIT (STRAWBERRIES, PEACHES, OR BLUEBERRIES)

4 CUPS WHIPPED CREAM

1. Slice cake into ½-inch-thick pieces. Place 1 layer of cake in the bottom of a glass serving dish.
2. Cover cake with custard, followed by fruit. Continue layering, finishing with whipped cream.

YIELD: 6–8 servings
PREPARATION TIME: 10–15 minutes
COOKING TIME: Follow the package instructions for the custard or pudding

# Cape Hatteras Lighthouse
## HATTERAS ISLAND, NORTH CAROLINA

THIS LIGHTHOUSE—NOW THE TALLEST IN THE COUNTRY—HAS BENEFITED FROM THE GOVERNMENT'S attention since its establishment at the beginning of the nineteenth century.

In 1803, Alexander Hamilton was instrumental in allocating funds for the first lighthouse on this spot. But some decades later, the building was considered too short to shine far enough out to sea for the increased shipping traffic and larger ships. This fact came to the attention of the newly created Lighthouse Board of the United States in 1852. Shortly afterward, the tower was raised 150 feet. Soon after that, Confederate soldiers damaged it to hinder Union activities on the coast, but the Union army put it back in service in 1862.

After the war, the lighthouse was deemed too damaged to repair. So a new lighthouse was built and defined with barber-pole striping; this is now the tallest lighthouse in America, at 208 feet. However, the coastline changed over the years, and since it had no pilings underneath it, the lighthouse was in serious danger by the end of the twentieth century. So in 1999, the Coast Guard moved the entire lighthouse back 2,900 feet. Now this lighthouse, which has protected so many ships, is itself protected and preserved.

# FAMILY SUPPER

Imagine a family supper on any weekday: cucumbers and onions from local gardens, and a family favorite for a cool evening—pork with dumplings. There's no special dessert tonight, just a piece of a simple prune cake with frosting.

CUCUMBERS AND RED ONION SALAD
PORK STEW WITH CORNMEAL DUMPLINGS
SIMPLE FROSTED CAKE

## CUCUMBERS AND RED ONION SALAD

*This smells of summer and good things to come.*

3 CUCUMBERS, PEELED, SPLIT LENGTHWISE, SEEDED, AND SLICED (ABOUT 4 CUPS)
1 SMALL RED ONION, SLICED THIN
½ CUP CIDER VINEGAR
¼ CUP SUGAR
3 TABLESPOONS CHOPPED FRESH MINT
1 TEASPOON SALT
⅛ TEASPOON FRESHLY GROUND BLACK PEPPER

1. Place the cucumber and onion in a bowl.
2. Combine the vinegar, sugar, mint, salt, and pepper. Add to cucumbers and toss.

YIELD: 4–6 servings
PREPARATION TIME: 10 minutes

## PORK STEW WITH CORNMEAL DUMPLINGS

*The Lexington firemen loved this dish best of all the recipes they sampled when we were testing for this book.*

3 POUNDS PORK BUTT, CUT INTO 1-INCH CUBES
2 TEASPOONS SALT, DIVIDED
½ TEASPOON FRESHLY GROUND BLACK PEPPER, DIVIDED
7 TABLESPOONS VEGETABLE OIL, DIVIDED
2 ONIONS, CHOPPED
2 CELERY STALKS, CHOPPED
3 CARROTS, CHOPPED
½ CUP PEAS, FRESH OR FROZEN
½ POUND SWEET POTATO, PEELED AND CUBED
2 TABLESPOONS CHOPPED FRESH THYME
4 CUPS BEEF STOCK
CORNMEAL DUMPLINGS (RECIPE FOLLOWS), FOR TOPPING

1.  Season pork with 1 teaspoon salt and ¼ teaspoon black pepper.
2.  Heat a large pot over medium-high heat. Add 4 tablespoons of oil and cook the pork in batches until browned. Take care to not burn the fond (the brown bits left in the bottom of the pot from cooking the pork). Remove the pork and set aside.
3.  Add 3 tablespoons of oil to the pan and sauté the onions, celery, and carrots for 10 to 15 minutes, or until vegetables are tender.
4.  Add the fresh peas (if using), sweet potatoes, thyme, remaining salt and pepper, and stock. Bring to a simmer, cover, and cook for 35 minutes. If using frozen peas, add now . Spoon the Cornmeal Dumpling batter on top of stew, re-cover, and cook for 10 minutes.

YIELD: 6–8 servings
PREPARATION TIME: 15–20 minutes
COOKING TIME: 1 hour 10 minutes

*Cornmeal Dumplings*

¾ CUP CORNMEAL
1¼ CUPS ALL-PURPOSE FLOUR
2½ TEASPOONS BAKING POWDER
¼ TEASPOON SALT
1 TABLESPOON CHOPPED FRESH SAGE
1 TABLESPOON CHOPPED FRESH ROSEMARY
2 TABLESPOONS BUTTER, MELTED
1 EGG, BEATEN
1 CUP BUTTERMILK

1.  Combine the cornmeal, flour, baking powder, salt, sage, and rosemary in a bowl.
2.  Stir together the butter, egg and buttermilk. Pour into the flour mixture and mix to form a batter.

YIELD: About 3½ cups (about 6 dumplings)
PREPARATION TIME: 10 minutes

## SIMPLE FROSTED CAKE

*A great cake for a simple supper. No one will guess the secret ingredient because it's simply a good, moist cake on its own. If there's any left over, cover and leave it in the pan for a breakfast treat the next day.*

6 TABLESPOONS BUTTER, SOFTENED
1 CUP SUGAR
3 EGGS
1 TEASPOON VANILLA EXTRACT
2 CUPS ALL-PURPOSE FLOUR
2 TEASPOONS BAKING POWDER
½ TEASPOON SALT
1 CUP PURCHASED ORANGE ESSENCE PRUNES, ROUGHLY CHOPPED, LIGHTLY PACKED

1. Preheat oven to 325°F. Grease a 13×9-inch pan.
2. Put the butter in a mixing bowl. On medium speed, cream together the butter and sugar with electric mixer. Add eggs, 1 at a time, allowing them to fully incorporate. Mix in vanilla. Turn down the mixer speed.
3. In a separate bowl, mix together the flour, baking powder, and salt. Slowly add the flour mixture to the butter mixture, alternately with the prunes, and blend until smooth.
4. Pour into prepared cake pan and bake for 25 minutes, or until an inserted cake tester comes out clean. Do not overbake. Cool cake in pan to room temperature, then frost in pan (Frosting recipe follows).

YIELD: 8–10 servings
PREPARATION TIME: 15–20 minutes
BAKING TIME: 25 minutes

*Frosting*

3 CUPS POWDERED SUGAR
2 TABLESPOONS BUTTER, SOFTENED
3 TABLESPOONS MILK
1 TEASPOON VANILLA EXTRACT
1 TEASPOON ALMOND EXTRACT
¼ TEASPOON SALT

1. With an electric mixer, cream together the butter with the powdered sugar for a few seconds. Pour in the milk, vanilla, and almond, and mix completely. Add salt and whip until smooth.
2. Spread on top of cooled cake in pan.

YIELD: About 1½ cups
PREPARATION TIME: 5 minutes

# Morris Island Lighthouse
FOLLY BEACH, SOUTH CAROLINA

MORRIS ISLAND LIGHTHOUSE HAS A LONG AND LIVELY HISTORY THAT IS BEING carried on to this day. In 2008, the first phases of its "extreme preservation" were completed, and the work continues.

The first lighthouse here was actually a pitch fire that was lit each evening, to guide Colonial ships along the seacoast in 1673. An octagonal tower was built in 1767, and its height was raised in 1801. It was destroyed during the Civil War, when a very bloody battle was fought in the area; the site of the lighthouse was close to the strategically important Fort Sumter.

By 1864, the Union navy's blockade was crippling the South. In a harbor near Morris Island Light, several brave and desperate Confederate soldiers folded themselves into a tiny underwater vessel—the first submarine ever used in a war. They propelled themselves toward a Union ship and pushed a torpedo into its side. But the resulting explosion also destroyed the submarine, and neither the men nor their craft were ever recovered.

After the war, the lighthouse was rebuilt, and in peacetime, keepers' families lived here too. There was pure water available nearby for drinking. Through the nineteenth and into the twentieth century, a father and his sons might catch as much fish and seafood as they needed; one boy who lived at the lighthouse recalled using a pitchfork to spear flounder in tide pools.

# CAROLINA COUNTRY GATHERING

Family is important in this culture—keeping the family together, and reuniting with extended family whenever possible. A feeling of abundance is the underlying theme of this menu. Not only did local people have plenty of seafood, but when relatives got together, they would make their own versions of pulled pork and chicken pie, too. Pecan cookies, often served with pitchers of sweet tea, are a favorite local dessert.

FRIED OYSTERS WITH RELISH MAYONNAISE

RELISH MAYONNAISE

COLE SLAW

CAROLINA RED RICE

SHRIMP AND GRITS

CAROLINA PULLED PORK

BEAUFORT CHICKEN PIE

PECAN NUT CRUNCHIES

## FRIED OYSTERS WITH RELISH MAYONNAISE

*The oysters must be fresh. Eat them as soon as they are ready.*

1 PINT SHUCKED OYSTERS
½ CUP BUTTERMILK
1 TEASPOON GARLIC POWDER
1 TEASPOON ONION POWDER
1 CUP CORNMEAL
½ CUP ALL-PURPOSE FLOUR
1 TEASPOON SALT
¼ TEASPOON FRESHLY GROUND BLACK PEPPER
VEGETABLE SHORTENING, FOR FRYING
RELISH MAYONNAISE, (RECIPE FOLLOWS) FOR SERVING

1. Drain oysters.
2. Combine the oysters, buttermilk, garlic powder, and onion powder in a bowl.
3. In a separate bowl, mix together the cornmeal, flour, salt, and pepper.
4. Preheat the oven to 200°F. Oysters may need to be cooked in batches, and they can be kept warm.
5. Heat ½ inch vegetable shortening in a heavy pot over medium-high heat to 375°F.
6. Dredge the oysters in the cornmeal mixture.

7. Place the oysters in oil a few at a time. Cook until golden brown, about 2 to 3 minutes, turning over once. Drain on a rack. Place in a warmed oven while the rest of the oysters are being cooked. Serve hot.
8. Serve with Relish Mayonnaise

YIELD: 4 servings
PREPARATION TIME: 5–10 minutes
COOKING TIME: 2–3 minutes per batch

## RELISH MAYONNAISE

¾ CUP MAYONNAISE
¼ CUP CORN RELISH (SEE RECIPE ON PAGE 258)

1. Blend ingredients well.

YIELD: 1 cup
PREPARATION TIME: less than 5 minutes

## COLE SLAW

*This dish is very colorful, and the red cabbage gives it a slight peppery flavor.*

½ POUND RED CABBAGE, THINLY SLICED
½ POUND SAVOY CABBAGE, THINLY
   SLICED
1 ONION, SLICED
1 CUP SLICED FENNEL BULB
2 SCALLIONS, SLICED
½ RED BELL PEPPER, SLICED
½ CUP CHOPPED FRESH PARSLEY
½ CUP CHOPPED FRESH BASIL
¼ CUP CIDER VINEGAR
2 TABLESPOONS SUGAR
1 CUP MAYONNAISE
2 TABLESPOONS BROWN MUSTARD
2 TEASPOONS CELERY SEED
1 TABLESPOON SALT
1 TEASPOON FRESHLY GROUND BLACK PEPPER

1. Combine the cabbages, onion, fennel, scallions, bell pepper, parsley, and basil.
2. Toss the cabbage mixture with the vinegar and sugar.
3. In a separate bowl, mix together the mayonnaise, mustard, celery seed, salt, and pepper. Combine the mayonnaise and cabbage mixtures and serve.

YIELD: 10–12 servings
PREPARATION TIME: 20–25 minutes

## CAROLINA RED RICE

*Where we grew up, this was sometimes known as "Spanish rice" but this preparation is pure Carolina.*

2 TABLESPOONS VEGETABLE OIL
4 SLICES BACON, DICED
½ ONION, DICED
4 CELERY STALKS, DICED
1 CLOVE GARLIC, MINCED
1 CUP LONG GRAIN RICE
1 (15-OUNCE) CAN DICED TOMATOES, DRAINED
1 TABLESPOON CHOPPED FRESH, OR 1 TEASPOON DRIED, MARJORAM
1 TABLESPOON CHOPPED FRESH PARSLEY
2 CUPS CHICKEN STOCK
2 TEASPOONS SALT
¼ TEASPOON FRESHLY GROUND BLACK PEPPER
2 TABLESPOONS BUTTER, SOFTENED

1. Heat oil in a heavy large pot over medium heat and sauté bacon for 3 to 4 minutes. Stir in onions, celery, and garlic. Cook for 20 minutes, or until vegetables are tender.
2. Rinse the rice 3 times, until the water runs clear.
3. Stir in rice, tomatoes, marjoram, parsley, stock, salt, and pepper. Cover, bring to a boil, and reduce to a simmer. Cook, covered, until all liquid is absorbed, about 25 to 30 minutes. Turn off heat, stir in the butter using a fork, and allow to rest, covered, for 5 minutes.

YIELD: 6 servings
PREPARATION TIME: 10–15 minutes
COOKING TIME: 45–50 minutes, with resting time

## SHRIMP AND GRITS

*Have it for breakfast, like the folks from Carolina do.*

1 CUP GRITS
2 CUPS MILK
2 CUPS CHICKEN STOCK
2 TABLESPOONS BUTTER
2 TEASPOONS SALT, DIVIDED
½ TEASPOON FRESHLY GROUND BLACK PEPPER, DIVIDED
½ POUND BACON, DICED
1 ONION, DICED
1 GREEN BELL PEPPER, DICED
2 CELERY STALKS, DICED
2 CLOVES GARLIC, MINCED
¼ TEASPOON CAYENNE PEPPER
1 BAY LEAF
1 TABLESPOON CHOPPED FRESH THYME
1 TABLESPOON ALL-PURPOSE FLOUR
2 CUPS BEEF STOCK
2 TABLESPOONS TOMATO PASTE
1 POUND SHRIMP, PEELED AND DEVEINED

1. Put the grits into a bowl of water, covering by ½ inch, and stir. Skim off any particles that float to the surface.
2. Pour the milk and chicken stock into a pot and bring to a boil. Slowly whisk in the grits. Continue to whisk until the mixture is smooth. Reduce heat to low and cook for 55 to 60 minutes. The grains should not feel hard when rubbed between 2 fingers. Mix in the butter, 1 teaspoon salt and ¼ teaspoon black pepper.
3. In a separate pan, sauté the bacon over medium heat for 4 to 6 minutes. Stir in the onion, bell pepper, celery, and garlic. Cook for 15 to 20 minutes, or until vegetables are tender. Stir in the cayenne, bay leaf, thyme, and flour. Cook for 2 minutes.
4. Pour in the beef stock and tomato paste. Simmer for 5 minutes. Stir in the shrimp. Cook until shrimp are opaque, about 4 to 5 minutes. Season with remaining salt and pepper.
5. Serve over the grits.

YIELD: 4 servings
PREPARATION TIME: 15–20 minutes
COOKING TIME: 55–60 minutes for the grits, and 20–25 minutes for the shrimp

## CAROLINA PULLED PORK

*There are as many recipes for pulled pork as there are people who love barbecue—so make any changes you want to make it your own. This recipe was developed for people who do not have a large smoker. Your kettle grill will work just fine. Serve on soft rolls or buns.*

1 CUP DRY RUB (RECIPE FOLLOWS)
6 POUNDS PORK SHOULDER
8 POUNDS HARDWOOD CHARCOAL
6 CUPS WOOD CHIPS, SOAKED IN WATER FOR 30–40 MINUTES
3 CUPS MOP (RECIPE FOLLOWS)
2 CUPS MUSTARD SAUCE (RECIPE FOLLOWS)
SOFT ROLLS OR BUNS FOR SERVING
TOP WITH COLE SLAW, FOR SERVING (SEE RECIPE ON PAGE 97)

1. Put on a pair of latex gloves. Rub the Dry Rub into the pork. Place pork on a rack and the rack on a sheet tray in the refrigerator. Cover lightly with plastic wrap. Refrigerate overnight.
2. Start the grill.
3. When the coals are hot, pile them to one side of the grill. Place a disposable aluminum bread pan next to the coals. Fill with water. This will help protect the meat from getting too much direct heat. If your rack has a hinged top for coal replenishment, position the opening over coals.
4. Place the pork opposite the coals. Put 1 cup of the wood chips on coals, and cover.
5. Position the lid vent over the pork. This will help draft the smoke over the pork.
6. Open the bottom vent all the way and the top vent ¼ or less. If you have a thermometer on or in the grill, it should read around 225°F. Smoke the pork for at least 6 to 7 hours, replenishing the water, coals, and wood chips as needed. Start new coal in a chimney starter. Apply Mop liberally every 30 minutes.
7. Check the internal temperature of the pork. When ready, it will read 165°F. Remove from grill and place, covered with foil, on a plate. When cool enough to handle, separate and shred the meat using 2 forks.
8. Mix in Mustard Sauce. Serve on buns topped with Cole Slaw.

YIELD: 10–12 servings
PREPARATION TIME: Less than 5 minutes to rub pork, and 10–15 minutes to prepare to
  serve.
REFRIGERATION TIME: Overnight
SMOKING TIME: 6–7 hours

*Dry Rub*

½ CUP BROWN SUGAR
½ CUP PAPRIKA
1 TABLESPOON GARLIC POWDER
1 TABLESPOON GROUND FENNEL SEED
1 TABLESPOON DRIED OREGANO
1 TABLESPOON FRESHLY GROUND BLACK PEPPER
¼ CUP SALT

1. Combine all the ingredients.

YIELD: 1½ cups

*Mop*

1 CUP WATER
1½ CUPS CIDER VINEGAR
3 TABLESPOONS WORCESTERSHIRE SAUCE
2 TABLESPOONS FRESHLY GROUND BLACK PEPPER
1 TABLESPOON SALT
½ CUP VEGETABLE OIL

1. Combine all the ingredients.

YIELD: 3 cups

*Mustard Sauce*

1 CUP CIDER VINEGAR
6 TABLESPOONS BROWN MUSTARD
¼ CUP HONEY
5 TEASPOONS WORCESTERSHIRE SAUCE
2 TEASPOONS TABASCO SAUCE
¼ CUP VEGETABLE OIL
2 TEASPOONS SALT

1. Mix all the ingredients together.

YIELD: About 2 cups

# BEAUFORT CHICKEN PIE

*A crispy top and a succulent center.*

8 CHICKEN THIGHS, BONELESS AND SKINLESS
3 ½ TEASPOONS SALT, DIVIDED
¼ TEASPOON PLUS ⅛ TEASPOON FRESHLY GROUND BLACK PEPPER, DIVIDED
5 TABLESPOONS VEGETABLE OIL, DIVIDED
2 ONIONS, DICED
2 CELERY STALKS, DICED
1 BELL PEPPER, DICED
1 CUP CORN KERNELS (ABOUT 2 EARS)
½ CUP CHICKEN STOCK
½ CUP WHITE WINE
¼ TEASPOON PLUS ⅛ TEASPOON GROUND MACE
1 BAY LEAF
6 CUPS COOKED RICE
2 EGGS, SLIGHTLY BEATEN
1 EGG
1 TEASPOON WATER

1. Cut the chicken into 1-inch pieces. Season with 1 teaspoon salt and ⅛ teaspoon pepper.
2. Heat 3 tablespoons of oil in a large saucepan. Cook the chicken, in batches, until golden brown. Remove and set aside.
3. Preheat the oven to 400°F.
4. Add an additional 2 tablespoons of oil to the saucepan and sauté the onions, celery, and bell pepper for 10 to 15 minutes. Stir in the corn and cook for an additional 5 minutes. Add the reserved chicken, stock, wine, ¼ teaspoon mace, bay leaf, 1 teaspoon salt, and ⅛ teaspoon pepper. Simmer for 5 minutes.
5. In a separate bowl, mix together the rice, 2 eggs, 1½ teaspoons salt, ⅛ teaspoon pepper, and ⅛ teaspoon mace. Layer half of the rice in the bottom of a casserole dish, spoon in the chicken, and top with remaining rice.
6. Bake in the oven for 30 minutes.
7. Mix remaining egg with water to make a wash. Brush top of rice with egg wash and place under the broiler for 5 to 6 minutes. Rotate dish to get even browning.

YIELD: 6–8 servings
PREPARATION TIME: 15–20 minutes
COOKING TIME: 60–70 minutes, not including rice

# PECAN NUT CRUNCHIES

*Ann's daughters loved eating these cookies and helped name them.*

1 ½ CUPS ALL-PURPOSE FLOUR
½ TEASPOON BAKING SODA
½ TEASPOON SALT
8 TABLESPOONS BUTTER, SOFTENED
½ CUP DARK BROWN SUGAR
½ CUP SUGAR

1 EGG, BEATEN
1 TEASPOON VANILLA EXTRACT
1 CUP PECAN PIECES
½ CUP RAISINS

1. Preheat the oven to 325°F.
2. Blend together the flour, baking soda, and salt.
3. Cream the butter in a mixer. Add both sugars, scraping down the sides as the mixer runs. Add egg and vanilla, and blend.
4. Slowly add the flour to the butter–sugar mixture.
5. Stir in the pecans and raisins. Drop teaspoonfuls of the batter onto a parchment-covered baking sheet. Bake for 15 minutes.

YIELD: 30–36 cookies
PREPARATION TIME: 15 minutes
COOKING TIME: 15 minutes per batch

# Saint Simons Lighthouse

SAINT SIMONS, GEORGIA

IMPORTED FROM MASSACHUSETTS, THE BUILDER OF THE FIRST LIGHTHOUSE on this spot became its keeper for twenty-seven years after it was lit in 1810. He built the lighthouse of a material called "tabby"—a type of cement made with sand, oyster shells, lime, and water. Despite its humble construction, the lighthouse endured until the Civil War, when, like many others, it was destroyed; this time by Confederate soldiers seeking to confuse Yankee ships off the coast.

After the war, rebuilding was tough. Many workers became sick and died, and even the contractor himself succumbed to an unnamed disease. The new St. Simons Lighthouse was finally completed and lit in 1872. But by 1880, St. Simons Light was said to be haunted, after a lighthouse keeper was shot and killed by his assistant. Some say the keeper haunts it, and some say it's the young assailant. But not during the daytime. Then it's safe to come visit the keeper's house, which has been restored and turned into a Victorian era museum.

# LATE SUMMER LUNCH

Here's a late summer menu to make and enjoy while reflecting on all the years St. Simons Lighthouse has spent guarding the Georgia coastline. This meal has a wealth of traditional dishes and local ingredients from the past two hundred years: a seafood boil, peanuts, black-eyed peas, sweet Vidalia onions, and succulent peaches for a simple but glorious finish.

PEANUT SOUP
BAKED VIDALIA ONIONS
BLACK-EYED PEAS AND BACON
LOW COUNTRY BOIL
MY FRIEND CATHY'S EASY PEACH COBBLER

## PEANUT SOUP
*A subtle peanut flavor that goes well with the chicken.*

2 TABLESPOONS BUTTER
1 ONION, DICED
2 CELERY STALKS, DICED
3 CHICKEN THIGHS, BONELESS AND SKINLESS
¼ CUP UNSALTED SMOOTH PEANUT BUTTER
4 CUPS CHICKEN STOCK
2 BAY LEAVES
¼ TEASPOON CAYENNE PEPPER
1 TEASPOON SALT
¼ TEASPOON FRESHLY GROUND BLACK PEPPER

1. Melt the butter in a saucepan. When the butter has stopped foaming, sauté the onions, celery, and chicken. Cook for 15 minutes, or until chicken is cooked through.
2. Stir in the peanut butter, stock, bay leaves, cayenne, salt, and pepper.
3. Cook for 30 to 35 minutes. Remove chicken and bay leaves. Discard bay leaves.
4. Dice or shred chicken to smallish pieces and return to pot.

YIELD: 4–6 servings
PREPARATION TIME: 10–15 minutes
COOKING TIME: 45–50 minutes

## BAKED VIDALIA ONIONS
*Georgia's own sweet onions, with a spark of additional flavors.*

2 LARGE VIDALIA OR OTHER SWEET ONIONS, PEELED AND HALVED
2 TABLESPOONS BUTTER
8 TEASPOONS WORCESTERSHIRE SAUCE

1 TEASPOON SALT
¼ TEASPOON FRESHLY GROUND BLACK PEPPER

1. Preheat the oven to 350°F.
2. Cut 4 pieces of aluminum foil, each 12 inches square. Center the onion halves on the foil.
3. Dot each onion with equal amounts of the butter, Worcestershire sauce, salt, and pepper.
4. Wrap onions in foil, and bake for 55 to 60 minutes.

YIELD: 4 servings
PREPARATION TIME: 10 minutes
COOKING TIME: 55–60 minutes

## BLACK-EYED PEAS AND BACON

*Use good-quality bacon. It will make a big difference.*

2 TABLESPOONS VEGETABLE OIL
1 POUND BLACK-EYED PEAS, SOAKED OVER-
    NIGHT IN WATER UNDER REFRIGERATION
½ POUND BACON, DICED
1 ONION, DICED
2 CLOVES GARLIC, MINCED
1 RED BELL PEPPER, DICED
2 CUPS CHICKEN STOCK
½ CUP MOLASSES
1 TABLESPOON SALT
1 TEASPOON FRESHLY GROUND BLACK PEPPER

1. Preheat the oven to 350°F.
2. Heat a large pot over medium heat. Add the oil and sauté the bacon, onion, garlic, and pepper for 15 minutes, or until the vegetables are tender.
3. Add the black-eyed peas, stock, molasses, salt, and pepper. Bring to a boil.
4. Transfer to an ovenproof dish and bake, covered, for 2–2½ hours.

YIELD: 8 servings
PREPARATION TIME: 10–15 minutes
SOAKING TIME: Overnight
COOKING TIME: 2½–3 hours

## LOW COUNTRY BOIL

*Every region has their own version of this one-pot meal.*

CRAB BOIL (FOLLOW DIRECTIONS ON PACKAGE)
3 POUNDS NEW POTATOES
3 POUNDS SMOKED KIELBASA SAUSAGE
8 EARS CORN, CUT IN HALF
4 POUNDS SHRIMP, UNPEELED
1½ CUPS BUTTER, MELTED FOR SERVING

1. Put 5 quarts of water, the crab boil, and the potatoes in a large pot. Cover and bring to a boil.
2. Boil for 5 minutes, and add the sausage and corn. Cook for 5 minutes more.
3. Add the shrimp and cook for 3 to 4 minutes.
4. Drain and serve with butter.

YIELD: 6–8 servings
PREPARATION TIME: 5–10 minutes
COOKING TIME: 15 minutes, not including bringing the water to a boil

## MY FRIEND CATHY'S EASY PEACH COBBLER

*This is quick, easy, and good. Great with whipped cream.*

4 TABLESPOONS BUTTER, MELTED
1 CUP SUGAR
1 CUP ALL-PURPOSE FLOUR
1½ TEASPOONS BAKING POWDER
¼ TEASPOON SALT
1 CUP MILK
1 (15-OUNCE) CAN SLICED PEACHES IN LIGHT SYRUP

1. Preheat the oven to 400°F.
2. Pour the melted butter into a baking dish.
3. In a bowl, mix the sugar, flour, baking powder and salt together. Blend in the milk. The mixture will appear lumpy. Pour the mixture into the baking dish. Do not stir.
4. Add the fruit and its juice to the dish, all at once. Do not stir.
5. Bake for 30 minutes, or until golden brown. The cobbler will rise up the sides.

YIELD: 4–6 servings
PREPARATION TIME: 5–10 minutes
COOKING TIME: 30 minutes

# St. John's Light
MAYPORT, FLORIDA

ST. JOHN'S IS THE YOUNGEST LIGHTHOUSE IN OUR GROUP, AND ONE OF THE most unusual in design. It was constructed in 1954, and now uses solar power for its beacon, which sits on the flat roof of this Art Deco-style square tower. St. John's Light Station replaced the St. John's Lightship that had been anchored offshore, which in turn replaced the St. John's River Lighthouse, a tower that still stands a couple of miles away. In 1967, the Coast Guard turned over this light to the U.S. Navy; it now stands inside a naval base in Mayport, Florida.

This area also has a history of conflict—albeit one more recent than the Civil War, which ruined so many other lighthouses along the southern coastline of the United States. In 1942, German spies were landed on the Florida coastline by a German U-boat. Their mission was to sabotage factories supplying the United States' war effort, but the men were apprehended before they could carry out their mission. One version of this story even has the Germans surrendering to a puzzled local policeman before he was aware of their landing.

More welcome immigrants to this part of Florida in earlier centuries include the Huguenots, who were succeeded by centuries of Spaniards and a wave of Menorcans, who remain proud of their Mediterranean heritage to this day. All fished for local catches; grouper is the most typical catch here.

# DINNER FOR COMPANY

Menorcans, who hail from an island in the Mediterranean, have added their food culture to the Southeast's native foods. This menu is a melding of several styles, true to this area.

*Segmenting citrus and removing the pith is called supreming.*

HEARTS OF PALM SALAD WITH GRAPEFRUIT VINAIGRETTE
SPICY SNAP BEANS WITH BUTTER, GARLIC, AND
    JALAPEÑO PEPPER
ROASTED POTATOES WITH CAPERS AND FETA
ROASTED GROUPER WITH VEGETABLE MEDLEY
KEY LIME PIE

## HEARTS OF PALM SALAD WITH GRAPEFRUIT VINAIGRETTE

*A retro classic, hearts of palm makes a nice comeback in this salad.*

2 CANS HEARTS OF PALM, SLICED INTO ¼-INCH DISCS
2 GRAPEFRUITS, SEGMENTED AND PITH REMOVED
1 SMALL RED ONION, SLICED THIN (ABOUT ½ CUP)
1 AVOCADO, SKINNED, PITTED, AND SLICED
1 RIPE TOMATO, SLICED
1 TEASPOON SALT
½ TEASPOON FRESHLY GROUND BLACK PEPPER
2 TABLESPOONS GRAPEFRUIT JUICE
6 TABLESPOONS EXTRA VIRGIN OLIVE OIL

1. Arrange the hearts of palm, grapefruit, onion, avocado, and tomato on a platter.
2. Season with the salt and pepper. Blend together the grapefruit juice and olive oil. Pour over salad.

YIELD: 6 servings
PREPARATION TIME: 15–20 minutes

## SPICY SNAP BEANS WITH BUTTER, GARLIC, AND JALAPEÑO PEPPER

*This can be a side dish for many different types of fish.*

1 ½ TEASPOONS SALT, DIVIDED
1 POUND SNAP BEANS
3 TABLESPOONS BUTTER
1 TABLESPOON VEGETABLE OIL
3 CLOVES GARLIC, SLICED
1 JALAPEÑO PEPPER, SEEDED AND DICED
¼ TEASPOON FRESHLY GROUND BLACK PEPPER

1. Remove the stem ends from the beans.
2. Bring a pot of water to a boil. Add 1 teaspoon of salt and the beans, and cook for 3 to 4 minutes. Drain and set aside.
3. Heat a pan on medium heat. Add the butter and oil. When the butter stops foaming, add the garlic and jalapeño. Sauté for 1 to 2 minutes.
4. Toss in the green beans and sauté for 6 to 8 minutes. Season with remaining salt and pepper.

**Note:** Wear latex gloves when cutting jalapeño peppers to prevent burning your fingers and spreading the heat to other foods.

YIELD: 4 servings
PREPARATION TIME: 10 minutes
COOKING TIME: 15 minutes

## ROASTED POTATOES WITH CAPERS AND FETA

*The Menorcan influence is obvious in this dish.*

4 RUSSET POTATOES
5 TABLESPOONS VEGETABLE OIL, DIVIDED
3 ONIONS, SLICED
¼ CUP CAPERS
½ CUP FETA CHEESE
¼ CUP EXTRA VIRGIN OLIVE OIL
1 ½ TEASPOONS SALT, DIVIDED
¼ TEASPOON FRESHLY GROUND BLACK PEPPER

1. Preheat the oven to 400°F.
2. Rub the potatoes with 2 tablespoons of oil. Bake until easily pierced with a fork, about 60 to 70 minutes.
3. While the potatoes are baking, heat a pan over medium-low heat. Add remaining oil. Stir in the onions and 1 teaspoon salt. Cook the onions until they are a golden brown, about 50 to 60 minutes. Stir occasionally.

4. Remove the potatoes from the oven and roughly chop into 1-inch pieces. Place in a metal or glass bowl and mix with the onions, capers, feta cheese, olive oil, remaining salt, and pepper.

YIELD: 4–6 servings
PREPARATION TIME: 5–10 minutes
BAKING TIME: 60–70 minutes

## ROASTED GROUPER WITH VEGETABLE MEDLEY
*Mediterranean flavors for a Florida fish.*

4 TABLESPOONS VEGETABLE OIL (PLUS 2 TABLESPOONS, OPTIONAL)
1 MEDIUM EGGPLANT, CUT INTO ½-INCH CUBES
3 CLOVES GARLIC, MINCED
1 MEDIUM RED ONION, DICED
1 SMALL FENNEL BULB, CHOPPED
1 RED BELL PEPPER, SEEDED AND DICED
1 YELLOW SQUASH, DICED
1 ZUCCHINI, DICED

4 PLUM TOMATOES, CHOPPED
2 TABLESPOONS CAPERS
5 ANCHOVY FILLETS, MASHED
1 TABLESPOON RED WINE VINEGAR
½ CUP CHOPPED FRESH PARSLEY
1 TABLESPOON FRESH OREGANO
¼ CUP PINE NUTS, TOASTED
6 GROUPER FILLETS (ABOUT 6 OUNCES EACH)
2½ TEASPOONS SALT, DIVIDED
½ TEASPOON FRESHLY GROUND BLACK PEPPER, DIVIDED

1. Preheat the oven to 400°F.
2. Heat the oil in a large sauté pan over high heat. Sauté the eggplant until it begins to brown, about 5 to 10 minutes (Eggplant soaks up oil quickly, so more oil may need to be added. If the pan needs more oil, add 2 tablespoons.) Reduce heat to medium-high and add garlic, onions, fennel, and ½ teaspoon of salt. Cook 10-15 minutes or until vegetables are tender.
3. Stir in the bell pepper, squash, zucchini, and tomatoes. Sauté for 10 minutes. Stir in the capers, anchovies, vinegar, parsley, oregano and pine nuts. Continue cooking for 5 minutes. Season with 1 teaspoon salt and ¼ teaspoon pepper.
4. Season the grouper with remaining salt and pepper. Lay fillets on top of the vegetables and put pan in the oven. Bake for 15-20 minutes.

YIELD: 6 servings
PREPARATION TIME: 15–20 minutes
COOKING TIME: 30–35 minutes on the stovetop, and 15–20 minutes in the oven

## KEY LIME PIE
*Tangy and creamy, the way it should be.*

1 (14-OUNCE) CAN SWEETENED CONDENSED MILK
4 EGG YOLKS
½ CUP KEY LIME JUICE
1 (9-INCH) GRAHAM CRACKER PIE CRUST (RECIPE FOLLOWS)

1. Preheat the oven to 350°F. Adjust the rack to the middle of the oven.
2. Blend together condensed milk, egg yolks, and lime juice.
3. Fold thickened mixture into the graham cracker pie crust and bake for 15 minutes. The center will be set and will move like gelatin.
4. Allow pie to cool, then refrigerate for at least 1 hour before serving.

YIELD: 6 servings
PREPARATION TIME: 5 minutes
COOKING TIME: 15 minutes

*Graham Cracker Pie Crust*

1 ½ CUPS FINELY CRUSHED GRAHAM CRACKERS
4 TABLESPOONS BUTTER, MELTED

1. Combine ingredients.
2. Press into a 9-inch pie plate. Refrigerate for at least 30 minutes.

YIELD: 1 (9-inch) pie crust
PREPARATION TIME: 10 minutes
REFRIGERATION TIME: 30 minutes

# PUERTO RICO AND THE U.S. VIRGIN ISLANDS REGION

*P*irates, traders, and settlers from a dozen nations in Europe and Africa initially defined the population of the Virgin Islands and Puerto Rico—following the South American Indians who had arrived centuries before.

The name of Puerto Rico, a series of islands in the Caribbean, means "rich port" in Spanish. The Commonwealth of Puerto Rico has a rich heritage, originating with the Taino Indians, who were followed by waves of Spanish and African settlers.

Further south, the Virgin Islands were probably named in tribute to the Virgin Mary, an important religious figure in the lives of Christopher Columbus and the Spanish traders who settled there after Columbus "discovered" the West Indies. Following the Caribe Indians, the Spanish, Danes, Dutch, French, and English also colonized the Virgin Islands. When slavery was finally abolished in the mid-1800s, the European plantation owners brought over workers from other continents: people from India, for instance, who contributed their curries to the local food culture.

Lighthouses were a late addition to this region. National security in the early twentieth century seems to have been their impetus along with safety for the shipping trade. For the same reason, many lighthouses became obsolete when radar and other modern technologies became the norm. Although some lighthouses in this region have been restored in the past few years, others are among the saddest and most neglected of America's noble beacons.

A hundred years ago, lighthouse keepers living in a subtropical climate could depend on nature to deliver produce and fresh fish year-round. The few native fruits and squashes formed a major component of common cuisine, as well as lobster, conch, red snapper, cod and other seafood, some chicken, and goat for special occasions. Early on, the people of the islands used a bit of sugar cane for sweetening, but much of it was cooked into molasses and exported to the North for the production of rum.

These territories became part of the United States at the turn of the twentieth century. In the early- to mid-1900s, many Americans emigrated from the mainland to these desirable subtropical islands. Much of their cooking has remained essentially static, which gives this cuisine a retro feel today.

# Faro Los Morrillos de Cabo Rojo

MORRILLOS PENINSULA, PUERTO RICO

THIS LIGHTHOUSE, WHICH DATES FROM 1882, LOOKS OUT OVER THE MONA Passage, a dramatic strait between the Atlantic Ocean and the Caribbean Sea. It was built by the Spanish, who controlled Puerto Rico at that time. It was restored once, in 1986, but after that the lighthouse was not well-maintained, and deteriorated rapidly and quite seriously for the next 15 years.

In 2002, Los Morrillos got a second chance at life when the city of Cabo Rojo decided to spend millions of dollars renovating the lighthouse, which is now inside the Cabo Rojo National Wildlife Refuge, a well-planned national park. The lighthouse renovation was completed in 2004, and the park now also contains miles of walkways for natural observation and photography. It is a sanctuary for migratory and native birds.

Puerto Rican-grown foods are the basis of most people's daily meals, but in this cuisine they are often overlaid by recipes from the mainland. Meat is a must on feast days, but Spanish-oriented side dishes and classic adobo spicing are also common at the table. And Puerto Ricans definitely have a sweet tooth, which is often incorporated into meals in more than one course.

# Menu para el Día de Acción de Gracias (Thanksgiving Menu)

It seems appropriate to be grateful for Los Morrillos' renovation. And, as part of the United States of America, Puerto Rico also celebrates Thanksgiving Day—though with its own take on the traditional turkey dinner. For instance, this dressing for the turkey is meat-based, and it is seasoned with adobo, a must-have seasoning for many Puerto Rican dishes.

Cocktel de Fruta Fresca (Fresh Fruit Cocktail)

Ensalada Fresca (Green Salad)

Arroz con Gandules (Rice and Pigeon Peas)

Batata Mameya Majada (Mashed Sweet Potatoes with Garlic)

Pavo Relleno al Horno (Roasted Turkey with Puerto Rican Beef Dressing)

Picadillo Para Relleno (Puerto Rican Beef Dressing)

Adobo

Dulce de Lechoza con Queso Blanco (Sweet Papaya with White Goat Cheese)

## COCKTEL DE FRUTA FRESCA (FRESH FRUIT COCKTAIL)

*This is a great way to start a meal—fresh fruit drinks to stimulate the appetite.*

24–36 OUNCES FRESH FRUIT JUICE (BANANA, PAPAYA, GUAVA, OR PINEAPPLE)

1. Serve chilled in 6-ounce wine glasses for a more festive holiday presentation.

YIELD: 4–6 servings
PREPARATION TIME: Less than 5 minutes

## ENSALADA FRESCA (GREEN SALAD)

*In this recipe, a green salad literally means a collection of wonderful fresh green vegetables. If you want something a little different than oil and vinegar, try the Thousand Island Dressing (recipe follows).*

½ POUND HARICOTS VERTS (GREEN BEANS) STEM ENDS REMOVED
2 AVOCADOS
4 CUPS CHOPPED ROMAINE LETTUCE
2 TABLESPOONS WHITE WINE VINEGAR
6 TABLESPOONS EXTRA VIRGIN OLIVE OIL
1½ TEASPOONS SALT, DIVIDED
¼ TEASPOON FRESHLY GROUND BLACK PEPPER

1. Bring a pot of water to a boil. Add 1 teaspoon salt and the haricots verts, and cook for 2 to 3 minutes. Remove and immediately plunge into ice cold water.

2. Cut the avocados in half lengthwise. Remove the pit, peel, and cube.
3. Place haricots verts, romaine, and avocados in a bowl.
4. Mix together the vinegar, olive oil, the remaining salt, and pepper. Pour over the salad and toss.

YIELD: 4–6 servings
PREPARATION TIME: 5 minutes

*Thousand Island Dressing*

¼ CUP KETCHUP
¼ CUP MAYONNAISE
¼ CUP SWEET PICKLE RELISH
⅛ TEASPOON SALT
PINCH OF FRESHLY GROUND BLACK PEPPER

1. Combine all the ingredients in a bowl and mix.

YIELD: About ¾ cup
PREPARATION TIME: Less than 5 minutes

## ARROZ CON GANDULES (RICE AND PIGEON PEAS)

*Pigeon peas are found in many dishes in Puerto Rico. Alcaparrado and sofrito can be found in the Latin American section of the grocery store.*

1½ POUNDS OF PORK, DICED
1 TABLESPOON ADOBO (SEE RECIPE ON PAGE 120)
4 TABLESPOONS VEGETABLE OIL
1 ONION, DICED
1 GREEN BELL PEPPER, DICED
2 CLOVES GARLIC, DICED
½ CUP ALCAPARRADO (WITH PITTED OLIVES)
½ CUP SOFRITO
¼ POUND HAM, DICED
½ CUP DICED TOMATOES
2 CUPS RICE
2 (15-OUNCE) CANS PIGEON PEAS, DRAINED AND RINSED
¼ CUP CHOPPED FRESH CILANTRO
1 TEASPOON SALT
¼ TEASPOON FRESHLY GROUND BLACK PEPPER

1. Bring 5 cups of water to a boil, add the pork and adobo. Cook for 20 minutes. Reserve pork and liquid. Add water to reserved liquid to yield 5 cups.
2. Heat a pot over medium heat. Add the oil. Cook the pork, onions, bell pepper, and garlic for 10 minutes, or until vegetables are tender, stirring occasionally.
3. Mix in the alcaparrado, sofrito, ham, tomatoes, and rice. Pour in reserved liquid and bring to a boil. Reduce to a simmer and cook for 20 minutes until water is absorbed.
4. With a fork, stir in the peas, cilantro, salt, and pepper. Cover and allow to rest for 5 minutes.

YIELD: 6 servings
PREPARATION TIME: 15–20 minutes
COOKING TIME: 50–60 minutes

## BATATA MAMEYA MAJADA (MASHED SWEET POTATOES WITH GARLIC)

*Garlic is an interesting change from mainland American recipes, which normally pair something sweet with sweet potatoes. Batatas can be found in the Latin American section of the grocery store.*

2 POUNDS BATATAS OR SWEET POTATOES
2 CLOVES GARLIC, MINCED
5 TABLESPOONS BUTTER, SOFTENED
2 TEASPOONS SALT, DIVIDED
¼ TEASPOON FRESHLY GROUND BLACK PEPPER

1. Peel the batatas and cut into equal-sized, about 1½-inch cubes.
2. Put the batatas into a pot of water with 1 teaspoon of salt. Bring to a boil and cook until easily pierced with a fork.
3. Put the batatas in bowl, add the garlic and butter, and mash using a hand masher. Season with remaining salt and pepper.

YIELD: 4-6 servings
PREPARATION TIME: 10 minutes
COOKING TIME: 45–50 minutes

## PAVO RELLENO AL HORNO (ROASTED TURKEY WITH PUERTO RICAN BEEF DRESSING)

*An American classic roast turkey with a Spanish-influenced meat dressing—what richness! Sofrito can be found in the Latin American section of the grocery store.*

1 TURKEY (12-14 POUNDS)
2½ GALLONS PLUS 2 CUPS WATER, DIVIDED
4 CUPS KOSHER SALT
2 CUPS SUGAR
2 TABLESPOONS ADOBO (SEE RECIPE ON PAGE 120)
2 ONIONS, CHOPPED
1 HEAD OF GARLIC, SMASHED
1 CUP SOFRITO
PUERTO RICAN BEEF DRESSING, FOR SERVING (RECIPE FOLLOWS)

1. Place the turkey in a container large enough for it to be submerged in water. You can use a large plastic bucket from your hardware store. Be sure to scrub it well beforehand.
2. Mix together 2 ½ gallons water, salt, and sugar. Pour over the turkey. Make sure the turkey is completely submerged. If the turkey is not completely submerged, add more water. Follow the ratio of 2 cups of salt and 1 cup of sugar per gallon of water. Refrigerate the turkey overnight.
3. Remove the turkey from the brine and dry with paper towels.

4. Preheat the oven to 325°F.
5. Season the turkey with adobo inside and out. Fill the cavity with the onions, garlic and sofrito.
6. Place the turkey, breast side down, in a roasting pan. A v-shaped rack works best. Otherwise, set the turkey on a rack and use balls of aluminum foil to keep turkey centered. Add remaining water.
7. Roast for 1½ to 2 hours; basting every 20 to 30 minutes. Remove the turkey from the oven and turn over using paper towels. Continue to cook until a thermometer reads 170°F when inserted into the thigh. If the breast is not browned, increase temperature to 450°F and roast for an additional 10 minutes.
8. Remove the turkey from the oven and place on a carving platter. Cover loosely with foil, and let rest for 20 minutes.
9. Carve and serve with Puerto Rican Beef Dressing.

YIELD: 12 servings
REFRIGERATION TIME: Overnight
PREPARATION TIME: 15–20 minutes
ROASTING TIME: 2–2½ hours


*Puerto Rican Beef Dressing*

4 CUPS PICADILLO PARA RELLENO (RECIPE FOLLOWS)
1 CUP TOASTED ALMONDS
1 CUP CUBED BREAD
1 CUP DRIPPING FROM TURKEY

1. Combine all the ingredients in a pan, over medium heat. Cook for 5 to 10 minutes, or until hot.

YIELD: 12 servings
PREPARATION TIME: 5 minutes
COOKING TIME: 5–10 minutes


## PICADILLO PARA RELLENO (PUERTO RICAN BEEF DRESSING)
*This meat dressing is used as a filling for a number of Puerto Rican dishes. Recaito can be found in the Latin American section of the grocery store.*

2 TABLESPOONS VEGETABLE OIL
1½ POUNDS GROUND CHUCK
4 OUNCES HAM, CHOPPED FINE
1 ONION, DICED
1 RED BELL PEPPER, DICED
½ CUP DICED TOMATOES
¼ CUP TOMATO SAUCE
½ CUP WATER
¼ CUP CHOPPED MANZANILLA OLIVES
1 TABLESPOON CAPERS
¼ CUP RAISINS

3 TABLESPOONS RECAITO
1¼ TEASPOONS SALT
¼ TEASPOON FRESHLY GROUND BLACK PEPPER

1. Heat a pan over medium heat. Add oil and cook ground chuck and ham for 10 minutes, or until brown, stirring occasionally
2. Mix in onions and bell pepper and continue to cook for 15 minutes, or until vegetables are tender, stirring occasionally.
3. Stir in tomatoes, tomato sauce, water, olives, capers, raisins, recaito, salt, and pepper. Cover and simmer for 25 to 30 minutes, stirring occasionally. If it becomes too dry, add ¼ cup water.

YIELD: 4 cups
PREPARATION TIME: 10–15 minutes
COOKING TIME: 50–60 minutes


## ADOBO

*You can buy it at the store, but most brands have MSG. For a healthier version, make it yourself.*

1 MEASURE EACH OF GARLIC POWDER, ONION POWDER, AND DRIED OREGANO
½ MEASURE EACH OF SALT AND FRESHLY GROUND BLACK PEPPER

1. Stir ingredients together and save in a plastic container with lid. This is great for just about anything
2. Sprinkle on all meats, fish, even omelets and eggs.


## DULCE DE LECHOZA CON QUESO BLANCO (SWEET PAPAYA WITH WHITE GOAT CHEESE)

1 UNRIPENED Meradol RED PAPAYA (ABOUT 3 POUNDS)
2 CUPS WATER
2 CUPS SUGAR
1 CINNAMON STICK
QUESO BLANCO FOR SERVING

1. Peel papaya and cut in half. Remove seeds and slice papaya into ¼-inch slices. Cut in half crosswise.
2. Put papaya into a pot and cover with water. Simmer for 10 minutes.
3. Remove papaya from water. Discard water. Pour water and sugar into pot. Bring to a boil, then reduce to a simmer. Return papaya to the pot and add cinnamon stick. Simmer, stirring frequently, for 35 to 40 minutes until mixture has reduced and papaya is shiny. Remove papaya and continue to reduce liquid to a syrupy consistency. Remove from heat.
4. Add papaya back to liquid. Cool and refrigerate overnight.
5. Serve papaya with queso blanco crumbled on top. Pour papaya syrup over all.

YIELD: 4–5 cups
PREPARATION TIME: 10–15 minutes
COOKING TIME: 45 minutes

# Faro de Arecibo

PORT ARECIBO, PUERTO RICO

COMPLETED IN 1898, THIS IS THE LAST LIGHTHOUSE CONSTRUCTED BY THE Spanish while they governed Puerto Rico. It is on the north coast, overlooking shipping lanes in the Atlantic Ocean from a high, rocky perch.

Restored in 2002, Faro de Arecibo is now part of a cultural "theme park," the Arecibo Lighthouse & Historical Park, where displays illustrate Puerto Rico's cultural history from the Spanish "conquest" in 1493 to the beginning of the Spanish-American War in 1898.

Recipes from this area are a compilation of the region's Spanish heritage with contributions from twentieth-century mainland America. But on holidays, people often revert to their earliest memories; in this case, foods that reflect the strong Spanish culture that ruled the island, melded with native-grown foods for four hundred years. Beans and salt cod are Spanish-based staples, as are the islands' own fresh fruits, which are often made into sweet juice drinks.

# Menú de Cuaresma (Semana Santa) (Holy Week Menu)

During Holy Week before Easter, people are encouraged to think more about spiritual matters and to eat lightly. Rather than eat meat, they prepare meals with fish, eggs, and dairy.

Bebida Champola de Guayaba (Creamy Guava Drink)

Caldo Santo (Blessed Broth)

Frijoles y Calabaza (Beans with Squash)

Bacalao a la Vizcaína (Salt Cod Stew)

Flan de Queso

## BEBIDA CHAMPOLA DE GUAYABA (CREAMY GUAVA DRINK)

*A refreshing drink that can be tailored to your sweet tooth.*

2 (12-ounce) cans evaporated milk
24 ounces guava nectar
½ cup sugar
1 teaspoon vanilla extract
2 cups ice

1. Pour evaporated milk, guava nectar, sugar, and vanilla into blender. Blend for 15 to 30 seconds.
2. Add ice and blend until ice is mostly dissolved.
3. If at the beach simply pour over crushed ice.

YIELD: 4–6 servings
PREPARATION TIME: 5 minutes

## CALDO SANTO (BLESSED BROTH)

*This can be a one-pot meal, or it can be served in small portions at the start of the meal. Annatto seeds, recaito, alcaparrado, cassava, yautio, batata, and name can be found in the Latin American section of a grocery store.*

3 cups coconut milk
2 tablespoons annatto seeds
¼ cup recaito
2 cups water
¼ cup alcaparrado
1 small cassava, diced (about ½ cup)
1 small yautio (taro root), diced (about ½ cup)

1 small batata (sweet potato), diced (about ½ cup)
1 small name, diced (about ½ cup)
½ pound prepared salt cod, shredded (recipe follows)
½ pound shrimp, peeled and deveined
½ pound red snapper, skinned and cubed

1 TEASPOON SALT
¼ TEASPOON FRESHLY GROUND
  BLACK PEPPER

¼ CUP FRESH CILANTRO
2 TABLESPOONS CAPERS

1. Pour the coconut milk into a pot. Stir in the annatto seeds and bring to a simmer. Cook for 5 minutes, or until the milk achieves a red color.
2. Add the recaito, water, alcaparrado, cassava, yautio, batata, name, and salt cod. Simmer for 20 minutes, until the root vegetables are tender.
3. Mix in the shrimp, snapper, salt, and pepper. Cook for 5 minutes.
4. Finish by stirring in the cilantro and capers.

YIELD: 4–6 servings
PREPARATION TIME: 15–20 minutes
COOKING TIME: 30–35 minutes

## Salt Cod

**Note:** This dish requires the cod to be soaked for 3 days.

6 OUNCES SALT COD

1. Put cod into a bowl and cover with water. Refrigerate for 3 days, changing the water each day. This will remove most of the salt.
2. Pick through the cod, removing any skin and bones. Break the cod up into small pieces.

YIELD: About ½ pound prepared cod
SOAKING TIME: 3 days

# FRIJOLES Y CALABAZA (BEANS WITH SQUASH)

*Simply put it all in a pot, and you are done. Sofrito can be found in the Latin American section of the grocery store.*

1 (15-OUNCE) CAN PINTO BEANS,
  DRAINED AND RINSED
2 CANS WATER
4 TABLESPOONS SOFRITO
½ CUP TOMATO SAUCE
½ CUP DICED TOMATOES
½ RED BELL PEPPER, DICED

1 ONION, DICED
1 CLOVE GARLIC, SLICED
1 CHICKEN BOUILLON CUBE
1 CARROT, DICED
1 CUP SWEET POTATO, PEELED
  AND DICED

1. Put all the ingredients into a pot, bring to a boil, and reduce to a simmer. Cook, stirring occasionally, until the carrots and potato are soft and the liquid has reduced by half.

YIELD: 4–6 servings
PREPARATION TIME: 5–10 minutes
COOKING TIME: 20–25 minutes

## BACALAO A LA VIZCAÍNA (SALT COD STEW)

*A traditional recipe for salt cod, according to our favorite abuela (grandma), Lucia Osorio Cruz, in Puerto Rico.*

¼ CUP VEGETABLE OIL
1 POUND PREPARED SALT COD (SEE RECIPE FOR CALDO SANTO [BLESSED BROTH] ON PAGE 122; USE DOUBLE THE AMOUNT)
2 ONIONS, SLICED
1 POUND POTATOES, COOKED AND SLICED
½ CUP TOMATO SAUCE
½ CUP WATER
½ CUP MANZANILLA OLIVES, PITTED
1 TABLESPOON CAPERS
8 CLOVES GARLIC, MINCED
1 BAY LEAF
1 TEASPOON DRIED OREGANO
2 RED BELL PEPPERS, SLICED
½ CUP RAISINS
¾ CUP EXTRA VIRGIN OLIVE OIL, DIVIDED

1.  Heat vegetable oil in a large skillet over medium heat.
2.  Layer the cod, onions, and potatoes in pan.
3.  Pour the tomato sauce, water, olives, capers, garlic, bay leaf, oregano, peppers, raisins, and ½ cup olive oil over the cod. Bring to a boil and reduce to a simmer.
4.  Cover and cook for 30 to 35 minutes.
5.  Drizzle with remaining olive oil.

YIELD: 4–6 servings
PREPARATION TIME: 3 days for cod and 15–20 minutes for remainder of stew
COOKING TIME: 15–20 minutes for the potatoes, and 30 minutes for the finished dish

## FLAN DE QUESO

*More like cheesecake than a flan.*

2 CUPS SUGAR, DIVIDED
6 TABLESPOONS WATER
6 EGGS, SLIGHTLY BEATEN
1 (12-OUNCE) CAN EVAPORATED MILK
1 (14-OUNCE) CAN SWEETENED CONDENSED MILK
1 TEASPOON VANILLA EXTRACT
1 (8-OUNCE) PACKAGE CREAM CHEESE
ZEST OF 1 LEMON

1. Place 1 cup sugar and the water into a microwave-safe bowl (not plastic, because the liquid will become very hot). Microwave on high for 8 to 9 minutes, watching carefully, until the mixture achieves a caramel color.
2. Remove and pour into a 9-inch cake pan.
3. Preheat the oven to 300°F.
4. Mix together the eggs, evaporated milk, condensed milk, and vanilla.
5. Using an electric mixer, cream the remaining sugar, cream cheese, and lemon zest until smooth. With mixer going, slowly add the egg mixture until completely incorporated.
6. Pour into prepared cake pan. Place pan into a larger container and set on oven rack. Fill larger container with boiling water ½ to ¾ of the way up the side of the cake pan.
7. Bake for 50 to 60 minutes. The center is set when it moves like gelatin.
8. Cool and refrigerate for at least 4 hours. To unmold, dip the pan quickly into hot water and run a knife around the edge. Place a serving platter on top and invert. Tap lightly on the pan and remove pan.

YIELD: 8–12 servings
PREPARATION TIME: 15–20 minutes
COOKING TIME: 8–9 minutes for the caramel, and 50 to 60 minutes in the oven
REFRIGERATION TIME: 4 hours

# Faro de Punta Higuera

PUERTO RICO

THE LIGHTHOUSE AT PUNTA HIGUERA NEAR RINCÓN, PUERTO RICO, WAS built BY the Spanish in 1892, during their final decade of constructing lighthouses in these islands; their efforts ended in 1898 with the Spanish-American War. After the U.S. took over Puerto Rico, there was some confusion in the spelling of this lighthouse's name, which sometimes also appears in records as "Jiguero" or "Point Jiguero." For this reason, it's hard to figure out the exact cause of the lighthouse's destruction in 1918—earthquake, tsunami, or some combination of the two.

In any case, the lighthouse was rebuilt in 1922, and although it suffered in the latter part of the twentieth century, it has since been restored and stands proudly within a park popularly known as "El Faro Park." In 1968, the first annual World Surfing Contest was held in Rincón. The size of the waves here gives an indication of how important the lighthouse's beacon is to navigators of these seas. Many park visitors also come to watch humpback whale migration in the winter; in addition, the whales are studied scientifically from this location. And even more people come simply for the spectacular view from this point of land, far above the crashing surf.

# Menú para un Día en la Playa (Menu for a Day at the Beach)

With Puerto Rico's mild climate, almost any holiday or weekend can be celebrated with a picnic outing—even in winter. This is a typical menu to take to the beach. Prepare it beforehand, or make it on a nearby grill. Fresh-squeezed juices are considered a necessity when spending a day in the sun, so pick your favorite to start the meal: pineapple, orange, guava…

Bolas de Queso con Galletas Saladas (Spam and Cheese Balls on Crackers)

Antipasto de Tuna con Galletas Saladas (Tuna Salad on Crackers)

Tostones de Platano (Twice-Fried Plantains) with Platano Dipping Sauce

Alcapurias de Carne (Meat-Filled Taro Root Fritters)

Grilled Red Snapper

Mojo Isleno

Guava Paste with Queso Blanco

## BOLAS DE QUESO CON GALLETAS SALADAS (SPAM AND CHEESE BALLS ON CRACKERS)

*Try it—you'll like it!*

1 pound cream cheese
1 can Hormel Classic Spam
2 tablespoons adobo (see recipe on page 120)
Pineapple preserves
Ritz crackers

1. Mix together the cream cheese, spam, and adobo. Roll into round balls. Top with the pineapple preserves.
2. Serve with crackers.

YIELD: 100–125 pieces
PREPARATION TIME: 10 minutes
ASSEMBLY TIME: 20–25 minutes

**Note:** Another simpler presentation is to spread the cheese mixture on a platter, top with pineapple preserves, and present it as a dip.

## ANTIPASTO DE TUNA CON GALLETAS SALADAS (TUNA SALAD ON CRACKERS)

*Ed's Italian aunts made something very similar when he was growing up.*

2 TABLESPOONS VEGETABLE OIL
1 ONION, DICED
1 RED BELL PEPPER, DICED
1 CARROT, DICED
2 CANS ALBACORE CHUNK TUNA, PACKED IN WATER
2 TABLESPOONS TOMATO SAUCE
2 TABLESPOONS KETCHUP
½ TEASPOON SALT
⅛ TEASPOON FRESHLY GROUND BLACK PEPPER
RITZ CRACKERS, FOR SERVING

1. Heat a pan on medium heat. Add the oil and cook the onion, bell pepper, and carrot slowly for 10 minutes, or until vegetables are tender.
2. Stir in the tuna, tomato sauce, ketchup, salt, and pepper.
3. Serve on Ritz crackers

YIELD: 2 cups
PREPARATION TIME: 10 minutes
COOKING TIME: 10 minutes

## TOSTONES DE PLATANO (TWICE-FRIED PLANTAINS) WITH PLATANO DIPPING SAUCE

*Eat them while they are hot.*

VEGETABLE SHORTENING, FOR FRYING
4–5 GREEN PLANTAINS
½ TEASPOON ADOBO (SEE RECIPE ON PAGE 120)
½ TEASPOON SALT
⅛ TEASPOON FRESHLY GROUND BLACK PEPPER
PLATANO DIPPING SAUCE (RECIPE FOLLOWS)

1. Heat ½ inch vegetable shortening in a heavy pot over medium-high heat to 375°F.
2. Peel the plantains and slice into 1-inch discs. Put the plantains into oil and fry until golden brown, about 2 to 3 minutes, turning over once.
3. Remove from the oil and drain on a rack.
4. Place plantain slices on work surface or cutting board and flatten the cooked plantains using the bottom of a pan, a can, or in a tostonera (tostone press).
5. Refry the flattened plantains until golden brown and crisp, about 2 to 3 minutes.
6. Remove from oil and season with the adobo, salt, and pepper. Serve with Platano Dipping Sauce.

YIELD: 24–30 pieces
PREPARATION TIME: 5–10 minutes
COOKING TIME: 2–3 minutes per batch

*Platano Dipping Sauce*

1 CLOVE GARLIC, MINCED
1 TABLESPOON ADOBO (SEE RECIPE ON PAGE 120)
¼ CUP EXTRA VIRGIN OLIVE OIL
½ CUP TOMATO SAUCE
¼ CUP KETCHUP

1.  Mix all the ingredients.

YIELD: 1 cup
PREPARATION TIME: Less than 5 minutes

## ALCAPURIAS DE CARNE (MEAT-FILLED TARO ROOT FRITTERS)

*The color of these fritters comes from the achiote seeds which are turned into a paste to flavor and color the oil.*
*Yautia can be found in the Latin American section of the grocery store.*

2 POUNDS YAUTIA (TARO ROOT)
2 TABLESPOONS ACHIOTE OIL (RECIPE FOLLOWS)
1½ TEASPOONS SALT, DIVIDED
1 CUP PICADELLO PARA RELLENO (SEE RECIPE ON PAGE 119)
VEGETABLE SHORTENING, FOR FRYING

1.  Peel the yautia and grate by hand or dice. Put in a food processor and blend until a paste
    is formed. Mix in the Achiote Oil and 1 teaspoon of salt. Remove from processor and put
    in a bowl.
2.  Wet hands and place 2 tablespoons of batter in the palm of your hand. Spread the mixture
    to a ¼-inch thickness. Place 2 teaspoons of the picadello para relleno in the center and fold
    the edges up, sealing in the meat. If there are places where the meat is seen, cover with
    more batter. Form into a ¾-inch-round cylinder that is 1½ to 2 inches in length.
3.  Heat ½ inch vegetable shortening in a heavy pot over medium-high heat to 375°F.
4.  Fry the alcapurias until golden brown, about 7 to 10 minutes. Drain on a rack and season
    with remaining salt.

YIELD: 16 alcapurias
PREPARATION TIME: 30 minutes
COOKING TIME: 7–10 minutes per batch

*Achiote Oil*
*Achiote seeds can be found in the Latin American section of the grocery store.*

1 CUP VEGETABLE OIL
½ CUP ACHIOTE SEEDS (ANNATTO SEEDS)

1. Heat the oil on low heat. Add the seeds and heat until the oil becomes a deep red.

YIELD: 1 cup
COOKING TIME: 5 minutes

## GRILLED RED SNAPPER

*This is a very popular island fish. Great for the grill.*

VEGETABLE OIL, TO COAT GRILL RACK
6 RED SNAPPER FILLETS (ABOUT 6 OUNCES EACH)
1½ TEASPOONS SALT
½ TEASPOON FRESHLY GROUND BLACK PEPPER
MOJO ISLENO (RECIPE FOLLOWS) FOR SERVING

1. Start the grill.
2. When the coals are red hot, clean and oil the grill rack, and position the rack 4 inches from heat. The coals are the right temperature if you can only hold your hand above the rack for a count of 2.
3. Cut several slices through the skin of the fish to prevent it from curling. Season with the salt and pepper.
4. Place the fillets, skin side down, on the hot grill and cover. Turn over after 3 to 4 minutes. When turning, lift gently with tongs and a metal spatula. If grill is clean, fillets should turn easily. Grill for another 3 to 4 minutes. (This cooking time is good for fillets that are 1 inch thick.)
5. Serve with Mojo Isleno.

YIELD: 6 servings
PREPARATION TIME: 5 minutes for the fish
COOKING TIME: 6–8 minutes

## MOJO ISLENO

4 TABLESPOONS VEGETABLE OIL
1 ONION, DICED
1 RED BELL PEPPER, DICED
4–6 CLOVES GARLIC, MINCED
3 TABLESPOONS RED WINE VINEGAR
1 (15-OUNCE) CAN WHOLE TOMATOES, DRAINED, SEEDED AND CHOPPED
2 TABLESPOONS CAPERS
¼ CUP CHOPPED SPANISH OR MANZANILLA OLIVES
1 BAY LEAF
½ TEASPOON SALT
½ TEASPOON FRESHLY GROUND BLACK PEPPER
¼ CUP WATER

1. Heat a pan over medium heat. Add the oil. Cook the onion and bell pepper for 10 minutes, or until vegetables are tender. Mix in the garlic and cook for 2 to 3 minutes.

2. Stir in the vinegar, tomatoes, capers, olives, bay leaf, salt, and pepper.
3. Reduce heat to low and simmer until the mixture is thick. Add water and reduce for 5 minutes.

Yield: 2 cups
PREPARATION TIME: 10–15 minutes
COOKING TIME: 30 minutes

## GUAVA PASTE WITH QUESO BLANCO
*This a great contrast in flavors—sweet and salty.*

1 (21-OUNCE) CAN GUAVA PASTE
½ POUND QUESO BLANCO

1. Open and remove guava from the can. Slice into ¼-inch strips, about 1 inch long. Arrange on a plate along with the queso. Eat the guava and queso together.

YIELD: 10–12 servings
PREPARATION TIME: 5 minutes

# Buck Island Lighthouse
ST. THOMAS, U.S. VIRGIN ISLANDS

THE DANES BUILT BUCK ISLAND LIGHTHOUSE IN 1913 ON A SMALL ISLAND off St. Thomas, which had been reserved by the Danish crown under the king's personal jurisdiction during the nineteenth century. In 1917, the United States bought St. Thomas from Denmark for defensive purposes. This precipitated decades of American emigration to the island's very desirable climate.

Currently, the lighthouse is decaying, but its surroundings have taken on new life as a marine national park that protects an extensive and fascinating coral reef and provides a home for many species of fish and turtles, and pelicans and other birds.

Though Denmark ruled St. Thomas for some time before it became part of the United States, neither Danish nor American cuisine has highly impacted the majority of its natives. They tend to eat locally grown vegetables and fruit in addition to seafood from local waters. There are also goats on Buck Island, brought over to the lighthouse area by early settlers.

# ISLAND SUPPER

Supper for native residents of St. Thomas is very local—seafood, plantains, callaloo, and goat meat all come from this island. And fresh, locally grown fruit is a typical dessert.

CALLALOO SOUP

FRIED PLANTAINS

CURRIED GOAT

CUBED MANGO

## CALLALOO SOUP

*Callaloo greens are the leaves of the taro root. Other greens work just fine.*

1 POUND CONCH, DICED
5 TABLESPOONS VEGETABLE OIL, DIVIDED
½ POUND SMOKED HAM, CUBED
1 ONION, SLICED
2 CLOVES GARLIC, MINCED
1 QUART WATER
2 KNORR VEGETABLE BOUILLON CUBES
2 FRESH THYME SPRIGS
1 BAY LEAF
1 CHILE PEPPER, SCOTCH BONNET, OR HABANERO
1 POUND SWEET POTATOES, PEELED AND CUBED
10 OUNCES OKRA, FRESH OR FROZEN (IF FRESH, CUT INTO ½-INCH CUBES)
1 POUND CALLALOO OR 10 OUNCES BAGGED SPINACH
2 TEASPOONS SALT, DIVIDED

1. Place the conch in food processor. Process until the conch is in clumps that resemble small peas.
2. Heat 3 tablespoons of oil in a pot. Stir in ham, onions, and 1 teaspoon salt. Cook for 10 minutes, or until onions are tender. Stir in remaining oil, garlic, and conch, and cook for 5 minutes.
3. Pour in the water, bouillon cubes, thyme, bay leaf, pepper, and sweet potatoes. Cover and bring to a simmer. Cook for 20 minutes. Taste occasionally to test spiciness. Remove pepper when desired spiciness is reached.
4. Stir in the okra and cook for 5 minutes. Add the callaloo and cook until wilted.
5. Season with remaining salt.

YIELD: 6–8 servings
PREPARATION TIME: 10–15 minutes
COOKING TIME: 40–45 minutes

## FRIED PLANTAINS

*When the skin is black, the starches in the plantains are changing to sugar. That is when they are perfect for this dish.*

6 RIPE PLANTAINS (THEY SHOULD BE BLACK)
3 TABLESPOONS VEGETABLE OIL
6 TABLESPOONS BUTTER
1 TEASPOON SALT
¼ TEASPOON FRESHLY GROUND BLACK PEPPER

1. Peel plantains and slice in half lengthwise.
2. Heat the oil in a pan. Add the butter, allowing to melt. When the butter stops foaming, place plantains in the pan.
3. Cook for 3 to 4 minutes per side, or until golden brown. Season with the salt and pepper.

YIELD: 4–6 servings
PREPARATION TIME: 5 minutes
COOKING TIME: 6–8 minutes

## CURRIED GOAT

*Goat has a milder flavor than lamb. Get kid or young goat meat. Serve with cooked White Rice (see recipe on page 159).*

2 POUNDS GOAT MEAT, CUT INTO 1-INCH CUBES
1 TABLESPOON SALT, DIVIDED
½ TEASPOON FRESHLY GROUND BLACK PEPPER, DIVIDED
6 TABLESPOONS VEGETABLE OIL, DIVIDED
2 ONIONS, DICED
3 CLOVES GARLIC, MINCED
2 TEASPOONS SWEET CURRY POWDER
2 TEASPOONS HOT CURRY POWDER
2 BAY LEAVES
1 TABLESPOON FRESH THYME
¼ CUP COCONUT MILK
2 CUPS BEEF STOCK
1 TABLESPOON WHITE WINE VINEGAR

1. Season the goat with half the salt and pepper. Heat 4 tablespoons of oil in a large pot. Cook the goat in batches until nicely browned.
2. Remove the goat. Add remaining oil and sauté the onions for 10 to 15 minutes. Stir in the garlic and curry powders, and cook for 2 to 3 minutes. Add the reserved goat, bay leaves, thyme, coconut milk, stock, vinegar, and remaining salt and pepper. Simmer for 60 minutes, or until the goat is tender.

YIELD: 4 servings
PREPARATION TIME: 10–15 minutes
COOKING TIME: 1 hour and 15 minutes

## CUBED MANGO

*This is all about cutting and presenting a mango.*

2 RIPE, BUT FIRM, MANGOS

1. Wash the outside of the mango.
2. Place the mango on a cutting board. The mango will settle on its side. This is the direction the seed runs. The seed is ½ to ¾ of an inch thick.
3. Slice each mango in half lengthwise, taking into account the size of the seed.
4. Pick up half of each mango, flesh side facing you, and cut a checkerboard pattern into the flesh (but not through the skin). Repeat with each mango half.
5. Pick up the halves, and with the flesh facing you, gently push from underneath. The fruit will rise up and be ready to eat.
6. The flesh that is still on the seed can be removed by carefully cutting it away from the fibrous center. Be careful, because it is slippery.

YIELD: 4 servings
PREPARATION TIME: 10–15 minutes

# Ham's Bluff Lighthouse

ST. CROIX, U.S. VIRGIN ISLANDS

WHEN DENMARK RULED THIS ISLAND, IT WAS PART OF THE DANISH WEST
Indies; the Danes built this lighthouse on St. Croix in 1915. After the U.S. pur-
chased the island in 1917, it became part of the United States Virgin Islands. Ham's
Bluff Light is a striking lighthouse made of cast iron and painted solid white, except
for stripes at the top and bottom. It was administered by the U.S. Coast Guard until
1981, when the land it sits on was transferred to the U.S. Navy. In 2003, the Coast
Guard nominated this lighthouse for inclusion in the National Register of Historic
Places. Currently, Ham's Bluff is reported to be in "severe disrepair." Despite this
fact, the light itself functions, and it is solar powered.

Due to its location on government property, very few people have access to Ham's
Bluff Light. In 2004, lighthouse aficionados put this nearly hundred-year-old beacon
on an endangered watch, which Lighthouse Digest dauntingly calls its "Doomsday List."

Life in the Caribbean can be much more casual than up north; many mainland-
ers have emigrated here for just this reason. Tourism and restaurants notwithstanding,
native meals remain, by necessity, very locally based, with available staples like conch,
cornmeal, and okra.

# Virgin Island Lunch

Fish and cornmeal became the ingredients of a traditional lunch here centuries ago. And you must have conch fritters when you're in the Caribbean. The ice cream is a new treat.

Conch Fritters with Conch Dipping Sauce

Salt Cod and Potato Salad

Fungi and Okra (Creamy Cornmeal and Okra)

Grilled Lobsters with Mango and Papaya Salsa

Rum–Raisin Ice Cream

## CONCH FRITTERS WITH CONCH DIPPING SAUCE

*If you can not find conch, use quahogs or large clams.*

1 ONION, CHOPPED (ABOUT 1 CUP)
1 RED BELL PEPPER, SEEDED AND CHOPPED (ABOUT 1 CUP)
1 GREEN BELL PEPPER, SEEDED AND CHOPPED (ABOUT 1 CUP)
2 JALAPEÑO PEPPERS, SEEDED AND CHOPPED
1 POUND CONCH, CHOPPED
2 EGGS, SLIGHTLY BEATEN
⅓ CUP MILK
1 CUP ALL-PURPOSE FLOUR
1½ TEASPOONS BAKING POWDER
1 TEASPOON SALT
VEGETABLE SHORTENING, FOR FRYING
CONCH DIPPING SAUCE (RECIPE FOLLOWS) FOR SERVING

1. Place the onion, bell peppers, and jalapeño in a processor and pulse 10 times. Remove and place in a bowl.
2. Place the conch in the processor. Process until the conch resembles ground beef. Remove and combine with vegetables. Mix in the eggs and milk.
3. Mix together the flour, baking powder, and salt. Blend into the conch mixture.
4. Preheat the oven to 200°F. Fritters may need to be cooked in batches, and they can be kept warm.
5. Heat ½ inch of vegetable shortening in a heavy pot over medium-high heat to 360°F.
6. Spoon walnut-sized portions of batter into the hot oil, being careful not to overcrowd the pot. Cook for 2 to 3 minutes, turning over until browned on all sides.
7. Drain on a rack. Place in a warmed oven while the balance of the batter is being cooked. Serve hot, alongside Conch Dipping Sauce.

YIELD: 30–32 pieces
PREPARATION TIME: 15–20 minutes
COOKING TIME: 2–3 minutes per batch

*Conch Dipping Sauce*

½ CUP MAYONNAISE
¾ CUP KETCHUP
JUICE OF 1 LIME
2 TABLESPOONS PICKAPEPPA SAUCE

1. Combine all the ingredients.

YIELD: 1½ cups
PREPARATION TIME: Less than 5 minutes

## SALT COD AND POTATO SALAD

*Salt cod and potatoes are the basis for many Mediterranean-influenced dishes that made their way to the Caribbean.*

1 POUND BABY YUKON GOLD POTATOES
2 TEASPOONS SALT, DIVIDED
12 OUNCES PREPARED SALT COD (RECIPE FOL-
      LOWS)
4 LARGE ROMAINE LETTUCE LEAVES, CHOPPED
4 SCALLIONS, SLICED INTO THREADS
4 HARD-BOILED EGGS, SLICED
1 AVOCADO, SLICED IN HALF LENGTHWISE,
      PITTED, AND PEELED
3 TABLESPOONS WHITE WINE VINEGAR
9 TABLESPOONS EXTRA VIRGIN OLIVE OIL
½ TEASPOON FRESHLY GROUND BLACK PEPPER

1. Put the potatoes in a pot of cold water with 1 teaspoon salt. Cook until tender and can be pierced
   with a fork. Remove from water, let cool, and slice in half.
2. Place the cod, potatoes, romaine, scallions, eggs, and avocado in a bowl.
3. Mix together the vinegar, olive oil, remaining salt, and pepper. Pour over salad and toss.

*Salt Cod*

**Note:** this recipe requires 3 days for preparation

9 OUNCES SALT COD
1 BAY LEAF

1. Put cod into a bowl and cover with water. Refrigerate for 3 days, covered with plastic wrap,
   changing water each day. This will remove most of the salt.
2. Pick through cod removing any skin and bones.
3. Bring a pot of water to a boil. Add salt cod and bay leaf and simmer for 15 minutes. Remove cod and break cod into pieces.

YIELD: About 12 ounces prepared cod
SOAKING TIME: 3 days
COOKING TIME: 15 minutes


## FUNGI AND OKRA (CREAMY CORNMEAL AND OKRA)

*Cornmeal and okra are commonly used throughout the American South as well.*

3 TABLESPOONS VEGETABLE OIL
1 ONION, DICED
1 CLOVE GARLIC, DICED
10 OUNCES OKRA, FRESH OR FROZEN (IF FRESH, CUT INTO ½-INCH CUBES)
1 TEASPOON SALT, DIVIDED
¼ TEASPOON FRESHLY GROUND BLACK PEPPER, DIVIDED
4 CUPS WATER, DIVIDED
1 KNORR VEGETABLE BOUILLON CUBE
1 CUP CORNMEAL
2 TABLESPOONS BUTTER

1. Heat the oil in a sauté pan. Stir in the onion, garlic, okra, ½ teaspoon salt, and ⅛ teaspoon pepper. Sauté for 10 to 15 minutes, or until vegetables are tender. Set aside.
2. In a bowl, mix the cornmeal with 2 cups of water and the vegetable cube. In a separate pot, bring 2 cups of water to a boil. Stir in the cornmeal mixture, mixing all the time to prevent lumping. Reduce heat to low and cook for 20 minutes. The cornmeal should be smooth, with no grainy feel when rubbed between your 2 fingers.
3. Stir in the vegetables, remaining salt, pepper, and butter. Cook for 5 minutes.

YIELD: 6 servings
PREPARATION TIME: 10–15 minutes
COOKING TIME: 35–40 minutes


## GRILLED LOBSTERS WITH MANGO AND PAPAYA SALSA

*Lobster is very popular on St. Thomas. Here it only make culinary sense to serve it with a tropical salsa.*

4 LOBSTERS (1½ TO 2 POUNDS EACH)
VEGETABLE OIL, TO COAT GRILL RACK
8 TABLESPOONS EXTRA VIRGIN OLIVE OIL
1½ TEASPOONS SALT
½ TEASPOON FRESHLY GROUND BLACK PEPPER
MANGO AND PAPAYA SALSA (RECIPE FOLLOWS) FOR SERVING

1. Start the grill.
2. Split the lobsters in half lengthwise. Remove anything that is dark green in color. This is the stomach and intestine.
3. Crack the claws with a nut cracker or the back side of a knife.
4. When the coals are red hot, clean and oil the grill rack, and position the rack 4 inches from heat. The coals are the right temperature if you can only hold your hand above the rack for a count of 3.

5. Drizzle 1 tablespoon of the olive oil on each lobster half, and season with the salt and pepper.
6. Place the lobsters, shell side down, on the grill. Replace cover and grill for 4 minutes. Turn over and grill for another 4 to 5 minutes, or until the thickest part of the tail is opaque and firm.
7. Serve with Mango and Papaya Salsa.

YIELD: 4 servings
PREPARATION TIME: 10–15 minutes
COOKING TIME: 10–15 minutes

*Mango and Papaya Salsa*

1 MANGO, PEELED, PITTED, AND DICED
2 SCALLIONS, DICED
1 CUP DICED PAPAYA
1 TEASPOON DICED JALAPEÑO PEPPER
½ CUP CHOPPED FRESH CILANTRO
1 TEASPOON PICKAPEPPA SAUCE
JUICE OF 1 LIME
¼ TEASPOON SALT
⅛ TEASPOON FRESHLY GROUND BLACK PEPPER

1. Put mango in a blender and purée. Combine rest of the ingredients with the puréed mango.

YIELD: About 1 cup
PREPARATION TIME: 15 minutes

## RUM–RAISIN ICE CREAM
*Very, very rummy and very, very yummy.*

½ CUP SUGAR, DIVIDED
1 CUP WHOLE MILK
1 CUP HEAVY CREAM
4 EGG YOLKS
¼ CUP RAISINS
¼ CUP DARK RUM

1. Heat ¼ cup of sugar, the milk, and cream over medium heat in a heavy saucepan. Cook until the sugar has dissolved, bubbles begin to form around the edge, and steam begins to come off the surface. Remove from heat. Watch carefully because it will boil over.
2. Whisk the egg yolks and remaining sugar together in a bowl. Continue to whisk and slowly add ½ cup of the milk mixture to the egg yolks. When blended, add back to the saucepan, whisking constantly. Turn heat to medium-low and whisk until mixture thickens and coats the back of a spoon, about 5 to 7 minutes. Do not allow to boil.
3. Strain the mixture and refrigerate for 2 hours or until chilled.

4. In a separate bowl, combine the raisins and rum. Cover and allow raisins to rehydrate for at least 1 hour at room temperature.
5. Strain the raisins and reserve 2 tablespoons of rum. Mix raisins and reserved rum into chilled milk mixture and put into an ice cream maker. Follow manufacturers' instructions.

YIELD: 3 cups
PREPARATION TIME: 5 minutes
COOKING TIME: 15–20 minutes
REFRIGERATION TIME: 2 hours
CHURNING TIME: See manufacturer's instructions

# GULF COAST REGION

*A long the Gulf of Mexico, you can find everything from swamps to desert and from large cities to farmland in Florida, Alabama, Mississippi, Louisiana, and Texas. The ports on this body of water—and the adjacent rivers and lakes—are used for a bit of everything: local boating, domestic and international shipping, fishing, and shrimping.*

*Various tribes of American Indians lived in these regions five hundred years ago, when Spanish explorers traveled up through Florida from the sea. The Spanish also surged into Texas from Mexico. And in between, with the passing of the centuries, the French held sway in their Louisiana Territory.*

*Here, the early lighthouse-type markers were primitive wooden poles and stands, as on the northeast coast. But in the nineteenth century, with increased shipping trade, greater visibility was required. Soon tall, sturdy towers began to shine their beacons out over the Gulf from Florida on coastal islands, in river deltas and along the shoreline all the way to Mexico.*

*Being in the subtropics made it more difficult to store food, but the lighthouse keepers and their families were compensated by enjoying fresh fruits and vegetables year-round. For those without much else, there were squashes, greens and corn, plenty of hog products, and crawfish, and along the coast it was shrimp, shrimp, shrimp. In the French-oriented New Orleans area, these foods evolved into their own style of haute cuisine, while out in the countryside things got spicier—we now call it Cajun style.*

*As always, lighthouse keepers had ready sources of fresh fish; here, it was Gulf fish, such as pompano, trout, flounder, and redfish. Fresh eating was healthy eating. The lighthouse families had an additional significant health advantage in the days before window screens and air conditioning. Rather than being stuck in congested, hot, and often unsanitary towns, keeper families lived along the shore, in the path of fresh ocean breezes.*

# Cape St. George Lighthouse
LITTLE ST. GEORGE ISLAND, FLORIDA

THE ENGLISH FOLLOWED THE SPANISH IN OCCUPYING THE LAND HERE AND establishing farming plantations very early in the country's history. The first Cape St. George Lighthouse was put up in 1833 to guide ships up the Apalachicola and Chatahoochee Rivers, to and from plantations shipping out their cotton crops. Water currents soon undermined its foundations. A second lighthouse was built further inland, but it was blown down in 1851. The next lighthouse was built in 1852, but the light was extinguished during the Civil War so the Yankees wouldn't see it; it was relit in 1865 and shone throughout the rest of the nineteenth century and most of the twentieth, as well.

Yet by the first part of this century, severe storms and hurricanes again put the lighthouse in jeopardy, and alarms were raised about the condition of Cape St. George Light, with good reason. The lighthouse actually tumbled down in 2005, to the distress of the local community. Determined to save the light, they mobilized, personally donated money, and raised grant money, and rebuilt their cherished Cape St. George Light. The light was reopened to the public in December 2008.

In this area of the country, menus have been more influenced by availability than fashion; this region was traditionally inhabited by rural people who made their living off the land and the sea. Shrimp and fish, with a few local greens, are the basics of many people's suppers, at home or in restaurants, to this day.

## SUPPER ON THE PANHANDLE

Someone is always bringing home shrimp—enough for dinner. If you're lucky, there's local pompano, too. Add a few greens as a salad and/or a quick-fried side dish, and finish it off with a Florida citrus dessert. Eat outside, if it's not too buggy.

GREEN SALAD WITH ITALIAN DRESSING
QUICK-FRIED MUSTARD GREENS
SHRIMP BOIL
PAN-FRIED POMPANO
STUFFED FROZEN ORANGES

### GREEN SALAD WITH ITALIAN DRESSING

*This salad can be as retro or as modern as you want it, depending on what type of salad greens you use.*

4 CUPS MIXED SALAD GREENS, WASHED AND TORN INTO
    BITE-SIZE PIECES
1 CUCUMBER, PEELED, SPLIT LENGTHWISE, SEEDED, AND
    SLICED
1 TOMATO, SLICED INTO WEDGES
ITALIAN DRESSING (RECIPE FOLLOWS), FOR SERVING

1. Combine all the ingredients in a salad bowl. Toss with Italian Dressing.
2. Serve immediately.

YIELD: 4 servings.
PREPARATION TIME: 5–10 minutes.

*Italian Dressing*

¼ CUP RED WINE VINEGAR
¾ CUP EXTRA VIRGIN OLIVE OIL
1 TEASPOON DRIED OREGANO
1 TEASPOON DRIED BASIL
½ TEASPOON GROUND FENNEL SEED
½ TEASPOON GARLIC POWDER

¼ TEASPOON SALT
⅛ TEASPOON FRESHLY GROUND BLACK PEPPER
¼ TEASPOON SUGAR

1. Combine all the ingredients and mix.

YIELD: 1 cup
PREPARATION TIME: Less than 5 minutes

## QUICK-FRIED MUSTARD GREENS

*Definitely for the true greens lover: a burst of flavor in your mouth.*

4 TABLESPOONS VEGETABLE OIL
2 CLOVES GARLIC, SLICED
1½ POUNDS MUSTARD GREENS, WASHED
    AND CHOPPED, STEMS REMOVED
2 TABLESPOONS CIDER VINEGAR
1 TEASPOON SALT
¼ TEASPOON FRESHLY GROUND BLACK
    PEPPER

1. Heat pan on high heat and add oil. Stir in garlic and cook for about 30 seconds, or until fragrant.
2. Mix in the greens and fry until wilted. Toss in the vinegar, salt, and pepper.

YIELD: 4 servings
PREPARATION TIME: 5–10 minutes
COOKING TIME: 2 minutes

## SHRIMP BOIL

*The Gulf's favorite supper. The shrimp must be fresh, right out of the sea. Have on hand sliced lemons, cocktail sauce, and horseradish, for serving.*

**Note:** Shrimp boil is a commercial seasoning mixture that you use to season the boiling water.

2 BOTTLES DARK BEER
1 QUART WATER
½ CUP SHRIMP BOIL
3 POUNDS SHRIMP, PEELED AND DEVEINED

1. Bring the beer, water, and shrimp boil to a boil.
2. Stir in the shrimp, cover and return to a boil. Cook for 2 to 3 minutes.
3. Drain and serve immediately, with the sliced lemons, cocktail sauce, and horseradish.

YIELD: 6 servings
COOKING TIME: 2–3 minutes

## PAN-FRIED POMPANO

*Becky's husband Branko, who grew up in Florida, told us which fish to choose for this dish.*

6 POMPANO, RED SNAPPER, OR BONITA FILLETS (ABOUT 6 OUNCES EACH)
1 TEASPOON SALT
¼ TEASPOON FRESHLY GROUND BLACK PEPPER
VEGETABLE SHORTENING, FOR FRYING
¼ CUP CORNMEAL
¼ CUP ALL-PURPOSE FLOUR
LEMON WEDGES, FOR SERVING

1. Rinse and dry fillets. Season with the salt and pepper.
2. Melt shortening in a large skillet to a depth of ¼ inch. Turn heat to medium.
3. Combine cornmeal and flour. Dredge pompano fillets in cornmeal mixture and shake off excess. Place on a rack and refrigerate for 10-15 minutes, or while oil comes up to 350°F.
4. Preheat the oven to 200°F. Fillets may need to be cooked in batches, and they can be kept warm.
5. Remove fillets from refrigerator. Redredge in cornmeal mixture, shake off excess, and carefully place fillets in oil. Avoid overcrowding. Cook for 2 to 3 minutes per side, until golden brown. Place on a rack and keep warm in oven if cooking in batches.
6. Serve with lemon wedges.

YIELD: 6 servings
PREPARATION TIME: Less than 5 minutes
REFRIGERATION TIME: 10–15 minutes
COOKING TIME: 4–6 minutes per batch


## STUFFED FROZEN ORANGES

*Not difficult to make, and very impressive to serve.*

11–12 ORANGES
1 CUP GRANULATED SUGAR
1 OUNCE TRIPLE SEC
¾ CUP HEAVY CREAM

1. Cut the oranges in half and carefully scoop out 6 halves, reserving the pulp. The orange halves will serve as dishes. Place them in the freezer.
2. Juice remaining orange halves and reserved pulp until you have 4 cups of juice. Pour the juice and sugar into a pot and simmer until sugar has dissolved. Add triple sec.
3. Pour into a 13×9-inch pan and place in freezer. Ice crystals will begin to form after 30 to 45 minutes. Stir with a fork, breaking up the ice crystals. Continue to stir every 15 minutes, for 2½ to 3 hours.
4. During the last 15 minutes, whip the cream to stiff peaks.
5. Transfer the orange ice to a bowl and fold in the whipped cream. Spoon into prepared frozen orange cups and serve immediately or return to the freezer. If frozen, soften in refrigerator 30 minutes before serving.

Yield: 6 servings
PREPARATION TIME: 20 minutes
COOKING TIME: 5 minutes
FREEZER TIME: 2½–3 hours

# Biloxi Lighthouse

BILOXI, MISSISSIPPI

ALONG THE GULF COAST, MISSISSIPPI SHARES A CULTURAL HERITAGE WITH its neighbors, Alabama and Louisiana. By the nineteenth century, Biloxi was one of a network of shipping hubs connecting mainland river ports with shipping lines in the Gulf of Mexico. Built in 1848, Biloxi Light is distinguished by having a female lighthouse keeper from just after the Civil War until 1920—when her daughter took over.

Currently, Biloxi Light is the only intact lighthouse in the state of Mississippi, perhaps because it was the first cast-iron lighthouse in the state. Its location is also unique, as a busy road was built right around it: Biloxi Lighthouse is now located on the median strip of Highway 90.

From Native Americans to Africans, local residents left their imprint on farm-influenced cuisine in Mississippi during the past few centuries. Often subsistence farmers with only small amounts of local crops, they depended on a few vegetables like corn and sweet potatoes for their meals, occasionally adding the embellishment of scallions or peanuts—and a chicken, when available.

# SUNDAY FAMILY SUPPER

Chicken was a prized element of special Sunday family suppers during most of this country's history. Traditional side dishes and even desserts were concocted from locally raised greens, vegetables and herbs, and staples such as beans, corn, and squash.

BRAISED GREENS STEMS
HOPPIN' JOHN
CHEDDAR CHEESE AND SCALLION GRITS
CHICKEN, PEANUT, AND SWEET POTATO STEW
SWEET POTATO PIE

## BRAISED GREENS STEMS

*This is a great recipe for the thick stems that are left over when making many of the recipes in this book.*

2 TABLESPOONS VEGETABLE OIL
2 SLICES BACON, DICED
1 ONION, SLICED
2 CLOVES GARLIC, SLICED
STEMS FROM 2½–3 POUNDS GREENS
¼ TEASPOON CHILE FLAKES
¼ TEASPOON SALT
1 CUP BEEF STOCK

1. Heat a pan over medium heat. Add the oil and cook the bacon for 4–5 minutes. Stir in the onion and garlic, and cook for 10 minutes or until vegetables are tender.
2. Add the stems, chile flakes, and salt. Sauté for 2 minutes.
3. Pour in the stock, and simmer until stems are tender. Add more stock, as needed. Cook until the stock has almost evaporated.

YIELD: 4 servings
PREPARATION TIME: 5–10 minutes
COOKING TIME: 40–50 minutes, depending on the type of stems

## HOPPIN' JOHN

*This dish is a combination of African, Caribbean, and French cuisine.*

3 TABLESPOONS VEGETABLE OIL
4 SLICES BACON, DICED
2 ONIONS, DICED
2 CELERY STALKS, DICED
1 GREEN BELL PEPPER, DICED
2 CLOVES GARLIC, MINCED

1 CHILE, SERRANO, OR JALAPEÑO PEPPER, DICED
1 POUND BLACK-EYED PEAS, SOAKED OVERNIGHT IN WATER UNDER
   REFRIGERATION
4 CUPS CHICKEN STOCK
1 CUP RICE
2 TEASPOONS SALT
½ TEASPOON FRESHLY GROUND BLACK PEPPER

1. Heat a large pot over medium heat. Add the oil and cook the bacon 4 to 5 minutes.
2. Stir in the onions, celery, green pepper, garlic, and pepper. Sauté for 20 to 25 minutes. Add the black-eyed peas and stock. Cover, bring to a boil, and reduce to a simmer.
3. Cook for 40 to 45 minutes. Stir in rice, salt, and pepper. Re-cover, bring back to a boil, reduce to a simmer, and cook until rice is done, about 20 minutes.

YIELD: 8–10 servings
PREPARATION TIME: 10–15 minutes
SOAKING TIME: Overnight
COOKING TIME: 1½ hours

## CHEDDAR CHEESE AND SCALLION GRITS
*Spark up the traditional cheese grits with the color and flavor of fresh green onions (scallions).*

2 CUPS MILK
2 CUPS WATER
1 CUP GRITS
¾ CUP GRATED CHEDDAR CHEESE
2 TABLESPOONS BUTTER, SOFTENED
4 SCALLIONS, CHOPPED
¼ TEASPOON GARLIC POWDER
¾ TEASPOON TABASCO SAUCE
2 TEASPOONS SALT
½ TEASPOON FRESHLY GROUND BLACK PEPPER

1. Place the grits in a bowl with water, covering by ½ inch. Stir the grits and skim off any particles that float to the surface.
2. Bring the milk and water to a boil.
3. Gradually pour grits into milk, whisking all the time.
4. Reduce the heat to low, and stir occasionally. Add ½ cup water if the grits begin to look too stiff. The grits should be smooth. Cook for 60 minutes.
5. Fold in the cheese, butter, scallions, garlic powder, Tabasco sauce, salt, and pepper.
6. Stir until the cheese has melted. Serve immediately.

YIELD: 6 servings
PREPARATION TIME: 5 minutes
COOKING TIME: 1 hour and 10 minutes

## CHICKEN, PEANUT, AND SWEET POTATO STEW

*An African-influenced Southern stew with a beautiful combination of flavors.*

3 TABLESPOONS VEGETABLE OIL
6 CHICKEN THIGHS, BONELESS
  AND SKINLESS
1 TABLESPOON SALT, DIVIDED
½ TEASPOON FRESHLY GROUND
  BLACK PEPPER, DIVIDED
1 ONION, DICED
1 RED BELL PEPPER, DICED
2 CLOVES GARLIC, SLICED
½ CUP DRY WHITE WINE

1 POUND SWEET POTATOES, PEELED
  AND DICED (ABOUT 3 CUPS)
1½ CUPS UNSALTED ROASTED
  PEANUTS
1 (15-OUNCE) CAN WHOLE
  TOMATOES, DRAINED, SEEDED
  AND CHOPPED
4 CUPS CHICKEN STOCK
1 TEASPOON GRATED FRESH
  GINGER
1 TEASPOON DRIED THYME

1. Heat the oil in a large pan. Season the chicken with 1½ teaspoons salt and ¼ teaspoon pepper.
2. Fry the chicken until golden brown, about 10 minutes. Cook in batches so as not to over-crowd the pan. Remove the chicken and set aside. Stir in the onion, bell pepper, and garlic, and cook for 10 minutes, or until vegetables are tender. Cube the chicken and return to the pot. Pour in the wine and simmer until liquid is reduced by half. Add the sweet potatoes, peanuts, tomatoes, stock, ginger, thyme, and remaining salt and pepper.
3. Cover and simmer for 30 to 35 minutes.

YIELD: 4 servings
PREPARATION TIME: 20–25 minutes
COOKING TIME: 50–60 minutes


## SWEET POTATO PIE

*Ed's friend Ann helped him test many of these recipes. Her family finished this pie before dinner.*

2 CUPS MASHED COOKED SWEET POTATOES (ABOUT 1 POUND)
2 EGGS, BEATEN
1 CUP SOUR CREAM
½ CUP BROWN SUGAR
1 TEASPOON CINNAMON
½ TEASPOON NUTMEG
4 TABLESPOONS BUTTER, MELTED
¼ CUP RAISINS
¼ TEASPOON SALT
1 (9-INCH) RICH PIE CRUST (RECIPE FOLLOWS), UNBAKED

1. Blend all the ingredients, except the crust, in a bowl until smooth.
2. Pour into the unbaked pie crust and bake for 10 minutes at 450°F. Reduce the temperature to 350°F, cover with a sheet of foil, and continue baking for 45 additional minutes. The pie is done when a cake tester comes out clean.
3. Remove from oven and let cool on a rack, but hide from your family until ready to serve!

YIELD: 6 servings
PREPARATION TIME: 10–15 minutes
COOKING TIME: 50–55 minutes, not including the cooking time for the sweet potatoes.


*Rich Pie Crust*

1½ CUPS ALL-PURPOSE FLOUR
⅛ TEASPOON SALT
¾ CUP VEGETABLE SHORTENING, COLD
3 TABLESPOONS COLD WATER
2 EGG YOLKS, LIGHTLY BEATEN

1. Mix the flour and salt in a bowl and cut the shortening into the flour with 2 knives or a pastry blender, until the mixture is in clumps the size of peas. Gradually add the water and egg yolks, and blend together.
2. Form the pie dough into a ball, cover with plastic wrap, and refrigerate for 30 minutes.
3. Lightly flour work surface. Roll out the pie dough to be 1 inch larger than the pie plate. Fold the dough over rolling pin and place in the pie plate. Unfold to cover the entire plate. Fold the extra dough under, and crimp the edges.

YIELD: 1 (9-inch) pie crust
PREPARATION TIME: 15–20 minutes
REFRIGERATION TIME: 30 minutes

# Tchefuncte River Lighthouse
MADISONVILLE, LOUISIANA

THOUGH OTHERS HAD LIVED AND EXPLORED HERE, THE FRENCH WERE THE first to colonize this area of North America. They named it after their monarch, King Louis XIV, in the late 17th century. The king's name remained in the "Louisiana Purchase" and was finally immortalized in the name of this state—Louisiana—when it became part of the United States in 1812.

North of New Orleans, Lake Pontchartrain was a gathering place for American ships preparing for the Battle of New Orleans in the War of 1812; it was then a shipping outlet to the Gulf of Mexico. The lake's shore also functioned as a shipyard during World War II.

The first lighthouse was built here in 1837. After its light was darkened during the Civil War, an entirely new light was constructed in 1867. Tchefuncte River Lighthouse now protects recreational boaters and fishermen plying the shallows of the lake at the mouth of the Tchefuncte River, and it is being actively restored as of this writing.

In the United States, there is no more French-influenced culture than that of the New Orleans area. Both food and music can be lively, smooth, or hot—your choice. Delectable local seafood and French cuisine merge together here in recipes for rich oyster and shrimp concoctions, flavorful rice dishes, and meltingly sweet desserts that have become famous around the world.

# LUNCHTIME FEAST

There's no sense in going to Louisiana if you're not going to enjoy the food: rich and spicy, but always fresh from the sea and the land. Here are some classics—and one new dish to perk up the menu.

OYSTERS ROCKEFELLER

OKRA SOUP

EGGPLANT NAPOLEON

SHRIMP ETOUFFÉE

OVEN-FRIED CATFISH

BANANAS FOSTER

## OYSTERS ROCKEFELLER

*This is a historic delicacy, so rich it was named for the mega-wealthy Rockefeller family at the turn of the century.*

| | |
|---|---|
| 2 TABLESPOONS VEGETABLE OIL | ¼ TEASPOON FRESHLY GROUND |
| 2 (10-OUNCE) BAGS OF FRESH | BLACK PEPPER |
| SPINACH | ¼ TEASPOON CAYENNE |
| ½ CUP WATER | 8 TABLESPOONS BUTTER, MELTED |
| ½ CUP CHOPPED FRESH PARSLEY | ½ CUP BREAD CRUMBS |
| 4 SCALLIONS, CHOPPED | ¼ TEASPOON SALT |
| ½ TEASPOON GROUND ANISE OR | 2 DOZEN OYSTERS |
| FENNEL SEED | ROCK SALT |
| ½ TEASPOON DRIED THYME | EXTRA VIRGIN OLIVE OIL, FOR |
| 1 TABLESPOON HORSERADISH | SERVING |
| 1 TABLESPOON ANCHOVY PASTE | |

1. Heat a pan on high. Add the vegetable oil and spinach, and let cook. Pour in water, tossing and stirring while cooking. Remove from the pan and cool. Squeeze out any excess liquid.
2. Put the spinach, parsley, scallions, anise seed, thyme, horseradish, and anchovy paste, pepper, and cayenne pepper in a food processor fitted with the metal blade. Pulse 10 times until the mixture is combined, but not puréed.
3. With the machine running, add the butter and bread crumbs. Taste, and add salt, if desired. The anchovy paste may provide enough salt.
4. Preheat the oven to 450°F.
5. Line a baking sheet with rock salt or crumpled aluminum foil. This will keep the oysters

level. Open the oysters, then loosen oysters from the shell, leave in the shell, and place on salt or foil. (Oysters can be first put in the freezer for 20 minutes, making them easier to shuck.)

6. Bake the oysters for 5 to 7 minutes. Remove from the oven. Spoon the spinach mixture on to the oysters and return to the oven for another 5 minutes.

7. Finish by spooning 1 teaspoon of the olive oil on each oyster.

YIELD: 24 oysters
PREPARATION TIME: 5–10 minutes
COOKING TIME: 3–4 minutes for the spinach mixture, and 10–12 minutes in the oven

## OKRA SOUP

*This is one of Becky Sue's favorites.*

4 TABLESPOONS VEGETABLE OIL, DIVIDED
6 SLICES BACON, DICED
1 ONION, DICED
2 CELERY STALKS, DICED
1 GREEN BELL PEPPER, DICED
1 CLOVE GARLIC, MINCED
2 POUNDS OKRA, SLICED (FROZEN MAY BE USED)
1 (28-OUNCE) CAN PEELED WHOLE TOMATOES, SEEDED AND CHOPPED
6 OUNCES HAM, DICED
2 BAY LEAVES
2 TABLESPOONS FRESH, OR 2 TEASPOONS DRIED, THYME
4 CUPS CHICKEN STOCK
¼ CUP CHOPPED FRESH PARSLEY
1 TEASPOON SALT
¼ TEASPOON FRESHLY GROUND BLACK PEPPER

*If you are looking for a way to reuse these cans, check out the Boston Brown Bread recipe on page 19.*

1. Heat 2 tablespoons oil in a pot over medium heat. Fry the bacon for 3 minutes, stirring occasionally so as not to burn.

2. Stir in the onions, celery, and bell pepper. Sauté for 10 minutes, or until all the vegetables are tender. Mix in the garlic, okra, and remaining oil. Cook for 10 minutes.

3. Blend in the tomatoes, ham, bay leaves, thyme, stock and parsley. Simmer for 40 to 45 minutes. Season with the salt and pepper.

YIELD: 8–10 servings
PREPARATION TIME: 20 minutes
COOKING TIME: 60–65 minutes

## EGGPLANT NAPOLEON

*Clean, distinct flavors in a colorful presentation. Finishing with a pinch of fleur de sel and a drizzle of good extra virgin olive oil is mandatory.*

2 MEDIUM EGGPLANTS
2 MEDIUM TOMATOES
1 ONION
1 ZUCCHINI
1 YELLOW SQUASH
1 TEASPOON DRIED OREGANO
1 TEASPOON DRIED THYME
1 TEASPOON PAPRIKA
1 TEASPOON SALT
¼ TEASPOON FRESHLY GROUND BLACK PEPPER
1 TABLESPOON VEGETABLE OIL
6–12 FRESH BASIL LEAVES, DEPENDING ON SIZE
½ CUP EXTRA VIRGIN OLIVE OIL
1 TEASPOON FLEUR DE SEL, FOR SERVING

1. Slice the eggplant into eighteen ¼-inch discs. Slice the tomatoes into twelve ¼-inch slices. Slice the onion, zucchini, and yellow squash into very thin discs.
2. Combine the oregano, thyme, paprika, salt, and pepper together in a small bowl and mix.
3. Preheat the oven to 375°F.
4. Line a 13×9-inch baking dish with aluminum foil and coat with 1 tablespoon of vegetable oil. Lay down 6 eggplant discs, top each with 1 tomato slice. Add a few pieces of onions, zucchini and squash. Sprinkle with a bit of herb mixture and drizzle each with ½ teaspoon olive oil. Follow with 2 more layers of eggplant, tomato, etc. Top each stack with an eggplant slice, then 1 or 2 basil leaves and ½ teaspoon olive oil. Insert a toothpick in the center of each stack. This will hold it together while it cooks. Cover with aluminum foil and bake for 60 minutes.
5. Remove from the oven and discard the toothpicks.
6. Drizzle with remaining olive oil, and sprinkle with a pinch of fleur de sel.

YIELD: 6 servings
PREPARATION TIME: 25–30 minutes
BAKING TIME: 60 minutes

## SHRIMP ETOUFFÉE

*This dish is another classic of Louisiana. If you happen to be lucky enough to get fresh crawfish, use it instead of shrimp. Always serve on a bed of steaming White Rice.*

⅔ CUP VEGETABLE OIL
¾ CUP ALL-PURPOSE FLOUR, DIVIDED
4 TABLESPOONS BUTTER
1 CUP DICED ONION
1 CUP DICED GREEN BELL PEPPER
1 CUP DICED CELERY STALKS
2 CLOVES GARLIC, CHOPPED

2 CUPS VEGETABLE STOCK
1 CUP CLAM JUICE
1 CUP OR 1 (15-OUNCE) CAN DICED TOMATOES, DRAINED
¼ TEASPOON NUTMEG
1 BAY LEAF
1 TEASPOON DRIED THYME
1 TEASPOON SALT
¼ TEASPOON FRESHLY GROUND BLACK PEPPER
2½ POUNDS FRESH SHRIMP, PEELED AND DEVEINED
WHITE RICE (RECIPE FOLLOWS) FOR SERVING.

1. Pour the oil into a small pot and gradually stir in ½ cup of the flour. Cook over medium heat, stirring continuously, until the flour achieves a medium brown color, about 15 to 20 minutes. Transfer to a larger pot. This is your dark roux.
2. Stir the onions, green peppers, celery, and garlic into the dark roux. Cook for 15 to 20 minutes, until the vegetables are soft.
3. In a separate pan, melt the butter and mix in remaining flour and cook for 2 minutes. Set aside. This is your light roux.
4. Blend the vegetable stock into the dark roux, along with the clam juice, tomatoes, nutmeg, bay leaf, thyme, salt, and pepper. Bring to a boil, stir in the reserved light roux, reduce to a simmer and cook for 5 minutes. Add the shrimp and cook for 3 minutes, until opaque.
5. Serve with White Rice.

YIELD: 8 servings
PREPARATION TIME: 45 minutes with peeling shrimp
COOKING TIME: 60–70 minutes

*White Rice*

2 CUPS LONG-GRAIN WHITE RICE
½ TEASPOON SALT

1. Rinse rice by putting it in a bowl of water, gently agitating, then draining. Repeat a total of 3 times. This will help keep the grains separate.
2. Put the rice and salt into a pot with a tight-fitting lid. Fill with water to cover the rice by ½ inch. Cover, bring to a boil, and reduce to the lowest temperature.
3. Cook for 12 minutes, remove from heat, and allow to rest, covered, for 15 minutes.
4. Fluff with a fork and serve.

YIELD: 8 servings
PREPARATION TIME: 5 minutes
COOKING TIME: 12 minutes
RESTING TIME: 15 minutes

## OVEN-FRIED CATFISH

*Catfish is an underappreciated fish; it's sweet and delicate. Eat and enjoy.*

6 CATFISH FILLETS (ABOUT 6 OUNCES EACH)
2 TEASPOONS SALT
½ TEASPOON FRESHLY GROUND BLACK PEPPER
1 CUP CORNMEAL
VEGETABLE OIL, FOR FRYING
3 TABLESPOONS BUTTER

1. Rinse the fillets under cold water, pat dry and season both sides with salt and pepper.
2. Dredge the fillets in cornmeal.
3. Preheat the oven to 350°F.
4. Heat a sauté pan to medium heat and add enough oil to cover the bottom of the pan. Heat oil for 1 to 2 minutes. Put the butter in the pan and allow to melt and begin to foam. Carefully place the fillets in the pan. Sauté fillets for 3 to 4 minutes. Carefully remove fillets, turn over, and place on a baking sheet. Put baking sheet in oven for 6 to 8 minutes.

YIELD: 6 servings
PREPARATION TIME: 5–10 minutes
COOKING TIME: 10–15 minutes

## BANANAS FOSTER

*The classic New Orleans dessert—even better than you imagined. Serve on Vanilla Ice Cream.*

4 TABLESPOONS BUTTER
¼ CUP BROWN SUGAR
½ TEASPOON CINNAMON
6 RIPE FIRM BANANAS, SLICED LENGTHWISE
¼ CUP DARK RUM
¼ CUP BANANA LIQUEUR
VANILLA ICE CREAM, FOR SERVING (SEE RECIPE PAGE ON PAGE 240)

1. Melt the butter on low heat in a large pan. Stir in sugar and cinnamon and let simmer until sugar has melted. Place bananas, cut side down, in the pan. Remove pan from heat and add rum and banana liqueur. Return to the heat, tilt pan to ignite liquor, or use a long match if using an electric stove. Using a long spoon, carefully baste the bananas with the mixture.
2. Sauté for 4–5 minutes.
3. Serve on Vanilla Ice Cream.

Yield: 6 servings
Preparation time: 5 minutes
Cooking time: 10 minutes

**Note:** this does not include Vanilla Ice Cream recipe times

# Sabine Pass Lighthouse
SABINE PASS, LOUISIANA

AT LOUISIANA'S WESTERN EDGE NEAR THE TEXAS BORDER, THE SABINE PASS Lighthouse is located in a modest gulfside community. Because it was constructed on wetlands, the lighthouse has extensions on its base that give it the distinct appearance of a rocketship.

First lit in 1857, the then-darkened lighthouse witnessed the Battle of Sabine Pass during the Civil War and weathered a great hurricane in 1886.

Shipping increased as oil was discovered nearby in the early twentieth century, and the lighthouse was still deemed necessary even after a nearby jetty into the Gulf was built.

In this area, the Spanish, French, and then the English arrived, mixing with the native populations, in some cases, and melding their cultural traditions. To augment their meager pay, the keepers and their children fished, shrimped, and hunted, and considered the bounty of land and sea to be generous. Usually, they were able to eat fairly well, if simply, on locally sourced foods—as did everyone else in the area. Occasionally, foodstuffs might be donated or shared, especially if a relative brought something from another part of the state—like alligator, perhaps.

# Big Dinner at the Lighthouse

Seafood, such as shrimp, oysters, and crabs, could be found in local waters. Still, it would have been a treat to have a delicacy from Cajun country for a special dinner. And for dessert—Pralines, just like in the Big Easy.

GRILLED OYSTERS IN THE SHELL

SMOTHERED OKRA

CRAB BAKE

ALLIGATOR GUMBO

PRALINES

## GRILLED OYSTERS IN THE SHELL

*Grilling the oysters saves you the hassle of opening the oysters, and they taste so good when they come off the grill.*

24 OYSTERS
PREPARED HORSERADISH
8 LEMON WEDGES
4 TABLESPOONS BUTTER, MELTED
¼ CUP GRATED PARMESAN CHEESE
HOT SAUCE

1. Start the grill.
2. When the coals are red hot, position the rack 4 inches from heat. The coals are the right temperature if you can only hold your hand above the rack for a count of 2.
3. Clean the oysters by scrubbing them under cold running water. Discard any with cracked or broken shells. Place oysters, rounded side down, on the grill, and cover. Cook until they begin to open, about 8 to 10 minutes. Remove them immediately. Open oysters the rest of the way using an oyster knife or flathead screwdriver. Use a towel to protect your hand, and be careful to save the liquid. Discard any oysters that do not open.
4. Place on a platter and serve with the prepared horseradish, lemon wedges, melted butter, Parmesan cheese, and hot sauce.

YIELD: 4 servings
PREPARATION TIME: 5–10 minutes
GRILLING TIME: 10 minutes

## SMOTHERED OKRA

*This dish will turn you into an okra lover, even if you never thought it could happen.*

1 POUND FRESH OKRA
4 TABLESPOONS BUTTER
2 TABLESPOONS VEGETABLE OIL

1 ONION, DICED
1 SMALL GREEN PEPPER, DICED
2 CELERY STALKS, DICED
1 CUP CORN KERNELS (ABOUT 2 EARS)
1 CUP OR 1 (15-OUNCE) CAN DICED TOMATOES
½ TEASPOON DRIED THYME
1 TEASPOON SALT
¼ TEASPOON FRESHLY GROUND BLACK PEPPER

1. Cut the stems off the okra, and chop the pods into rings. Set aside.
2. Melt the butter in a pan along with the oil.
3. Stir in the onion, green pepper, and celery. Cook for 10 to 15 minutes, or until vegetables are tender.
4. Add the okra and cook for 5 minutes. Blend in the corn, tomatoes, thyme, salt, and pepper. Simmer for 20 to 25 minutes, or until the mixture thickens, stirring occasionally. The vegetables will still retain their texture.

YIELD: 6–8 servings
PREPARATION TIME: 25–30 minutes
COOKING TIME: 20–25 minutes

## CRAB BAKE

*If you want this dish to sing, use only the freshest crabmeat. This is usually served with crackers or lettuce leaves, and maybe some hot sauce on the side.*

2 TABLESPOONS VEGETABLE OIL
1 ONION, DICED (ABOUT 1 CUP)
1 GREEN BELL PEPPER, DICED (ABOUT
   1 CUP)
2 CELERY STALKS, DICED (ABOUT 1 CUP)
1 POUND FRESH CRABMEAT
1 CUP MAYONNAISE
2 SCALLIONS, DICED
½ TEASPOON WORCESTERSHIRE SAUCE
½ TEASPOON SALT
⅛ TEASPOON FRESHLY GROUND BLACK PEPPER
1 CUP BREAD CRUMBS
2 TABLESPOONS BUTTER, MELTED

1. Preheat the oven to 350°F.
2. Heat a pan over medium heat. Add the oil and sauté the onion, bell pepper, and celery for 10 to 15 minutes, or until vegetables are tender and slightly brown.
3. Combine the cooked vegetables with the crabmeat, mayonnaise, scallions, Worcestershire sauce, salt, and pepper and put into a casserole.
4. Mix the bread crumbs and butter and spread on top of the crab mixture. Bake for 30 to 35 minutes.

YIELD: 4–6 servings
PREPARATION TIME: 10–15 minutes
COOKING TIME: 10–15 minutes to sauté the vegetables, and 30–35
 minutes in the oven

## ALLIGATOR GUMBO

*Yes, really! Serve over white rice.*

3 TABLESPOONS PLUS ⅔ CUP VEGETABLE OIL
2 POUNDS ALLIGATOR, CUT INTO 1-INCH CUBES
2½ TEASPOONS SALT, DIVIDED
½ TEASPOON FRESHLY GROUND BLACK PEPPER, DIVIDED
½ CUP ALL-PURPOSE FLOUR
1 POUND ANDOUILLE SAUSAGE OR OTHER HOT SAUSAGE,
 SLICED ½ INCH THICK
2 ONIONS, DICED (ABOUT 2 CUPS)
1 GREEN BELL PEPPER, DICED (ABOUT 1 CUP)
2 CELERY STALKS, DICED (ABOUT 1 CUP)
4 CLOVES GARLIC, CHOPPED
1 QUART VEGETABLE STOCK
1 (28-OUNCE) CAN WHOLE TOMATOES, SEEDED AND
 CHOPPED
1 CUP CHOPPED SUN-DRIED TOMATOES
2 BAY LEAVES
2 TEASPOONS DRIED THYME
2 TEASPOONS DRIED OREGANO
2½–3 TABLESPOONS FILÉ POWDER
WHITE RICE, FOR SERVING (SEE RECIPE ON PAGE 159)

1. Heat a large pot on medium-high heat. Add 3 tablespoons of oil. Season the alligator with 2 teaspoons salt and ¼ teaspoon black pepper,
   and cook for 10 minutes. Remove the alligator and any liquid. Cover to
   keep warm.
2. Pour remaining oil into the pot and gradually stir in the flour. Cook
   the flour, stirring continuously, until it achieves a medium brown color,
   about 15 to 20 minutes. This is a dark roux.
3. Add the sausage, onions, bell pepper, celery and garlic and cook 15 to
   20 minutes, or until vegetables are tender. Continue to stir and scrape
   the bottom of the pot. Be careful not to burn.
4. Stir in the alligator, stock, canned tomatoes, sun-dried tomatoes, bay
   leaves, thyme, and oregano. Bring to a boil and reduce to a simmer.
   Cook for 50 to 60 minutes, scraping bottom of the pot often.
5. Remove from heat and stir in the filé powder and remaining salt and
   pepper. Allow to rest for 5 to 10 minutes.
6. Serve on White Rice.

YIELD: 8–10 servings
PREPARATION TIME: 20–25 minutes
COOKING TIME: 25–30 minutes for the roux, and 1–1½ hours for the
 gumbo

*You can make the roux in advance and refrigerate it. Also, Ed has made a roux by starting it on the stove and transferring it to the oven and baking it. Less attention is required, but it does take longer.*

## PRALINES

*We could not stop eating these. They melt in your mouth, ending with a satisfying crunch of toasted pecan.*

1½ CUPS PECAN PIECES
1 CUP BROWN SUGAR, FIRMLY PACKED
1 CUP SUGAR
½ CUP HALF-AND-HALF OR LIGHT CREAM
2 TABLESPOONS BUTTER
1 TEASPOON VANILLA EXTRACT

1. Preheat the oven to 350°F. Place the pecans on a baking sheet and bake for 10 minutes.
2. Insert a candy thermometer into a small pot. Pour in the brown sugar, sugar, half-and-half, and butter. Cook until the thermometer reads 236°F, about 5 to 7 minutes.
3. Remove from heat and stir in the vanilla. Let cool for 4 to 5 minutes.
4. Stir in pecans using a wooden spoon. Beat vigorously for about 3 minutes. When thick and not glossy, quickly spoon out 2–inch diameter pralines onto wax paper or a marble slab to cool.

YIELD: 15 large (2-inch) pralines
PREPARATION TIME: 5–10 minutes
COOKING TIME: 20 minutes with roasting nuts

# Bolivar Point Lighthouse

PORT BOLIVAR, TEXAS

BOLIVAR POINT LIGHT IS A GRAND OLD LIGHTHOUSE, ONE THAT MAY HAVE saved more lives on land than at sea. Built in 1871 near the booming city of Galveston, this lighthouse drew sightseers for decades. In the late summer of 1900, sailors who had been out in the Gulf warned that a major hurricane was approaching. Meteorologists had seen the storm signals too, although their science was much more primitive than today, but the public didn't pay much attention. So people went out to the beach to watch the winds whip up the tides. Dozens were caught there when the storm broke.

Lighthouse keeper Harry Claiborne opened the doors to the tower, and the terrified sightseers crowded in, each one climbing up as far as possible and standing trapped in the dark, airless stairway for hours while winds and harsh rains lashed the tower: they were frightened—even sickened—but safe. When the storm abated, 125 people came out and stared. Their city had been flattened.

Over one hundred years later, the lighthouse remains, but it is now privately owned. A historic and gracious Gulf city again grew up on Galveston Island, even though this area continues to be periodically victimized by hurricanes. Its proximity to Mexico gives its native dishes a decidedly Spanish flair. Citrus and chiles are basic accents. Shrimp and fish from the Gulf are staples—and favorites, by far, in the area.

# UPSCALE DINNER IN GALVESTON

In Texas, upscale dishes are appreciated even more when they're made with local ingredients. This is a postmodern take on a dinner of locally grown watermelon and chayote, with tuna from the Gulf, finishing with the newly popular Mexican classic Tres Leches Cake.

WATERMELON SALAD
CHAYOTE SLAW
GRILLED TUNA MARINATED IN CITRUS
TRES LECHES CAKE

## WATERMELON SALAD

*A surprisingly great combination of ingredients. Try it—you'll be more than pleased.*

8 CUPS CHOPPED SEEDLESS WATERMELON (1-INCH CUBES)
1 SMALL RED ONION, SLICED THIN (ABOUT ½ CUP)
1 RED BELL PEPPER, SEEDED AND SLICED THIN
½ CUP THINLY SLICED FRESH MINT
1 JALAPEÑO PEPPER, SEEDED AND DICED (OPTIONAL)
⅓ CUP MOLASSES DRESSING (RECIPE FOLLOWS), FOR SERVING
1 TEASPOON SALT
½ TEASPOON FRESHLY GROUND BLACK PEPPER

1. Combine the watermelon, onion, bell pepper, mint, and jalapeño in a bowl.
2. Pour the Molasses Dressing over the watermelon, season with salt and pepper, and toss.
3. Serve immediately.

YIELD: 8 servings
PREPARATION TIME: 15–20 minutes

*Molasses Dressing*

1 TABLESPOON MOLASSES
1 TABLESPOON BROWN SUGAR
JUICE OF 1 LIME (ABOUT 2 TABLESPOONS)
2 TEASPOONS LIME ZEST
2 TEASPOONS RICE WINE VINEGAR
2 TABLESPOONS EXTRA VIRGIN OLIVE OIL
1 TEASPOON PINK PEPPERCORNS, CRUSHED

1. Combine all the ingredients and blend well.

YIELD: About ⅓ cup
PREPARATION TIME: 10 minutes

## CHAYOTE SLAW
*Native Texan vegetables, dressed for dinner.*

3 CHAYOTES
1 SMALL GREEN BELL PEPPER, SEEDED AND DICED
½ POUND TOMATILLOS, DICED
3 SCALLIONS, DICED
2 AVOCADOS, PEELED, PITTED AND DICED
1 (15-OUNCE) CAN PINK BEANS, DRAINED AND RINSED
¼ CUP CHOPPED FRESH BASIL
¼ CUP CHOPPED FRESH CILANTRO
JUICE OF 1 LIME (ABOUT 2 TABLE-
    SPOONS)
½ CUP EXTRA VIRGIN OLIVE OIL
1 TEASPOON SALT
¼ TEASPOON FRESHLY GROUND BLACK
    PEPPER
1½ CUPS SLAW DRESSING (RECIPE
    FOLLOWS), FOR SERVING

1. Peel the chayote, cut in half, remove pit, and slice into strips.
2. Combine the chayote, bell pepper, tomatillos, scallions, avocado, beans, basil, and cilantro into a bowl. Toss with the lime juice, olive oil, salt, and pepper.
3. Mix in the Slaw Dressing.

YIELD: 8–10 servings
PREPARATION TIME: 20–25 minutes

*Slaw Dressing*

½ CUP SOUR CREAM
½ CUP MAYONNAISE
2 TABLESPOONS HEAVY CREAM
2 CLOVES GARLIC, MINCED
1 TEASPOON GROUND CUMIN
¼ CUP CHOPPED FRESH CILANTRO
¼ CUP CHOPPED FRESH BASIL
¼ TEASPOON SALT
⅛ TEASPOON FRESHLY GROUND BLACK PEPPER

1. Combine all the ingredients in a bowl and mix.

YIELD: About 1½ cups
PREPARATION TIME: 5 minutes

## GRILLED TUNA MARINATED IN CITRUS

*You'll find line-caught yellowfin, blackfin, and bluefin in the Gulf. Use this recipe with any of these fish.*

6 TUNA STEAKS (ABOUT 6–8 OUNCES EACH)
¼ CUP ORANGE JUICE (ABOUT 1 MEDIUM ORANGE)
¼ CUP LIME JUICE (ABOUT 2 LIMES)
¼ CUP LEMON JUICE (ABOUT 1 LEMON)
¼ CUP EXTRA VIRGIN OLIVE OIL
¼ CUP CHOPPED FRESH CILANTRO
VEGETABLE OIL, TO COAT GRILL RACK
1 TEASPOON SALT
¼ TEASPOON FRESHLY GROUND BLACK PEPPER

1. Start the grill.
2. Combine the juices, olive oil, and cilantro in a bowl. Mix well.
3. Pour over the tuna, cover and marinate for 30 minutes, under refrigeration.
4. When the coals are red hot, clean and oil the grill rack, and position the rack 4 inches from heat. The coals are the right temperature if you can only hold your hand above the rack for a count of 2.
5. Remove the steaks from the marinade and wipe dry. Season with salt and pepper. Place steaks on the hot grill. Turn over after 3 minutes. When turning, lift gently with tongs and a metal spatula. If the grill is clean, the steaks should turn easily. Grill for another 3 minutes.

YIELD: 6 servings
PREPARATION TIME: 15–20 minutes
MARINATING TIME: 30 minutes
COOKING TIME: 3 minutes per side for rare, 4–5 minutes per side for medium, and 6–7 minutes per side for well done, based on a steak that is 1¼ inches thick

## TRES LECHES CAKE

*This is a modern version of the traditional celebration cake that has recently become so popular. It still tastes decadently wonderful, but this recipe is actually low in fat.*

5 EGGS, SEPARATED
1 CUP PLUS 2 TABLESPOONS SUGAR, DIVIDED
⅔ CUP LOWFAT MILK, DIVIDED
1½ TEASPOONS VANILLA EXTRACT, DIVIDED
1 CUP ALL-PURPOSE FLOUR
1½ TEASPOONS BAKING POWDER
10 OUNCES SWEETENED CONDENSED MILK, LOWFAT OR NONFAT
10 OUNCES NONFAT EVAPORATED MILK
1 CUP WHIPPING CREAM, REGULAR OR NONFAT

1. Preheat the oven to 350°F.
2. Grease and flour 1 (9-inch) springform pan or 2 (8-inch) round cake pans.
3. Beat the egg yolks with ¾ cup sugar until light yellow and doubled in volume.
4. Beat in ⅓ cup milk and 1 teaspoon of vanilla.
5. Slowly add the flour and baking powder, and beat until incorporated.
6. Using a separate bowl beat egg whites with ¼ cup sugar just until firm.
7. Fold the egg whites into batter and fill springform or layer pans.
8. Bake 20–40 minutes (depending on pan size), or until the cake is golden brown and an inserted tester comes out clean.
9. Run the knife around the edge of the pan to loosen the cake. Cool for 15 minutes.
10. Mix together the sweetened condensed milk, evaporated milk, and remaining lowfat milk.
11. Place the cake on rimmed cake plate. If using 2 layers, place bottoms together, 1 on top of the other.
12. Prick deeply with a fork at least a dozen times. Pour the milk mixture very slowly over the cake, letting it absorb into the cake, in 5 or 6 passes.
13. Cover and refrigerate at least 4 hours or overnight.
14. Whip the heavy cream till thickened. Add the rest of the sugar and vanilla, and whip just until stiff.
15. Spread over the cake and serve immediately.

YIELD: 8–10 servings
PREPARATION TIME: 15–20 minutes for cake, and 5 minutes for mixing the three milks and whipping the cream
BAKING TIME: 20–40 minutes, depending on cake pan size
REFRIGERATION TIME: 4 hours

# Point Isabel Lighthouse
## PORT ISABEL, TEXAS

SEVERAL ADMINISTRATIVE CONFLICTS HAVE DOGGED THIS LIGHTHOUSE, from the problem of who owned the land it was built on, to later confusion over whether it is called Port Isabel or Point St. Isabel. In 1852, the first lighthouse was established on this spot—which was then called Brazos, Santiago—on a former military camp from the Mexican-American War. In the next decade, more battles were fought here during the Civil War. After the end of that conflict, the lighthouse was renovated and lit again in 1866.

Run down again in only a few years, it was renovated once more in 1881, only to be abandoned in 1888 when the U.S. government couldn't prove it owned the land because no title could be found. But ships needed the light's guidance, so the government finally purchased the land and reestablished the lighthouse in 1895.

It only remained lit until 1905, but the tower stands to this day, having been donated to the state by private owners in 1950. After renovation, replicas of the keepers' cottage were built that now house the city's chamber of commerce and visitor center. In fact, the image of Port Isabel Lighthouse has now become a vital part of the city's identity.

For the first few hundred years of European occupation, the region was owned by Spain and Mexico, before becoming part of the United States. This area is a gateway to Texas's interior, where ranching began in the early 1800s, and the cuisine is heavily Spanish or Mexican-influenced. Beans, rice, and chiles became mainstream here centuries ago, and the rest of the United States has jumped on the bandwagon of appreciation for these foods.

## COWBOY DINNER

We all think we know what we'd eat as a Texas cowboy, so we've created this menu to match our imaginations. This is as close as many of us will ever get to authentic Texan dishes and it's based on the area's locally available foods.

TEXAS CAVIAR
HERBED RICE
TEXAS CHILI
TEX-MEX PECAN PIE

### TEXAS CAVIAR

*A new Texas classic, great as an appetizer, a side, or a vegetarian main dish.*

2 (15-OUNCE) CANS BLACK-EYED
  PEAS, DRAINED
1 RED ONION, DICED
2 CLOVES GARLIC, MINCED
1 CELERY STALK, DICED
1 SMALL RED BELL PEPPER, DICED
1 TABLESPOON SEEDED AND DICED
  JALAPEÑO PEPPER

ZEST OF 1 LIME
¼ CUP LIME JUICE (ABOUT 2
  LIMES)
¾ CUP EXTRA VIRGIN OLIVE OIL
¼ CUP CHOPPED FRESH CILANTRO
1 TEASPOON SALT
¼ TEASPOON FRESHLY GROUND
  BLACK PEPPER

1. Combine the black-eyed peas, onion, garlic, celery, bell pepper, and jalapeño.
2. Toss with the zest, lime juice, and olive oil. Add the cilantro, salt, and pepper.

YIELD: 6 servings
PREPARATION TIME: 15–20 minutes

### HERBED RICE

*This rice is a good foil for Texas chili.*

1 CUP LONG GRAIN WHITE RICE
¼ TEASPOON SALT
½ TEASPOON DRIED THYME
½ TEASPOON DRIED OREGANO

1. Rinse rice by putting it in a bowl and covering it with water, gently agitating, and then draining. Repeat a total of 3 times. This will help keep the grains separate.
2. Put rice, salt, and herbs into a pot with a tight-fitting lid. Fill with water to cover the rice by ½ inch. Cover, bring to a boil, and reduce to the lowest temperature.
3. Cook for 12 minutes, remove from heat, and allow to rest, covered, for 15 minutes.
4. Fluff with a fork and serve.

YIELD: 4 servings
PREPARATION TIME: 5 minutes
COOKING TIME: 12 minutes
RESTING TIME: 15 minutes

## TEXAS CHILI

*Real chili—no beans! Great for a slow cooker.*

¼ CUP PLUS 2 TABLESPOONS VEGETABLE OIL,
    DIVIDED
4 POUNDS BEEF CHUCK, CUT INTO 1-INCH CUBES
2½ TEASPOONS SALT, DIVIDED
½ TEASPOON FRESHLY GROUND BLACK PEPPER,
    DIVIDED
2 ONIONS, CHOPPED
2 RED BELL PEPPERS, CHOPPED
3 CLOVES GARLIC, CHOPPED
5 TABLESPOONS TOMATO PASTE
1 CUP RED WINE
1 TABLESPOON DRIED OREGANO
1 TEASPOON CUMIN
2 TEASPOONS SMOKED PAPRIKA
1 TEASPOON PAPRIKA
1½ CHIPOTLE PEPPERS IN ADOBO SAUCE, SMASHED
1 JALAPEÑO PEPPER, SEEDED AND DICED
2 CUPS BEEF STOCK
1 CUP WATER

1. Heat a pot on medium-high. Pour in ¼ cup oil. Allow to heat up. Season the beef with 2 teaspoons salt and ¼ teaspoon pepper. Cook the beef in batches until browned.
2. Remove the beef and set aside. Reduce heat to medium and add remaining oil. Sauté the onions, bell pepper, and garlic for 10 to 15 minutes, or until vegetables are tender. Stir in the tomato paste and red wine. Cook until the wine is reduced by half, about 5 minutes. Stir in the reserved beef, with oregano, cumin, paprikas, chipotles, and jalapeño. Cook for 2 minutes.
3. Pour in the beef stock and water. Simmer for 3 hours.
4. Season with remaining salt and pepper.

YIELD: 8–10 servings
PREPARATION TIME: 15–20 minutes
COOKING TIME: 3–3½ hours

## TEX-MEX PECAN PIE

*This is the best pecan pie you'll ever eat, bar none—and it's made with native Texas-grown pecans.*

2 CUPS CHOPPED PECANS, TOASTED
1 CUP SUGAR
1 CUP DARK CORN SYRUP
3 EGGS, SLIGHTLY BEATEN
6 TABLESPOONS BUTTER, MELTED
½ CUP CHOCOLATE MORSELS
½ TEASPOON VANILLA EXTRACT
2 TEASPOONS GROUND MULATO OR ANCHO CHILE
¼ TEASPOON SALT
1 (9-INCH) PIE CRUST (RECIPE FOLLOWS), PREBAKED

1. Preheat the oven to 375°F.
2. Combine the pecans, sugar, corn syrup, eggs, butter, chocolate, vanilla, chile, and salt. Mix together until smooth.
3. Pour into the pie crust.
4. Bake for 40–45 minutes. Remove and allow to cool on a rack for 1 hour before serving.

YIELD: 6 servings
PREPARATION TIME: Less than 5 minutes
BAKING TIME: 40–45 minutes


*Pie Crust*

1½ CUPS ALL-PURPOSE FLOUR
⅛ TEASPOON SALT
¾ CUP SHORTENING, COLD
⅓ CUP COLD WATER

1. Mix the flour and salt in a bowl and cut the shortening into the flour with 2 knives or a pastry blender, until the mixture is in clumps the size of peas. Gradually add the water and blend together.
2. Form the pie dough into a ball, cover with plastic wrap, and refrigerate for 30 minutes.
3. Lightly flour work surface. Roll out the pie dough to be 1 inch larger than the pie plate. Fold the dough over rolling pin and place in the pie plate. Unfold to cover the entire plate. Fold the extra dough under, and crimp the edges.
4. With a fork, poke holes in the bottom of the crust, and place in the refrigerator for at least 10 minutes.
5. Preheat the oven to 450°F. Take the pie crust from the refrigerator, line the bottom with foil, and fill it with dried beans or rice. Bake for 15 to 20 minutes, or until lightly browned. Remove the pie crust from the oven, remove the foil and beans, and let cool on a rack.

YIELD: 1 (9-inch) pie crust
PREPARATION TIME: 15–20 minutes
REFRIGERATION TIME: 40 minutes
BAKING TIME: 15–20 minutes

# HAWAII AND CALIFORNIA REGION

Although their states have different cultural histories, Hawaiians and Californians both have an affinity for the pure and natural foods favored by their gentle climates and easy lifestyles. From the coastal fishing villages of the Hawaiian Islands to the organic farms of California, the people of these regions live by common ideals, respecting the land and the sea.

Hawaii's sheltered western Pacific beaches drew their first settlers from the South Pacific more than a thousand years ago. Humans also brought pineapples, coconuts, and other produce we now think of as "native Hawaiian." Toward the end of the eighteenth century, Europeans began to colonize the Hawaiian Islands, sending missionaries and traders from New England to this very different land, where a strong native culture still dominates the lifestyle. All the same, there are also solid Japanese and Chinese components in the cuisine today, as in the population.

In California, Spanish missionaries traveled northward along the coast during the eighteenth century, and then Native Americans were pushed back as Spanish and American settlers moved in. From place names to the continuing influx of Mexicans and Central Americans, a strong Spanish element lives on in California today. Further north, some aspects of Spanish cuisine made way for other European traditions brought in by ranchers, farmers, and gold prospectors. Later, San Francisco became a hub for Chinese and Japanese immigrants. Italians who arrived as seafarers in the twentieth century found a familiar climate to settle in. Toward the end of the 1900s, many Koreans, Vietnamese, Cambodians and other Asians also arrived.

When it's winter in the East and North, California supplies a taste of sunshine for everyone's menus, and Californians are accustomed to having the freshest of everything available to them, including avocados, tomatoes, lettuces, oranges, and other "seasonal" fruits and vegetables. Hawaii, as an island nation, may have fewer locally grown foods, but Hawaiians enjoy pineapples, coconuts, and papayas picked from their own trees and mahi mahi caught offshore the same day it's eaten. In keeping with the warmer climate, meals tend to be lighter, with sweet and savory salads and vegetable dishes dominating the menus.

# Makapu'u Lighthouse

OAHU, HAWAII

SHIPS OF ALL NATIONS LANDED ON THE HAWAIIAN ISLANDS FOR HUNDREDS OF years. They had come from America for many decades before ship captains began petitioning for a lighthouse in 1888. Yet there remained nothing to guide them along this northeastern part of Oahu until Makapu'u Light was finished in 1909. The point and the lighthouse there are said to be named for a Tahitian goddess with many eyes.

Although it is a small tower—only thirty-five feet high—it stands four hundred feet above sea level on a ledge blasted from lava rock. With the largest lens in the United States, its light can be discerned from twenty-eight miles out at sea; this is the beacon that tells ships from America they are near the end of their long crossing.

Oahu became the capital of Hawaii at the turn of the twentieth century, when Hawaii officially became part of the United States. Immigrants and visitors alike began flocking here in larger numbers, all leaving their imprint on the food culture. Polynesian, Japanese, and Chinese dishes became common in the cuisine of the general populace. Later, they also adapted—and adopted—foods from the United States mainland. We find South Pacific-style fresh fish or Hawaiian stewed pork dishes eaten in combination with American-style macaroni or Asian rice, and eggs and bacon (or Spam) served at breakfast alongside native papaya and mango.

## PLATE LUNCH

Today, the "plate lunch" is still a staple midday meal in many parts of Hawaii. It typically includes meat or fish, macaroni salad, and rice served on a divided, picnic-style plate. Main dishes reflect the islands' mix of cultures, with Korean pulgoki ("fire beef"), Japanese teriyaki beef, Chinese barbecued ribs, Hawaiian lomi-lomi salmon or kalua pork (pulled pork) enjoyed by natives and tourists alike. Asian rice dishes share the plate with typically American macaroni salads, and tropical fruits round out the lunch. Plate lunches are found everywhere, from local markets to fine hotels, and are often enjoyed on the beach or under a swaying palm tree.

ASIAN RICE

MACARONI SALAD

ROASTED GREEN PAPAYA

LOMI LOMI SALMON

KALUA PORK

FRIED BANANAS WITH MACADAMIA NUTS AND KONA COFFEE

### ASIAN RICE

*Go home. Cook rice. The start of every meal.*

3 CUPS SHORT-GRAIN OR SUSHI RICE
3 CUPS WATER
3 TABLESPOONS RICE WINE VINEGAR
3 TABLESPOONS SUGAR
2 TEASPOONS SALT

1. Rinse the rice in cold water until the water runs clear. Drain and allow to rest in a colander for 20 to 30 minutes.
2. Put the water and rice into a pot with a tight-fitting lid. Bring the water to a boil and reduce to the lowest setting. Cook for 15 minutes, or until all the water has been absorbed. Remove from heat and allow to rest, covered, for 10 minutes.
3. Put the vinegar, sugar and salt in a microwave-safe bowl. Microwave for 20 seconds, until the sugar and salt have dissolved.
4. Remove the rice from the pot and put it into a wide bowl. You will want to cool the rice as quickly as possible, while drizzling in the vinegar mixture and being careful not to smash the rice. If you can fan the rice, it will cool even quicker and achieve a glossy look.

YIELD: About 6 cups
PREPARATION TIME: Less than 5 minutes
RESTING TIME: 20–30 minutes
COOKING TIME: 25 minutes total

## MACARONI SALAD

*You can't have a plate lunch without macaroni salad.*

1 CUP GOOD-QUALITY MAYONNAISE
¼ CUP GRATED CARROTS
1 CELERY STALK, DICED
2 SCALLIONS, DICED
¼ CUP MILK
1 TEASPOON SALT
¼ TEASPOON FRESHLY GROUND BLACK PEPPER
3 CUPS COOKED ELBOW MACARONI

1. Mix all the ingredients except macaroni until blended. Then toss with noodles. Refrigerate for at least 1 hour.

YIELD: 6 servings
PREPARATION TIME: 10 minutes
COOKING TIME: 8–10 minutes for macaroni
REFRIGERATION TIME: 1 hour

## ROASTED GREEN PAPAYA

*Green papaya is eaten as a vegetable, not a fruit.*

3 GREEN HAWAIIAN PAPAYAS
4 TABLESPOONS BUTTER, DIVIDED
1½ TEASPOONS SALT
½ TEASPOON CHINESE FIVE-SPICE POWDER

1. Preheat the oven to 350°F.
2. Cut all 3 papayas in half lengthwise, and remove seeds.
3. Put 2 teaspoons of butter into each half, and season with salt and Chinese five-spice powder.
4. Roast for 50 to 60 minutes.

YIELD: 6 servings
PREPARATION TIME: 10 minutes
ROASTING TIME: 50–60 minutes

*Chinese five spice powder is a combination of star anise, fennel seed, Szechwan pepper, cinnamon, and ground clove.*

## LOMI LOMI SALMON
*A traditional accompaniment to your plate lunch.*

**Note:** This dish takes 24 hours to prepare.

1 1 POUND SALMON FILLET, 1 INCH THICK (WILL YIELD 10
    OUNCES SALT SALMON)
HAWAIIAN SALT OR SEA SALT
1 28-OUNCE CAN OR SIMILAR WEIGHT
1 RIPE TOMATO, DICED (ABOUT 1 CUP)
½ CUP DICED MAUI MAUI, OR OTHER SWEET, ONION
2 SCALLIONS, DICED
JUICE OF 1 LIME (ABOUT 2 TABLESPOONS)
¼ TEASPOON FRESHLY GROUND BLACK PEPPER
¼ CUP CRUSHED ICE

1. Using a glass plate large enough to hold the fillet easily, cover the bottom with salt. Place fillet, skin side down, on the salt, and cover the fillet with salt. Cover with plastic wrap, place another plate on top, and weigh down with a 28-ounce can. Refrigerate for 24 hours.
2. Remove the salmon from refrigerator and rinse under cold water. Taste a small piece. If too salty, place in a bowl, cover with water, return to refrigerator and allow to soak for several hours to remove saltiness. Check occasionally.
3. Remove the skin and cut the salmon into ½-inch cubes. Mix the tomato, onion, lime juice, and pepper into the salmon by hand and refrigerate.
4. Mix with a ¼ cup of crushed ice before serving.

YIELD: 4 servings
REFRIGERATION TIME: 24 hours
PREPARATION TIME: 10–15 minutes to combine ingredients

## KALUA PORK
*When this is done, it will melt in your mouth.*

4–5 POUNDS PORK BUTT
1 TABLESPOON HAWAIIAN SEA OR KOSHER SALT
3 TABLESPOONS LIQUID SMOKE
5–6 TI LEAVES (BANANA LEAVES CAN BE USED)
¼ CUP WATER
HEAVY-DUTY ALUMINUM FOIL

1. Preheat the oven to 325°F.
2. Lay a large piece of foil on a work surface. Cover the foil with ti leaves.
3. Rub the pork with the salt and liquid smoke.
4. Place the pork on the leaves. Pour in water, and wrap the pork and leaves tightly in foil.

*The ti plant, which is also known as the good luck plant, is an all-purpose plant. It is used in traditional Hawaiian cooking, and also to store food. Banana leaves are a good substitute.*

5. Place on baking sheet and put in the oven. Roast for 5 hours.
6. Remove from the oven, unwrap the pork, and place in a bowl along with the liquid. Shred the pork using 2 forks.

YIELD: 8–10 servings
PREPARATION TIME: 15–20 minutes
ROASTING TIME: 5 hours

## FRIED BANANAS WITH MACADAMIA NUTS AND KONA COFFEE

*An island version of Bananas Foster, without the rum.*

4 RIPE YELLOW BANANAS
3 TABLESPOONS BUTTER
3 TABLESPOONS RAW, OR LIGHT BROWN,
   SUGAR
2 TABLESPOONS KONA COFFEE
2 TABLESPOONS CHOPPED MACADAMIA
   NUTS, TOASTED, FOR GARNISH

1. Peel and slice the bananas in half and then lengthwise.
2. Heat a sauté pan on medium heat. Add the butter and sugar. When melted, add the bananas and cook for 3 minutes.
3. Pour in the coffee.
4. Serve on a platter, garnished with the macadamia nuts.

YIELD: 4–6 servings
PREPARATION TIME: 5–6 minutes
COOKING TIME: 10 minutes

# Lahaina Lighthouse

MAUI, HAWAII

SHIPS FROM THE UNITED STATES BEGAN TO VISIT THE HAWAIIAN ISLANDS in the late eighteenth century. Before the turn of the nineteenth century, the islands were unified under the invading King Kamehameha I, whose capital became Lahaina, a city on the island of Maui.

As many as five hundred ships would anchor here for the winter after whaling in Alaska during the summer months. At the same time, Hawaii began exporting sandalwood and sugar cane. Hawaii's first lighthouse, a small wooden structure, was built at the harbor in Lahaina in 1840.

But by 1845, the shipping industry's focus began to shift to Honolulu. However, enough ships continued to dock at Lahaina for a new lighthouse to be built on the edge of the marina in the early twentieth century. Lahaina Light has stood here since 1916, a beacon for military transports as well as tourist ships and local sailors. During World War II, there was a large contingent of ships anchored here; today, cruise ships flock to this lovely island with its legendary climate and relaxing lifestyle.

The sugar plantations brought immigrant workers from Asia as well as Europe— and later from the American mainland—all of whom contributed elements of their cuisines to the fresh Hawaiian-style meals with papayas, avocados, and fish. And, of course, pineapples, which were first planted here in the early twentieth century.

## Asian-Pacific Dinner

An Asian-influenced dinner is very common in the Hawaiian Islands. Desserts lean toward preferences of American tourists, such as a showy pineapple boat with some Chocolate Chip-Macadamia Nut Cookies, which have spread in popularity throughout the United States for the past twenty years.

Asian Chopped Salad

Shrimp Toast

Stir-Fried Baby Bok Choy

Grilled Mahi Mahi with Mango Salsa

Khao Pad Mu (Thai Fried Rice)

Hawaiian Fruit Salad in a Pineapple Boat

Chocolate Chip—Macadamia Nut Cookies

### ASIAN CHOPPED SALAD

*A combination of colorful Asian vegetables, fruit, and herbs.*

2 CUPS NAPA CABBAGE, SLICED THIN
1 CUP BOK CHOY, SLICED THIN
¼ POUND SNOW PEAS, HALVED
4 SCALLIONS, SLICED THIN
1 UNRIPE MANGO, PEELED AND SLICED
1 RED BELL PEPPER, SLICED THIN
1 CUP PAPAYA, DICED

¼ CUP ROUGHLY CHOPPED FRESH MINT
¼ CUP ROUGHLY CHOPPED FRESH BASIL
¼ CUP ROUGHLY CHOPPED FRESH CILANTRO
ASIAN DRESSING (RECIPE FOLLOWS), FOR SERVING

1. Combine all the salad ingredients into 1 large bowl.
2. Toss with the Asian Dressing and serve.

YIELD: 6 servings
PREPARATION TIME: 20 minutes

*Asian Dressing*

¼ CUP LIME JUICE (ABOUT 2 LIMES)
½ CUP VEGETABLE OIL
1 TEASPOON FISH SAUCE

1 TABLESPOON BROWN SUGAR
1 TABLESPOON GRATED FRESH GINGER
½ TEASPOON GARLIC CHILE PASTE

1. Blend together all the ingredients.

YIELD: About 1 cup
PREPARATION TIME: 5 minutes

## SHRIMP TOAST

*For those with a love for hot food, use garlic chile paste as a dip.*

½ POUND SHRIMP, PEELED AND DEVEINED
2 CLOVES GARLIC, MINCED
2 SCALLIONS, MINCED
1 TEASPOON MINCED FRESH GINGER
½ TEASPOON TOASTED SESAME SEED OIL
½ TEASPOON SALT
¼ TEASPOON FRESHLY GROUND BLACK PEPPER
VEGETABLE SHORTENING, FOR FRYING
8 SLICES FIRM WHITE BREAD

1. Put the shrimp, garlic, scallions, ginger, sesame seed oil, salt, and pepper into a food processor. Pulse 8 times, until the mixture is smooth.
2. Heat ½ inch vegetable shortening in a heavy pot over medium-high heat to 375°F. Trim the crusts off the bread, spread the shrimp mixture onto the bread, and cut into quarters.
3. Gently place the shrimp toast in the oil, shrimp side down, using a slotted spoon. Do not overcrowd. Turn over, cooking for 1 to 2 minutes per side.
4. Remove from oil, drain on rack, and serve immediately.

YIELD: 32 pieces
PREPARATION TIME: 15–20 minutes
COOKING TIME: 2–4 minutes per batch

## STIR-FRIED BABY BOK CHOY

*Be sure to use toasted sesame seed oil on this dish. It will make all the difference.*

1 POUND BABY BOK CHOY
3 TABLESPOONS VEGETABLE OIL
2 CLOVES GARLIC, SLICED
1 TABLESPOON CHOPPED FRESH GINGER

2 SCALLIONS, DICED
2 TEASPOONS TOASTED SESAME OIL
½ TEASPOON SALT
⅛ TEASPOON FRESHLY GROUND BLACK PEPPER

1. Cut bok choy into quarters, lengthwise, leaving the stem end intact. Rinse under cold water to ensure that all the grit has been removed. Drain and dry using a salad spinner.

2. Heat a large pan over medium-high heat. Add the oil and allow it to get hot for 1 minute. Cook bok choy, turning over occasionally, in the oil for 5 minutes, or until lightly browned. Add the garlic, ginger, and scallions and cook for 1 to 2 minutes. Stir to keep from burning.
3. Season with the sesame oil, salt, and pepper.

YIELD: 4 servings
PREPARATION TIME: 10–15 minutes
COOKING TIME: 7–10 minutes

## GRILLED MAHI MAHI WITH MANGO SALSA

*Mahi mahi and mango salsa have become mainstream in the last 10 years.*

VEGETABLE OIL, TO COAT GRILL
RACK
6 MAHI MAHI FILLETS (ABOUT 6
OUNCES EACH)
2 TEASPOONS SALT

½ TEASPOON FRESHLY GROUND
BLACK PEPPER
MANGO SALSA (RECIPE FOLLOWS),
FOR SERVING

1. Start the grill.
2. When the coals are red hot, clean and oil the grill rack, and position the rack 4 inches from heat. The coals are the right temperature if you can only hold your hand above the rack for a count of 2.
3. Season the fillets with the salt and pepper. Place the fillets on the hot grill and cover. Turn over after 3 minutes. When turning, lift gently with tongs and a metal spatula. If the grill is clean, fillets should turn easily. Grill for another 3 to 4 minutes, depending on thickness and desired doneness.
4. Serve with Mango Salsa.

YIELD: 6 servings
PREPARATION TIME: 5 minutes for fish
COOKING TIME: 6–8 minutes

*Mango Salsa*

1 MANGO, PEELED, PITTED AND DICED
1 SMALL RED ONION, DICED (ABOUT ¼ CUP)
1 JALAPEÑO PEPPER SEEDED AND DICED
1 CHERRY PEPPER, SEEDED AND DICED
½ CUP CHOPPED FRESH CILANTRO
1 TABLESPOON TOASTED SESAME SEED OIL
1 TEASPOON FISH SAUCE
JUICE OF 1 LIME

1. Take half of the diced mango and purée.
2. Combine the balance of the mango and the rest of the ingredients with the puréed mango.

YIELD: About 1 cup
PREPARATION TIME: 15 minutes

## KHAO PAD MU (THAI FRIED RICE)

*This is a bright, light-tasting fried rice.*
*It helps to have all the ingredients prepared before starting to cook.*

4 TABLESPOONS VEGETABLE OIL
3 CLOVES GARLIC, CHOPPED FINE
1 ONION, HALVED LENGTHWISE AND SLICED THIN
8 OUNCES LEAN GROUND PORK
2 EGGS, BEATEN
4 CUPS COOKED JASMINE RICE
2 TOMATOES, SEEDED AND CHOPPED
1 SMALL YELLOW PEPPER, HALVED LENGTHWISE AND SLICED THIN
2 SCALLIONS, SLICED THIN
2 TABLESPOONS FISH SAUCE
1 TEASPOON PALM, OR LIGHT BROWN, SUGAR
½ CUP CHOPPED FRESH CILANTRO

1. Heat a wok or heavy skillet on high. Add the oil. When the oil is hot (after about 30 seconds), stir fry the garlic until it begins to change color. Add the onion and stir fry for 1 minute. Stir in the pork and cook for 3 minutes, or until the pork is no longer pink. Mix in the eggs, then the rice.
2. Flatten the rice in the wok and up the sides. Turn it over and press again. Stir fry for another minute. Then add the tomatoes, yellow pepper, scallions, fish sauce, and sugar. Cook for 5 to 6 minutes. Toss with cilantro. Remove from heat.

YIELD: 4–6 servings
PREPARATION TIME: 20 minutes
COOKING TIME: 10 minutes

## HAWAIIAN FRUIT SALAD IN A PINEAPPLE BOAT

*Serving the fruit in a pineapple boat makes for a more festive occasion.*

1 PINEAPPLE
1 MANGO
1 PAPAYA
2 BANANAS
2 ORANGES
¼ CUP SWEETENED SHREDDED COCONUT

1. Slice the pineapple in half lengthwise, through the crown. Cut out the tough core and discard. Carefully remove the fruit and set aside.
2. Wash the outside of the mango. Place the mango on a cutting board. The mango will settle on its side. This is the direction the seed runs. The seed is ½ to ¾ of an inch thick.
3. Slice each mango in half lengthwise, taking into account the size of the seed.

*Many of the fruits we think are native to Hawaii were actually imported.*

*These are the approximate dates for when these fruits were introduced to Hawaii:*

*Banana and coconut, prior to 1778; mango, 1820; orange, 1840; pineapple, 1880; and papaya, 1911.*

4. Pick up half of each mango, flesh side facing you, and cut a checkerboard pattern into the flesh (but not through the skin). Repeat with each mango half.
5. Pick up the halves, and with the flesh facing you, gently push from underneath. Cut the cubes away from the skin and put in a bowl with the pineapple.
6. Peel, seed, and cube the papaya. Add to bowl.
7. Peel and slice the bananas and oranges. Combine with the rest of the fruit and toss.
8. Place the fruit inside the empty pineapple shells. Top with coconut.

YIELD: 4–6 servings
PREPARATION TIME: 15–20 minutes

## CHOCOLATE CHIP–MACADAMIA NUT COOKIES

*Hawaii's macadamia nuts have made this classic recipe more interesting, but the most fun part of this recipe is snacking on the "leftover" chips and nuts while baking.*

*The dough can be mixed, wrapped in plastic, and then refrigerated for 1 to 2 days (or frozen for up to a month) before baking. We like to make these cookies fairly small (about 2 to 3 inches) and not supersized like everything else is these days, so you can enjoy a few cookies and not take in too many calories.*

1 CUP BUTTER, SOFTENED
¾ CUP PACKED BROWN SUGAR
¾ CUP SUGAR
2 EGGS
1 TEASPOON VANILLA EXTRACT
2¼ CUPS ALL-PURPOSE FLOUR
½ TEASPOON BAKING POWDER
½ TEASPOON BAKING SODA
½ TEASPOON SALT
⅞ CUP SEMISWEET CHOCOLATE CHIPS
⅞ CUP MILK CHOCOLATE CHIPS
⅞ CUP UNSALTED MACADAMIA NUT HALVES, ROASTED

1. Preheat the oven to 375°F.
2. Cream the butter and sugars until fluffy. Add the eggs and vanilla and beat well.
3. In a separate bowl, combine the flour, baking powder, baking soda and salt.
4. Add the flour mixture to the butter–sugar mixture, and beat well.
5. Add the chocolate chips and nuts, and mix by hand to incorporate.
6. Drop by rounded tablespoonfuls on a greased cookie sheet. Bake 9 to 12 minutes, or until browned. Cool on a rack.
7. Serve at room temperature. Store airtight when completely cool, if you haven't already eaten them all!

YIELD: 5–7 dozen, depending on cookie size
PREPARATION TIME: 20 minutes
BAKING TIME: 9–12 minutes per batch

# Point Vicente Lighthouse
RANCHO PALOS VERDES, CALIFORNIA

POINT VICENTE WAS NAMED AFTER A SPANISH MISSIONARY BY AN EXPLORER in the late 1700s. This time period marks the beginning of regular sea voyages in this part of the world. Many ships that traveled up and down this dangerous section of the Southern California coast were wrecked before the government finally built a lighthouse here in 1926. Point Vicente Light's white tower is so decorative, and its site is so picturesque, that it was used as a backdrop for Hollywood films from the industry's earliest days.

During World War II, the beacon, which shone twenty miles out to sea, was shrouded and dimmed so as not to provide any navigational help to possible enemies offshore. After the war, cars on the highway and neighbors in nearby houses were disturbed by the rebrightened rotating light, so its landward windows were painted white. It was then that people began to observe the hazy figure of a woman behind the windows: a ghostly presence, possibly the spirit of a former keeper's wife still tied to her mortal dwelling place.

# A Hollywood Meal

In Southern California, winter is the growing season for fruit and vegetable crops to supply many other regions of the country. Because fresh produce is available here year-round, Californians developed a cuisine based on vegetables and fruits, with little fish and meat. Then, Hollywood celebrities demanded special treatment—elegant dishes developed to tempt their delicate palates.

Cobb Salad

Honeydew Melon Avocado Soup with Crème Fraîche and Mint

Sautéed Ribbons of Zucchini, Yellow Squash, and Carrots

Pan-Fried Halibut

Pignoli Flan

## COBB SALAD

*This is a very authentic version of a Hollywood classic.*

2 cups chopped romaine lettuce
1 small bunch watercress, large stems removed
2 cups chopped iceberg lettuce
2 cups chopped chicory
½ teaspoon salt
¼ teaspoon freshly ground black pepper
2 avocados, peeled, pitted, and chopped
3 cups diced cooked chicken breast
8–10 slices bacon, cooked and crumbled
4 hard-boiled eggs, diced
3 tomatoes, diced
1 cup crumbled Roquefort cheese
¼ cup chopped fresh chives
¾ cup Cobb Salad Vinaigrette (recipe follows), for serving

1. Season the 4 different greens with salt and pepper, and toss.
2. Arrange the avocado, chicken, bacon, eggs, tomatoes, and Roquefort cheese on top of greens. Sprinkle the top with chives.
3. Drizzle Cobb Salad Vinaigrette on top and serve.

YIELD: 6–8 servings
PREPARATION TIME: 20–25 minutes

*Cobb Salad Vinaigrette*

¼ CUP RED WINE VINEGAR
½ TEASPOON SUGAR
2 TABLESPOONS LEMON JUICE
1 TEASPOON WORCESTERSHIRE SAUCE
¼ TEASPOON POWDERED MUSTARD
1 CLOVE GARLIC, MINCED
½ TEASPOON SALT
½ TEASPOON FRESHLY GROUND BLACK PEPPER
½ CUP EXTRA VIRGIN OLIVE OIL

1. Mix all the ingredients, except olive oil, together.
2. Whisk in olive oil.

YIELD: About ¾ cup
PREPARATION TIME: 10 minutes

## HONEYDEW MELON AVOCADO SOUP WITH CRÈME FRAÎCHE AND MINT

*An unlikely combination of two green fruits makes a surprisingly delicious soup.*

1 HONEYDEW MELON (ABOUT 3 POUNDS)
1 AVOCADO
JUICE OF 1 LIME
PINCH OF SALT
SUGAR (OPTIONAL)
¼ CUP FRESH MINT LEAVES, LOOSELY
    PACKED, DIVIDED
4 TABLESPOONS CRÈME FRAÎCHE

1. Remove the rind and seeds from the melon and cut into pieces. Pit and peel the avocado.
2. Place the seeded melon, avocado, lime juice, salt, sugar (if needed), and half the mint in a blender. Purée until smooth.
3. Slice remaining mint as thinly as possible. Garnish the soup with remaining mint and a dollop of crème fraiche.

YIELD: 4 servings
PREPARATION TIME: 10 minutes

## SAUTÉED RIBBONS OF ZUCCHINI, YELLOW SQUASH, AND CARROTS

*A colorful, yet simple way to serve vegetables that are plentiful during many months of the year in nearly every part of the country.*

2 ZUCCHINI
2 YELLOW SQUASH
2 MEDIUM CARROTS, PEELED
3 TABLESPOONS EXTRA VIRGIN OLIVE OIL
1 CLOVE GARLIC, MINCED
1 TEASPOON CHOPPED FRESH THYME
½ TEASPOON SALT
⅛ TEASPOON FRESHLY GROUND BLACK PEPPER

1. Draw a vegetable peeler over the vegetables, making long ribbons. Ribbon the zucchini and squash only down to the seeds.
2. Heat a medium sauté pan over medium-high heat. Add the olive oil. When heated, add vegetables. After 1 minute, add the garlic and thyme.
3. Toss vegetables with salt and pepper while cooking for 3 to 5 minutes, or until just softened.

YIELD: 4 servings
PREPARATION TIME: 20 minutes
COOKING TIME: 5 minutes

*If the fish fillets are thin or tail pieces, they can be folded over to create a thicker fillet.*

## PAN-FRIED HALIBUT

*Halibut is sometimes best cooked simply.*

6 HALIBUT FILLETS (ABOUT 6 OUNCES EACH)
2 TEASPOONS SALT
¼ TEASPOON FRESHLY GROUND BLACK PEPPER
3 TABLESPOONS VEGETABLE OIL

1. Preheat the oven to 450°F. Place a rack in the oven at the lowest level.
2. Heat a large pan with an ovenproof handle over medium-high heat.
3. Season the fillets with salt and pepper.
4. Add the oil to the pan. Allow to heat up for 2 minutes.
5. Place the fillets in the pan, and cook for 5 minutes. Do not disturb. Place the pan in the oven and bake for 5 to 10 minutes. Fillets that are more than 1 inch thick will take 10 minutes.
6. Remove from oven, turn over, and serve.

YIELD: 6 servings
PREPARATION TIME: Less than 5 minutes
COOKING TIME: 10–15 minutes

## PIGNOLI FLAN

*Sprinkling pignolis (pine nuts) on top of this finished flan give this dish a touch of the great Southwest.*

1¾ CUPS SUGAR, DIVIDED
6 TABLESPOONS WATER
4 WHOLE EGGS
2 EGG YOLKS
4 CUPS HALF-AND-HALF OR LIGHT CREAM
¾ TEASPOON VANILLA EXTRACT
1½ CUPS PIGNOLIS (PINE NUTS), TOASTED

1. Place 1 cup of sugar and the water into a microwave-safe bowl (not a plastic bowl, because the liquid will become very hot). Microwave on high for 8 to 9 minutes, or until the sugar dissolves and the mixture achieves a caramel color.
2. Remove and pour the caramel into a 9-inch cake pan. Be very careful not to splash any on yourself.
3. Preheat the oven to 325°F.
4. Whisk together remaining sugar, eggs, and yolks.
5. Heat the half-and-half until warm. Remove from the heat and very slowly whisk into egg mixture, then blend in vanilla.
6. Pour the mixture into a prepared cake pan, then blend in vanilla.
7. Place the pan into a larger container and set on the oven rack. Fill the larger container with boiling water ½ to ¾ up the sides of the baking pan.
8. Bake for 50 to 60 minutes. The center is set when it moves like gelatin.
9. Cool and refrigerate for at least 4 hours. To unmold, dip the pan quickly into hot water and run a knife around the edge. Place a serving platter on top and invert. Tap lightly on the pan and remove. Sprinkle the pignolis on top.

YIELD: 6–8 servings
PREPARATION TIME: 5–10 minutes
COOKING TIME: 8–9 minutes for the caramel, and 50–60 minutes for the flan

# Oakland Harbor Lighthouse

OAKLAND, CALIFORNIA

OAKLAND HARBOR LIGHT WAS BUILT IN 1903 TO REPLACE AN EARLIER light that dated from 1890. Both were located on the eastern side of the Oakland Estuary, off San Francisco Bay. This light's wooden structure housed the families of lighthouse keepers until 1939, when they were billeted ashore. In 1965, the building was moved to its present location in an Oakland marina, and it became a restaurant. Quinn's Lighthouse Restaurant is named for an historic figure, Richard Turner Quinn, who emigrated from England in disgrace, spent some years as a reluctant pirate fighter, and later became the lighthouse keeper.

Today, it is a friendly place, its upstairs bar strewn with peanut shells, and well frequented by day sailors and boat dwellers. The dining areas also cater to families, and the restaurant serves holiday meals as a home-away-from home for travelers. The owner believes in heart-healthy cuisine (as the menu indicates), and he has also developed his own signature dishes, each marked with a little lighthouse.

# PACIFIC RIM LUNCH

In this part of California, there is ready access to all types of produce during much of the year. Gilroy, "the garlic capital of the world," and Castroville, "the artichoke capital of the world," are both Northern California towns. The West Coast is also home to scores of top innovative Asian chefs who update traditional dishes from China, Japan, Korea, Cambodia, and Vietnam and create contemporary Asian-fusion cuisine.

ARTICHOKES AND SESAME MAYONNAISE
ASPARAGUS WITH SOY SAUCE AND ORANGE JUICE DRESSING
VEGETARIAN SUMMER ROLLS
STEAMED MUSSELS WITH COCONUT MILK, CILANTRO, MINT, AND
     BASIL
ASIAN PEARS AND LYCHEE NUTS

## ARTICHOKES AND SESAME MAYONNAISE

*California is the artichoke capital of the United States; this recipe gives artichokes an Asian flavor.*

4 GLOBE ARTICHOKES
1 CUP SESAME SEED MAYONNAISE (RECIPE FOLLOWS)

1. Clean the artichokes by removing any leaves from the stem and using a scissor to cut away any thorns. Cut the artichokes in half, going through the stem.
2. Place the artichokes in a large steamer and cook for 35 to 45 minutes, or until a knife passes easily through the base.
3. Remove from the steamer and allow to cool. Remove the inedible "choke" before serving.

YIELD: 8 servings
PREPARATION TIME: 5–10 minutes
COOKING TIME: 35–45 minutes

*Sesame Seed Mayonnaise*

¾ CUP GOOD QUALITY MAYONNAISE
1 TABLESPOON TOASTED SESAME SEEDS
2 TEASPOONS TOASTED SESAME SEED OIL

1. Mix the mayonnaise, sesame seeds, and oil.

YIELD: 1 cup
PREPARATION TIME: less than 5 minutes

## ASPARAGUS WITH SOY SAUCE AND ORANGE JUICE DRESSING

*California meets Pacific rim flavors.*

1 BUNCH ASPARAGUS
2 QUARTS WATER
1⅛ TEASPOONS SALT, DIVIDED
½ CUP ORANGE JUICE
1½ TEASPOONS SOY SAUCE
ZEST OF 1 ORANGE
⅛ TEASPOON FRESHLY GROUND BLACK PEPPER

1. Clean asparagus by breaking or cutting off the fibrous ends.
2. Bring water to a boil. Add 1 teaspoon salt, then add the asparagus and cook for 4 to 5 minutes, or until barely tender.
3. Put the orange juice into a pan and reduce by half, about 3 minutes.
4. Combine the soy sauce and orange zest with the juice to make the dressing.
5. Remove the asparagus from the water and drain.
6. Toss with the dressing, season with remaining salt and pepper, and serve.

YIELD: 4 servings
PREPARATION TIME: 10 minutes
COOKING TIME: 15-20 minutes total for the asparagus and orange juice reduction

## VEGETARIAN SUMMER ROLLS

*Your vegetarian friends will love you for making this dish, and so will the meat lovers. It's got a lot of crunch and a little sweetness.*

½ CUP JULIENNED CARROT
½ CUP JULIENNED DAIKON RADISH
½ CUP JULIENNED NAPA CABBAGE
½ CUP BEAN SPROUTS
2 TABLESPOONS RICE WINE VINEGAR
2 TABLESPOONS MIRIN
2 TEASPOONS FISH SAUCE
2 TEASPOONS GRATED FRESH GINGER
12–14 SUMMER ROLL WRAPPERS (6 INCHES IN DIAMETER)
12–14 FRESH BASIL LEAVES
12–14 FRESH MINT LEAVES
12–14 FRESH CILANTRO SPRIGS
SUMMER ROLL DIPPING SAUCE (RECIPE FOLLOWS), FOR SERVING

1. Place the carrot, daikon radish, cabbage, and bean sprouts into a bowl. Toss with the vinegar, mirin, fish sauce, and ginger.

*A vegetable mandoline is a real time saver in this type of dish.*

2. Fill a bowl with hot water. Place a wrapper into the water and allow it to soften. Lay the wrapper flat on your work surface. Place 1 to 2 tablespoons of the vegetable mixture, 1 basil leaf, 1 mint leaf, and 1 cilantro sprig into the center. Fold the wrapper end closest to you over the vegetables. Next, fold the sides into the center and roll away from you, forming a cylinder. Repeat until all of the vegetable mixture is used. Change water when it becomes tepid.

YIELD: 12–14 summer rolls
PREPARATION TIME: 15–20 minutes
ASSEMBLY TIME: 15–20 minutes

*Summer Roll Dipping Sauce*

JUICE OF 2 LIMES
2 TABLESPOONS BROWN SUGAR
1 TEASPOON FISH SAUCE
¼ TEASPOON GARLIC CHILE PASTE

1. Combine all the ingredients and mix.

YIELD: ½ cup
PREPARATION TIME: 5 minutes

## STEAMED MUSSELS WITH COCONUT MILK, CILANTRO, MINT, AND BASIL

*Set up your ingredients, and you will be eating in 5 minutes.*

2 TEASPOONS SALT
8 OUNCES RICE NOODLES (FOLLOW PACKAGE INSTRUCTIONS FOR COOKING)
2 TABLESPOONS VEGETABLE OIL
2 CLOVES GARLIC, MINCED
1 TABLESPOON CHOPPED FRESH GINGER
2 POUNDS MUSSELS, CLEANED AND DEBEARDED
¼ CUP WHITE WINE

½ CUP COCONUT MILK
¼ CUP CHOPPED TOMATOES
JUICE OF 1 LIME
2 TABLESPOONS CHOPPED FRESH CILANTRO
2 TABLESPOONS CHOPPED FRESH MINT
2 TABLESPOONS CHOPPED FRESH BASIL
1 TEASPOON GARLIC CHILE PASTE
1 TEASPOON FISH SAUCE
2 SCALLIONS, SLICED, FOR GARNISH

1. Bring a large pot of water to a boil for the rice noodles. Add the salt. Follow the cooking instructions for the rice noodles.
2. Heat a covered pot over medium-high heat. Add the oil. After 1 minute, add the garlic and ginger and cook for 30 seconds.
3. Add the mussels. Remove the pan from the heat. Pour in the white wine and cover. Return to heat and cook until mussels begin to open, about 3 to 5 minutes.
4. Stir in the coconut milk, tomatoes, lime juice, cilantro, mint, basil, chile paste, and fish sauce.

5. Continue to cook for 2 minutes. Toss with rice noodles and garnish with scallions.

YIELD: 4 servings
PREPARATION TIME: 15–20 minutes
COOKING TIME: 10 minutes, not including the noodles

## ASIAN PEARS AND LYCHEE NUTS
*A simple dessert of Asian flavors.*

**Note:** There is a large pit in the center of the lychee nuts, so be careful not to bite down too hard.

1 POUND ASIAN PEARS
½ POUND LYCHEE NUTS
¼ CUP LEMON JUICE
1 TABLESPOON HONEY
4 TEASPOONS TOASTED SESAME SEED OIL
⅛ TEASPOON SALT

1. Wash, core, and cut the pears into thin slices.
2. Peel the tough outer skin off the lychee nuts.
3. In a bowl, mix together the lemon juice, honey, sesame seed oil, and salt to make a dressing.
4. Arrange the fruit on a platter or individual plates, and top with the dressing.

YIELD: 4 servings
PREPARATION TIME: 5 minutes

# East Brother Light Station

POINT RICHMOND, CALIFORNIA

RIVER AS WELL AS OCEAN SHIPPING MADE EAST BROTHER LIGHT A NECESSITY in 1874, so a small lighthouse was built with an attached two-story wooden keeper's house. It is located at the point where the Sacramento River flows into the San Pablo Straits, which lead to San Francisco Bay. And it's on solid rock—most of the site had to be leveled with dynamite.

In the late 1960s, Walter Fanning spearheaded the movement to repair the lighthouse and modernize the keeper's house, which was restored to its original Victorian elegance in 1980. As a child, Fanning often fished for striped bass and rock cod here while visiting his grandfather, who was East Brother Light's keeper during the early twentieth century. Today, the lighthouse also takes visitors: it's a bed-and-breakfast that serves dinner for guests, as well.

# ITALIAN DINNER

Here in California, fresh fruits and vegetables are available year-round, and this California menu takes full advantage of them. San Francisco's fishing and shipping industries lured immigrants from many nations. Italians brought their foods, farms, and lifestyles to a climate that reminded them of the familiar Mediterranean. They made fish stews and pastas with seafood and vegetables, contributing greatly to San Francisco's reputation as a restaurant capital.

WARM OLIVE SALAD WITH RUSTIC BREAD AND CHEESE

CIOPPINO

BAKED HALIBUT WITH TOMATOES, CAPERS, AND OLIVE VINAIGRETTE

PASTA WITH ENGLISH PEAS, PANCETTA, AND MINT

FIG TART

## WARM OLIVE SALAD WITH RUSTIC BREAD AND CHEESE

*No matter where you eat it—Italy, California or wherever—be sure you're outside, under a tree.*

1 POUND LIGHTLY BRINED OLIVES (⅓ POUND EACH OF BLACK AND GREEN
   CERIGNOLA OLIVES AND ⅓ POUND KALAMATA OLIVES)
4½ CUPS WATER, DIVIDED
¼ CUP EXTRA VIRGIN OLIVE OIL
4 CLOVES GARLIC, SLICED
1 MEDIUM ONION, SLICED
1 CUP SLICED FENNEL BULB
1 TEASPOON FENNEL SEED, CRUSHED
½ CUP DICED TOMATOES (FRESH OR CANNED)
2 TABLESPOONS TOMATO PASTE
½ LEMON, SLICED AND SEEDED
1 TEASPOON CHILE FLAKES
GOUDA, PARRANO, OR ASIAGO CHEESE AND RUSTIC BREAD SLICED, FOR
   SERVING

1. Blanch the olives in 4 cups boiling water. Drain.
2. Heat the olive oil in a pot on low heat. Sauté the garlic, onion, and fennel bulb and seeds for 15 to 20 minutes, or until vegetables are tender. Mix in the olives, tomatoes, tomato paste, lemon, chile flakes, and remaining water. Simmer for about 10 minutes, or until water is absorbed.
3. Serve warm or at room temperature with either Gouda, Parrano, or Asiago cheese and bread.

YIELD: 4–6 servings
PREPARATION TIME: 15–20 minutes (allow a few minutes longer if olives need to be pitted; pit olives by putting each on a cutting board and smashing it with a can and removing pit.)
COOKING TIME: 25–30 minutes

## CIOPPINO

*Serve with grilled sourdough bread that has been rubbed with garlic.*

½ CUP EXTRA VIRGIN OLIVE OIL
2 ONIONS, DICED
4 CELERY STALKS, DICED
1 FENNEL BULB, DICED
4 CLOVES GARLIC, SLICED
1 (28-OUNCE) CAN WHOLE PLUM
   TOMATOES, SEEDED
1 (8-OUNCE) CAN TOMATO SAUCE
1 TABLESPOON FRESH OREGANO
1 TABLESPOON FRESH THYME
12 SMALL CLAMS

1 POUND HALIBUT OR FIRM WHITE
   FISH, CUT INTO SERVING PIECES
½ POUND SHRIMP, PEELED AND
   DEVEINED
½ CUP CHOPPED FRESH BASIL
½ TEASPOON SALT
⅛ TEASPOON FRESHLY GROUND
   BLACK PEPPER
½ TEASPOON RED CHILE FLAKES
   (OPTIONAL)
GRILLED SOURDOUGH BREAD, FOR
   SERVING

1. Heat a large pot over medium heat. Add the olive oil and sauté the onions, celery, fennel, and garlic for 20 to 25 minutes, or until vegetables are tender.
2. Pour in the diced tomatoes and tomato sauce. Cover and bring to a boil and reduce to a simmer. Add the oregano and thyme. Cook for 20 minutes.
3. Add the clams and simmer for 8 to 10 minutes. Add the halibut and shrimp and simmer 2 to 3 minutes. Remove from heat and add basil, salt, pepper, and chile flakes (if using). Serve with grilled sourdough bread.

YIELD: 6 servings
PREPARATION TIME: 10–15 minutes
COOKING TIME: 55–60 minutes

## BAKED HALIBUT WITH TOMATOES, CAPERS, AND OLIVE VINAIGRETTE

*Katy Stewart, the innkeeper at East Brother Light Station, gave us this wonderful Mediterranean recipe that she serves to her dinner guests.*

½ CUP LEMON JUICE
2 TEASPOONS DIJON-STYLE MUSTARD
¾ CUP EXTRA VIRGIN OLIVE OIL
1 CUP QUARTERED CHERRY TOMATOES
⅔ CUP PITTED KALAMATA OLIVES
2 TABLESPOONS CAPERS
2 POUNDS HALIBUT STEAK, SKINNED, BONED, AND CUT INTO 4 PIECES
1 TEASPOON SALT
¼ TEASPOON FRESHLY GROUND BLACK PEPPER

1. Preheat the oven to 400°F.
2. Whisk together the lemon juice and mustard; add the olive oil in a slow stream until well blended. Stir in the tomatoes, olives, and capers, and add salt and pepper.
3. Arrange the fish steaks in a baking dish. Pour the lemon–tomato vinaigrette over the fish and bake for 7–9 minutes.

YIELD: 4 servings
PREPARATION TIME: 10–15 minutes
BAKING TIME: 7–9 minutes


## PASTA WITH ENGLISH PEAS, PANCETTA, AND MINT

*Wait for fresh peas—it's worth it.*

1 TABLESPOON PLUS ¼ TEASPOON SALT, DIVIDED
1 CUP FRESH ENGLISH PEAS
2 TABLESPOONS VEGETABLE OIL
4 OUNCES PANCETTA, CHOPPED
4 SHALLOTS, SLICED
12 OUNCES FRESH FETTUCCINE
¼ CUP FRESH MINT
¾ CUP CHICKEN STOCK
3 TABLESPOONS PARMESAN CHEESE
⅛ TEASPOON FRESHLY GROUND BLACK PEPPER

1. Bring a large pot of water to a boil and add 1 tablespoon salt. Blanch peas for 5 minutes. Remove peas and save the water to cook the pasta.
2. Heat a sauté pan over medium heat. Add the oil and pancetta. Cook for 5 minutes. Stir in the shallots and sauté for 10 minutes, or until tender.
3. Drop the pasta into the boiling water and stir. Cook for 2 to 3 minutes.
4. Add peas to pancetta and toss briefly till mixed..
5. Drain the pasta and toss with the peas. Add the mint, stock, and Parmesan cheese. Continue to toss until the sauce begins to thicken.
6. Season with remaining salt and pepper.

YIELD: 4–6 servings
PREPARATION TIME: 5–10 minutes
COOKING TIME: 15–20 minutes


## FIG TART

*You can use dried figs in a pinch. Reconstitute them in wine, or water with honey.*

12–15 FRESH FIGS
5 OUNCES GOAT CHEESE
1 (9-INCH) PREBAKED TART SHELL (RECIPE FOLLOWS)
2 TABLESPOONS CHOPPED FRESH MINT
⅛ TEASPOON CINNAMON
2 TABLESPOONS SLIVERED ALMONDS, TOASTED
4 TABLESPOONS HONEY, DIVIDED

1. Preheat the oven to 350°F.
2. Cut the figs in half, through the stem. Remove stems.
3. Spread the goat cheese on the bottom of the Tart Shell. Cover with the mint, cinnamon, almonds, and half the honey.
4. Arrange the cut figs in a spiral pattern—one circle with the cut side down and the next with the cut side up. Drizzle remaining honey on top of the figs.
5. Place in the oven and bake for 30 minutes.
6. Cool to room temperature before serving.

YIELD: 6–8 servings
PREPARATION TIME: 10–15 minutes
COOKING TIME: 30 minutes

*Tart Shell*

1½ CUPS ALL-PURPOSE FLOUR
⅛ TEASPOON SALT
¾ CUP VEGETABLE SHORTENING, COLD
3 TABLESPOONS COLD WATER
2 EGG YOLKS, LIGHTLY BEATEN

1. Mix the flour and salt in a bowl and cut the shortening into the flour with 2 knives or a pastry blender, until the mixture is in clumps the size of peas. Gradually add the water and yolks, and blend together.
2. Form into a ball, cover with plastic wrap, and refrigerate for at least 30 minutes.
3. Lightly flour your work surface. Roll out the dough to be 1 inch larger than the tart pan. Fold the dough in half and place in the pan. Unfold to cover the entire pan. Press dough into sides of pan until even with top of pan.
4. With a fork, poke holes in the bottom of the tart shell, and place in the refrigerator for at least 10 minutes.
5. Preheat the oven to 450°F. Remove the shell from the refrigerator, line the bottom with foil, and fill with dried beans or rice. Bake for 15 to 20 minutes, or until lightly browned.
6. Remove shell from oven, remove foil and beans, and let cool on a rack.

YIELD: 1 (9-inch) tart shell
PREPARATION TIME: 15–20 minutes
REFRIGERATION TIME: 40 minutes
COOKING TIME: 20 minutes

# Battery Point Lighthouse
CRESCENT CITY, CALIFORNIA

FIRST LIT IN 1856, BATTERY POINT LIGHTHOUSE WAS BUILT IN A CAPE COD style, but constructed of stone and brick to withstand the severity of the elements here on the border of California and Oregon. Battery Point Lighthouse has lived through a dramatic history from its inception, shortly after California became part of the United States, through the late twentieth century, when a tsunami wreaked havoc on nearby Crescent City.

There are dangers in visiting the lighthouse, even today. Legend says it is haunted by a ghost who has been heard climbing the tower in his heavy boots. And the lighthouse is cut off from the mainland during high tide twice every day. Visitors to Battery Point Island must plan carefully, because crossing can only be done on foot during certain hours—which change daily.

The Crescent City area became an early hub for the lumber industry, which was located to the north. Today, the ancient redwood forests are protected by national and state redwood park designations that extend down to the sea.

As did the Native Americans, the first settlers lived off crab and fish from the cold Pacific waters and berries from the woods. Gradually, the settlers increased the size of their farms to feed nearby cities that grew up after the Gold Rush, growing fresh vegetables and fruits year-round in this relatively mild climate.

# FARMER'S DINNER

This supper in Crescent City takes full advantage of the sea and local farms. Topping off the meal is a new California classic dessert that spread like wildfire when it was introduced in the 1970s.

CRAB LOUIS

GREEN BEANS WITH TOASTED PECANS

RED BLISS POTATOES WITH PARSLEY

CHICKEN UNDER A BRICK

CALIFORNIA MUD PIE

## CRAB LOUIS

*This dish originated along the Pacific coast with its lovely, fresh cool-water Dungeness crab.*

¾ CUP MAYONNAISE
2 TABLESPOONS CHILE SAUCE
¼ CUP DICED RED BELL PEPPER
2 TEASPOONS PREPARED HORSERADISH
1 SCALLION, SLICED
1 TABLESPOON LEMON JUICE

½ TEASPOON SALT
¼ TEASPOON FRESHLY GROUND
   BLACK PEPPER
2 CUPS DUNGENESS CRABMEAT
4–8 BOSTON OR BIBB LETTUCE
   LEAVES
4 HARD-BOILED EGGS, SLICED

1. Mix together the mayonnaise, chile sauce, bell pepper, horseradish, scallion, lemon juice, salt, and pepper.
2. Fold in the crabmeat.
3. Arrange the lettuce leaves on 4 plates, and top with the crabmeat mixture and sliced hard-boiled eggs.

YIELD: 4 servings
PREPARATION TIME: 10–15 minutes

## GREEN BEANS WITH TOASTED PECANS

*It's amazing how well the pecans work with the green beans and butter.*

1 POUND GREEN BEANS
1½ TEASPOONS SALT, DIVIDED
2 TABLESPOONS BUTTER
1 TABLESPOON VEGETABLE OIL
3 SHALLOTS, SLICED
½ CUP CHOPPED PECANS, TOASTED
¼ TEASPOON FRESHLY GROUND BLACK PEPPER

1. Remove the stem ends from the beans.
2. Bring a pot of water to a boil and add 1 teaspoon salt. Place the beans in water and cook for 3 to 4 minutes.
3. Heat a pan on medium heat. Add the butter and oil. When the butter stops foaming, add the shallots and reduce the heat to low. Cook for 6 to 8 minutes.
4. Drain the beans and put in the pan with the shallots. Mix together. Toss in the pecans and season with remaining salt and pepper.

YIELD: 4 servings
PREPARATION TIME: 10 minutes
COOKING TIME: 10 minutes

## RED BLISS POTATOES WITH PARSLEY

*Plenty of parsley and just enough butter create a super potato dish.*

2 POUNDS SMALL RED BLISS POTATOES
1½ TEASPOONS SALT, DIVIDED
4 TABLESPOONS BUTTER, MELTED
¼ CUP CHOPPED FRESH PARSLEY
¼ TEASPOON FRESHLY GROUND BLACK PEPPER

1. Put the potatoes in a pot with 1 teaspoon salt and cover with cold water. Bring to a boil and cook for 10 to 15 minutes, or until easily pierced with a fork.
2. Drain and return to pot. Mix in the butter, parsley, remaining salt, and pepper.
3. Put in a serving bowl.

YIELD: 4–6 servings
PREPARATION TIME: 5 minutes
COOKING TIME: 10–15 minutes

## CHICKEN UNDER A BRICK

*This is a fantastic way to cook a chicken; it's crispy on the outside, and tender in the middle.*

1 CHICKEN (4–5 POUNDS)
1 TABLESPOON CHOPPED FRESH THYME
1 TABLESPOON CHOPPED FRESH ROSEMARY
1 TABLESPOON CHOPPED FRESH SAGE
2 TABLESPOONS EXTRA VIRGIN OLIVE OIL
2 TEASPOONS SALT, DIVIDED
½ TEASPOON FRESHLY GROUND BLACK PEPPER, DIVIDED
3 TABLESPOONS VEGETABLE OIL

1. Wash the chicken and pat dry. Lay the chicken, breast-side down, on a cutting board. Using a kitchen scissors, cut along each side of the back bone. Remove the backbone. Press down on the leg sections of the chicken to flatten it.
2. Cut the chicken on either side of the sternum bone and pull it out. Using a paring knife, carefully remove the rib bones.

3. Mix together the herbs, olive oil, and half the salt and pepper. Tuck the mixture under the skin. Season the rest of the chicken with remaining salt and pepper. Allow to marinate for 1 hour or overnight in the refrigerator.
4. Preheat the oven to 450°F.
5. Wrap 2 bricks in several layers of aluminum foil.
6. Heat a large ovenproof skillet on medium-high heat. Add the vegetable oil and allow to heat up for 2 minutes.
7. Place the chicken, skin side down, in the skillet and place the bricks on top.
8. Cook for 10 minutes. Place skillet in the oven and roast for 60 minutes, or until internal temperature of chicken (at thigh) reaches 165°F.
9. Carefully loosen the chicken from the pan so as not to tear the skin. Cut the chicken into serving pieces.

YIELD: 4–6 servings
PREPARATION TIME: 20–25 minutes
MARINATING TIME: 60 minutes
COOKING TIME: 60 minutes

## CALIFORNIA MUD PIE

*This mud pie dessert is thought to have originated in Mississippi, but it was really northern California.*

8 SLICES SINGLE-LAYER CHOCOLATE FUDGE CAKE, UNFROSTED (SEE RECIPE ON PAGE 266)
VANILLA ICE CREAM, FOR TOPPING (SEE RECIPE ON PAGE 240)
BITTERSWEET HOT FUDGE SAUCE, FOR TOPPING (RECIPE FOLLOWS)

1. Slice the cake into 8 slices.
2. Top with a scoop of the Vanilla Ice Cream and spoon on the Bittersweet Hot Fudge Sauce.

YIELD: 8 servings
PREPARATION TIME: 5 minutes

*Bittersweet Hot Fudge Sauce*

4 OUNCES UNSWEETENED CHOCO-LATE, CHOPPED
3 TABLESPOONS BUTTER
1 TABLESPOON UNSWEETENED COCOA POWDER
⅔ CUP WATER
1¾ CUPS SUGAR
¾ CUP CORN SYRUP
1 TEASPOON VANILLA EXTRACT

1. Melt the chocolate and butter in a heavy pot over low heat. Whisk in the cocoa powder.
2. Stir in the water, sugar, and corn syrup. Bring to a boil and reduce to a simmer. Cook for 10 minutes.
3. Cool for 5 minutes, and then beat in the vanilla.
4. Serve warm.

YIELD: 2½ cups
PREPARATION TIME: Less than 5 minutes
COOKING TIME: 10 minutes

# PACIFIC NORTHWEST AND ALASKA REGION

Before Europeans began settling on this coast, ships with origins as diverse as Spain and Russia visited what is now the northwestern part of the United States: Oregon, Washington, and Alaska. Early explorers who surveyed these waters discovered rich stores of seafood and fish, and those who ventured into the forests found them filled with game. Sea and forest were being mined responsibly by the Native Americans who lived (or just summered) at the shore. They depended on the coastal region for food, clothing, and adornments; animal skins and whalebones were also used in housing.

Although Lewis and Clark's expedition came across the continent in the early 1800s, it wasn't until after the California Gold Rush of 1848 that there was a major influx of Europeans to this area. The Alaskan gold rush at the end of the nineteenth century further expanded U.S. interests to the north. By then Russians had already settled in the Alaskan mainland and islands, bringing their religion and building their churches in many fishing villages.

This coastland is stunningly beautiful—and it can be shockingly dangerous, with furious ocean-driven gales and currents. On peaceful days, the waters are a treasure of seafood and fish, with many kinds of crab and salmon dominating local menus. Adding to that are the native berries, apples, mushrooms, and nuts and the local cheeses—as well as a variety of other locally farmed fruits and vegetables, in season. A commitment to a responsible lifestyle pervades this area of the country, where people tend to live more in harmony with nature.

# Heceta Head Lighthouse

FLORENCE, OREGON

NOW AN EPICUREAN BED-AND-BREAKFAST, HECETA HEAD LIGHT WAS ONE of the most expensive lighthouses built in the late nineteenth century. The point it stands on was named for Don Bruno de Heceta, a Portuguese explorer who charted it for Spain in 1775.

A hundred years later, shipping was the only reliable way to move passengers and supplies up and down the United States' west coast, and a lighthouse was critically needed to warn ships off the rocks at this point. It took two years to build this lighthouse. After the materials were delivered by barges, they were offloaded, and mule-drawn wagons strained to cart the heavy loads two hundred feet up the cliffs.

Once it was lit in 1894, the light was maintained by a keeper with two assistants, who were sometimes marooned on this lonely outpost during the rainy season. The first head keeper had five daughters, so he created a small community here, with a post office, schoolhouse, and vegetable gardens to provide fresh food for the families.

Their isolation ended in the 1930s when the first construction crew arrived nearby to build this section of U.S. Route 101. Viewable from the highway, Heceta Head is one of the most picturesque—and most photographed—lighthouses on the West Coast.

While remaining a lighthouse, Heceta Head was turned into a bed-and-breakfast some years ago and restored to its original Queen Anne style. Chefs Carol and Mike Korgan took over this enterprise and built up its reputation as a gourmet vacation destination. Their daughter Michelle—also a chef—now runs it with her husband, Steve Bursey, and they maintain the family tradition with a seven-course breakfast.

Michelle uses many local and sustainable foods in her menus, including garden herbs and vegetables, locally grown beef and lamb, and artisanal cheeses. (Coincidentally, their *Lighthouse Breakfast Cookbook* was recently published.)

# MULTI-COURSE BREAKFAST

Michelle creates an elaborate breakfast for the guests of the bed-and-breakfast with dishes emphasizing local foods, using herbs and produce from her husband Steve's garden whenever possible.

YOGURT FRUIT FRAPPÉ

SAILOR'S BREAD WITH FRESH SEASONAL FRUIT

FRUIT AND JUNIPER GROVE FARM'S TUMALO TOMME

CHIVE CREPES WITH SMOKED SALMON AND HAND-PACKED RICOTTA CHEESE

SPINACH, KALE, AND JUNIPER GROVE FARM'S FETA FRITTATA

SUDAN FARMS GREEK LAMB SAUSAGE

## YOGURT FRUIT FRAPPÉ

*It is essential to use the best yogurt and very ripe fruit.*

1 CUP PLAIN YOGURT
½ CUP APPLE CIDER OR OTHER FRUIT JUICE
1¼ CUPS RASPBERRIES OR STRAWBERRIES
1–2 TABLESPOONS OF HONEY, DEPENDING ON SWEETNESS OF FRUIT
¼ TEASPOON VANILLA EXTRACT
4 SPRIGS FRESH MINT

1. Place all the ingredients, except the mint, in a blender and purée.
2. Serve in wine glasses with a sprig of mint.

YIELD: 4 servings
PREPARATION TIME: 5 minutes

## SAILOR'S BREAD WITH FRESH SEASONAL FRUIT

*This bread contains no dairy or eggs. Make it for your vegan friends; they'll be grateful and impressed. Legend has it this bread was made during long voyages, when eggs and butter were scarce, but spices were plentiful. Arrgh, and a little rum never hurt anyone!*

**Note:** Begin this recipe the day before baking.

2 CUPS PLUS 2 TABLESPOONS SUGAR, DIVIDED
¼ CUP COCOA
1 TABLESPOON GROUND CINNAMON
1½ TEASPOONS FRESHLY GROUND NUTMEG
1 TEASPOON GROUND ALLSPICE
1 TEASPOON GROUND CLOVES
2 TEASPOONS SALT
2 CUPS PLUS ½ CUP WATER, DIVIDED
¼ CUP SPICED RUM
1 CUP RAISINS
1⅔ CUPS VEGETABLE OIL
3 TABLESPOONS HONEY
2½ CUPS ALL-PURPOSE FLOUR
2½ CUPS CAKE FLOUR
3 TEASPOONS BAKING SODA
1½ TEASPOONS BAKING POWDER

1. Combine 2 cups of the sugar, the cocoa, cinnamon, nutmeg, allspice, cloves, and salt in a medium saucepan. Add 2 cups of the water, the rum, and raisins. Simmer over medium heat until hot but not boiling; remove from the heat. Cover the mixture and let stand at room temperature overnight.
2. The next day, preheat the oven to 350°F and oil 3 (8×4-inch) bread pans with baking spray.
3. Add the oil, remaining water, and honey to the cocoa mixture.
4. In a large mixing bowl, sift the flour, cake flour, baking soda, and baking powder together 3 times. Add the cocoa mixture and mix until combined.
5. Divide the mixture among the pans and sprinkle with remaining 2 tablespoons of sugar. Place the pans on a baking sheet and bake for 60 minutes, or until toothpicks inserted in the centers of breads come out clean. Let cool for 30 minutes; turn out and let rest on a rack until completely cool.

YIELD: 3 loaves
PREPARATION TIME: Overnight plus 15–20 minutes
COOKING TIME: 60 minutes

## FRUIT AND JUNIPER GROVE FARM'S TUMALO TOMME

*On your most decorative plate, place tomme or other mild local cheese and surround it with fresh berries or other fresh seasonal fruit. Use equal amounts of cheese and fruit.*

## CHIVE CREPES WITH SMOKED SALMON AND HAND-PACKED RICOTTA CHEESE

*This is an all-purpose dish. Good for breakfast, lunch, or as a dinner appetizer.*

4 CREPES (RECIPE FOLLOWS)
8 OUNCES SMOKED SALMON
1 CUP HAND-PACKED RICOTTA CHEESE
1 TEASPOON SALT
¼ TEASPOON FRESHLY GROUND BLACK PEPPER
CHIVE FLOWERS, FOR SERVING

1. Lay out crepes out on a work surface. Place 2 ounces of salmon on each crepe. Spread ¼ cup of ricotta cheese on top of salmon. Season with salt and pepper. Roll into a wrap. Cut in half using a serrated knife.
2. Serve sprinkled with chive flowers.

YIELD: 4 servings
PREPARATION TIME: 10 minutes

*Crepes*

½ CUP ALL-PURPOSE FLOUR
1 TEASPOON SALT
¼ TEASPOON FRESHLY GROUND
    BLACK PEPPER

2 LARGE EGGS, BEATEN
½ CUP MILK
¼ CUP FINELY CHOPPED CHIVES
1 TABLESPOON VEGETABLE OIL

1. Mix together the flour, salt, and pepper.
2. Whisk together the eggs, milk, and chives in a separate bowl. Pour the egg mixture into the flour and stir. Refrigerate for at least 30 minutes.
3. Heat a small nonstick sauté or crepe pan over medium heat. Add the oil and allow it to get hot. Test by putting a drop of the batter into the pan; it should sizzle.
4. Stir the batter. Ladle ¼ cup of batter into the pan. Rotate the pan so the batter covers the bottom of the pan. Cook for 1 to 2 minutes, or until the edges begin to curl and the top begins to look dry. Turn over and cook for 30 seconds more.
5. Slide the crepe onto a plate and repeat until all the batter is used.

YIELD: 4 crepes
PREPARATION TIME: 5–10 minutes
REFRIGERATION TIME: 30 minutes
COOKING TIME: 2–3 minutes per crepe

**Note:** This recipe can easily be double or tripled. The crepes can be made up to 3 days ahead, stacked with wax or parchment paper in between each one, and stored in a resealable plastic bag in the refrigerator.

# SPINACH, KALE, AND JUNIPER GROVE FARM'S FETA FRITTATA

*The people at Juniper Grove Farm have mastered the art of making feta. It is a creamy, full-flavored, and perfectly salted cheese. And because it is a salty cheese, no salt is added to the eggs. At Heceta Head, Steven grows beautiful bunches of rich Japanese kale and spinach in his kitchen garden. Michelle mixes them with farm-fresh eggs from Morning Glory Farm to make one of her signature dishes.*

12 LARGE EGGS
3 TABLESPOONS MAYONNAISE
1 TABLESPOON CLARIFIED BUTTER
2 TEASPOONS FINELY CHOPPED SHALLOT
3 MEDIUM KALE GREENS, RIBS REMOVED AND COARSELY CHOPPED
⅓ CUP BABY SPINACH
¼ CUP CRUMBLED FETA
¼ CUP CRÈME FRAÎCHE, FOR GARNISH
3 SUN-DRIED TOMATOES, JULIENNED, FOR GARNISH

1. In a large bowl, whisk the eggs with the mayonnaise until airy. Set aside.
2. Preheat the broiler to high. Heat a 10-inch nonstick skillet over medium heat. Add the butter and shallot; cook about 5 minutes, until tender. Add the kale and cook over medium-low heat until wilted and soft, about 5 minutes. Increase the heat to medium and add the eggs. Let them set a bit, but do not let them brown. (If they are getting brown, the temperature is too high.) With a rubber spatula, push the eggs from the bottom and sides and let the next layer of egg go to the bottom and set. Repeat until all the eggs are soft. Take the skillet off the heat.
3. Pile the spinach in the middle of the skillet and fold the eggs over the top to cover. Let the spinach steam in the eggs for about 2 minutes. Fold the spinach into the eggs, equally dispersing the spinach, but do not mix too much. Return the skillet to the heat for about 1 to 2 minutes to set the eggs. The frittata should easily come away from the pan. Sprinkle the feta over the top.
4. Place the skillet under the broiler with the handle sticking out of the oven. Broil until the feta starts to brown and the eggs are set. Run a rubber spatula around the skillet rim to loosen the sides. Tilt the skillet, and slide the frittata onto a serving platter. Cut into 6 pieces, and garnish each with the crème fraîche and sun-dried tomato. Using a pie server, serve 1 piece to each guest.

YIELD: 6 servings
PREPARATION TIME: 10–15 minutes
COOKING TIME: 10–15 minutes

# SUDAN FARMS GREEK LAMB SAUSAGE

*Sue and Dan Wilson raise lamb in Canby, Oregon. Every dish Michelle makes with their lamb just melts in your mouth. This sausage is outstanding with the Spinach, Kale, and Juniper Grove Farm's Feta Frittata.*

1 POUND GROUND LAMB
2 TABLESPOONS PINE NUTS
1 TABLESPOON FINELY CHOPPED KALAMATA OLIVES
1 TEASPOON MINCED FRESH MINT
½ TEASPOON FRESHLY GROUND BLACK PEPPER

1 TEASPOON SALT
¼ TEASPOON GROUND CINNAMON
¼ TEASPOON GROUND ALLSPICE
¼ TEASPOON LEMON ZEST
2 TABLESPOONS LEMON JUICE
2 TABLESPOONS VEGETABLE OIL

1. Mix the lamb, pine nuts, olives, mint, pepper, salt, cinnamon, allspice, zest, and lemon juice. Refrigerate 2 hours or overnight. Form the mixture into small patties
2. Heat heavy skillet on medium. Add the oil and heat. Add patties and brown on both sides, continuing until cooked through.

YIELD: 6-8 patties
PREPARATION TIME: 10 minutes
REFRIGERATION TIME: 2 hours
COOKING TIME: 10–15 minutes for a ½-inch thick patty

# Cape Meares Lighthouse

TILLAMOOK, OREGON

CAPE MEARES LIGHT HAS INFLUENCE FAR BEYOND ITS STATURE. ONLY THIRTY-EIGHT FEET high, it is located on a bluff two hundred feet above sea level, so its light can be seen for twenty-five miles out to sea. Built of brick-lined metal plates, this little lighthouse was completed in 1890. The light, along with its keeper's cottages, formed a small community that was largely cut off from the rest of the world for a couple of decades.

Originally, Native American Tillamooks inhabited this coast, and they were not always friendly to the Europeans and Americans who sailed up the coast in the mid-eighteenth century. Pioneers began arriving in this region by covered wagon during the latter half of the nineteenth century. In the early twentieth century, they created larger and larger settlements along this beautiful coastline. A nearby town called Bay City was established in 1912, effectively ending Cape Meares Light's years of isolation.

Despite later development, the coastline of Oregon is still home to many species of birds, fish, and sea mammals. Today, many birders come to Cape Meares to see peregrine falcons and other rare raptors and sea birds.

# Artisanal Vegetarian Lunch

Oregon's most famous cheese is Tillamook cheddar, produced by a 100-year-old farmers' cooperative that also makes ice cream, butter, sour cream, and yogurt from its non-HGH cows' milk. Lately, Oregon specialty crops, such as hazelnuts, mushrooms, and wine grapes, have taken center stage in the food world across the country. This is a hearty lunch that just happens to be vegetarian.

Tillamook Cheese Fondue with Crusty White Bread
Cauliflower with Garlic Brown Butter
Wild Mushroom Patties
Pears Poached in Green Tea

## TILLAMOOK CHEESE FONDUE WITH CRUSTY WHITE BREAD

*Try this fondue. It's so simple, but it has a great taste.*

2 tablespoons butter
2 tablespoons all-purpose flour
1 cup dark beer or lager
½ pound Tillamook cheese, grated
Small loaf of sourdough bread, cubed, for serving
2 Gala apples, cored and cubed, for serving

1. Melt the butter in a heavy saucepan. Stir in the flour and cook for 2 minutes. Whisk the beer into the pot until it thickens.
2. Stir the cheese into the beer a little at a time, stirring constantly until cheese has melted.
3. Serve with the cubed bread and apples.

YIELD: 4–6 servings
PREPARATION TIME: 10–15 minutes
COOKING TIME: 10 minutes

## CAULIFLOWER WITH GARLIC BROWN BUTTER

*The cauliflower just soaks up the flavors of the garlic and brown butter.*

1 head of cauliflower (about 1½–2 pounds)
2 tablespoons vegetable oil
4 tablespoons butter, cut into cubes
4 cloves garlic, sliced
½ teaspoon salt
¼ teaspoon freshly ground black pepper
¼ cup chopped fresh parsley
1 tablespoon Parmesan cheese

1. Bring a large pot of water to a boil.
2. Separate the cauliflower into 1-inch florets. Position a steam basket above the water and steam the cauliflower for 10 minutes.
3. Heat a pan on medium heat; add the oil to the pan. Melt the butter in the pan.
4. Put the garlic in a pan and cook for 2 minutes. Add the cauliflower, increase heat to medium-high, and mix. Cook for 5 to 8 minutes, tossing frequently, until the garlic and cauliflower begin to brown. Season with the salt and pepper. Sprinkle on the parsley and Parmesan cheese. Toss and serve.

YIELD: 4 servings
PREPARATION TIME: 10–15 minutes
COOKING TIME: 10 minutes to steam the cauliflower, and 5–8 minutes to sauté

## WILD MUSHROOM PATTIES

*A crispy exterior with an earthy, robust flavor.*

3 TABLESPOONS BUTTER
2 CUPS WILD MUSHROOMS, DICED (ABOUT ½ POUND)
1 SHALLOT, DICED
1 TEASPOON LEMON ZEST (ABOUT 1 LEMON)
1 CUP FRESH BREAD CRUMBS
1 EGG, BEATEN
2 TABLESPOONS HEAVY CREAM
¼ CUP CHOPPED FRESH PARSLEY
1 TEASPOON SALT
⅛ TEASPOON FRESHLY GROUND BLACK PEPPER
½ CUP PANKO BREAD CRUMBS
4 TABLESPOONS VEGETABLE OIL

1. Pulse the mushrooms in a processor until they resemble breadcrumbs.
2. Melt the butter in a pan. Sauté the mushrooms and shallots over medium heat for 10 minutes or until vegetables are tender. Let cool.
3. Stir in the lemon zest, fresh bread crumbs, egg, cream, parsley, salt, and pepper. Form into 8 patties. Coat with the panko bread crumbs.
4. Heat the oil in a pan over medium heat for 1 minute. Sauté the patties for 3 to 4 minutes on each side.

YIELD: 4–6 servings
PREPARATION TIME: 15–20 minutes
COOKING TIME: 6–8 minutes

# PEARS POACHED IN GREEN TEA

*An elegance of flavors.*

6 BOSC PEARS, FIRM AND RIPE
2 QUARTS BREWED GREEN TEA
3 STAR ANISE PODS
1 CINNAMON STICK
½ CUP HONEY
PEEL OF 1 LEMON

1. Peel the pears. Cut each in half lengthwise, and remove the core and the blossom end using a melon baller, spoon, or paring knife.
2. In a saucepan, bring the tea, star anise, cinnamon stick, honey, and lemon peel to a simmer. Add the pears and cover with a piece of parchment paper.
3. Cook until the pears are easily pierced with a paring knife (approximately 15 minutes). Remove the pears and strain the solids from the liquid. Return the liquid to the pot and reduce, over high heat, to a syrupy consistency, about 20 minutes.
4. Arrange the pears on plate and spoon the sauce over top.

YIELD: 6 servings
PREPARATION TIME: 10–15 minutes
COOKING TIME: 15–20 minutes for the pears, and 20 minutes for the reduction

# Point No Point Lighthouse
HANSVILLE, WASHINGTON

ALTHOUGH THIS LIGHT DATES FROM THE WINTER OF 1880, POINT NO
Point's Puget Sound location had already become famous by then. The Point No
Point Treaty, which began to end the Indian wars in this part of the country, was
signed here in 1855, and the treaty is the basis of much of what has happened in
regard to Native Americans in the region ever since.

The native people had called the peninsula by a name that meant "long nose."
European mariners gave it their own spin when, time after time, they mistook it for
a point with a deeper harbor—or a point in another part of Puget Sound, depending on which story you hear. This was the first lighthouse on Puget Sound; the same
architect also designed West Point Light, which is closer to Seattle. It is a small and
pleasing group of buildings, very welcoming in its proportions and effective as a light
station to this day. The U.S. Lighthouse Society recently moved its headquarters to
the keeper's duplex here.

The first keepers brought in all their supplies by boat, including a cow that was
slipped over the side of a boat so it could swim safely to shore; the cow was needed
for milk for the lighthouse keeper's new baby.

The sound was also very generous. Coast Guard keepers in the 1960s reported that they always looked forward to salmon season, because they could just throw a line into the water from the beach and catch a fish for dinner.

The keepers also had their own garden between the duplex and the lighthouse. During World War I, all keepers were encouraged to grow their own food to help the war effort, and they kept it up for many years afterward. Even now, small farms continue to grow many types of vegetables for local consumption. The Olympic Peninsula's foods are much the same as they have been for centuries: a treasure of fish, mushrooms, berries, and bays full of oysters, geoduck clams, shrimp, and crab. It's all evidence of the truth behind the saying, "When the tide is out, the table is set."

# From Sea, Farm, and Forest

Beginning with Oregon's native roasted filberts for nibbling, this meal continues with local vegetables, seafood, and the best authentic Northwestern method of cooking salmon—on a piece of cedar or alderwood that infuses the fish with heady aromas.

ROASTED FILBERTS WITH BUTTER AND SPICES
LENTIL SOUP WITH MANILA CLAMS
ROASTED ROOT VEGETABLES
CEDAR-PLANKED SALMON
APPLE TART

## ROASTED FILBERTS WITH BUTTER AND SPICES

*Set out dishes of these lightly spiced nuts before the guests arrive.*

**Note:** Prepare them the day before, so the nuts have time to absorb the butter.

2 CUPS FILBERTS
2 TABLESPOONS BUTTER, MELTED
½ TEASPOON GROUND ALLSPICE
¼ TEASPOON SALT
¼ TEASPOON CAYENNE PEPPER

1. Preheat the oven to 350°F.
2. Put the filberts on a baking sheet and roast for 8 to 10 minutes. Watch closely during the last several minutes, so they don't burn.
3. Remove from the oven and place on a clean dishtowel. Close the towel around the nuts and rub the nuts vigorously to remove the skins.
4. Put the cleaned nuts in a bowl and toss with the butter, allspice, salt, and cayenne.

5. Put the nuts in a covered container at room temperature and allow the butter to be absorbed into the nuts overnight.

YIELD: 2 cups
PREPARATION TIME: Less than 5 minutes
COOKING TIME: 8–10 minutes
RESTING TIME: Overnight

## LENTIL SOUP WITH MANILA CLAMS

*Serve in small bowls as a starter, or this can also be the main course of a meal.*

2 TABLESPOONS VEGETABLE OIL
2 ONIONS, DICED
3 CARROTS, PEELED AND DICED
2 CELERY STALKS, DICED
1 FENNEL BULB, DICED
2 CLOVES GARLIC, DICED
2 CUPS DRIED LENTILS (1 POUND)
1 TABLESPOON FRESH, OR 1 TEASPOON
    DRIED, OREGANO
¼ CUP CHOPPED FRESH PARSLEY
½ CUP DICED TOMATOES
5 CUPS VEGETABLE STOCK
¼ TEASPOON FRESHLY GROUND BLACK
    PEPPER
2 DOZEN CLAMS, CLEANED
CRUSTY BREAD, FOR SERVING

1. Heat the oil in a large pot over medium heat. Cook the onions, carrots, celery, fennel, and garlic for 10 to 15 minutes, or until vegetables are tender.
2. Stir in the lentils, oregano, parsley, tomatoes, stock, and pepper.
3. Cover and cook for 25 minutes or until lentils are tender. Add the clams and recover. Cook for 5 to 7 minutes, or until clams open. Discard any clams that have not opened. Serve with crusty bread.

YIELD: 6–8 servings
PREPARATION TIME: 10–15 minutes
COOKING TIME: 40–45 minutes

## ROASTED ROOT VEGETABLES

*They are as sweet as candy.*

1 ONION, QUARTERED
2 CARROTS, PEELED, AND CUT INTO 1-INCH PIECES
1 SMALL TURNIP, PEELED, AND CUT INTO ¾–1-INCH CUBES
1 YUKON GOLD POTATO, CUT INTO ¾–1-INCH CUBES
1 SMALL RUTABAGA, PEELED, AND CUT INTO ¾–1-INCH
    CUBES
¼ CUP VEGETABLE OIL
2¼ TEASPOONS SALT, DIVIDED
¼ TEASPOON FRESHLY GROUND BLACK PEPPER
2 TABLESPOONS BUTTER
2 TABLESPOONS CHOPPED FRESH SAGE, ROSEMARY, OR
    THYME, OR A MIX OF THE THREE

1. Preheat the oven to 400°F. Place a heavy baking sheet in the oven to heat up.
2. Toss all the vegetables together with the vegetable oil, 2 teaspoons of salt, and the pepper.
3. Place on a baking sheet and bake for 50 to 60 minutes, or until vegetables are tender. Turn the vegetables over halfway through the cooking time to ensure even browning. Check doneness by piercing a potato or turnip with a fork.
4. Melt the butter with herbs in a microwave on low setting.
5. Put the vegetables in a bowl and toss with the butter mixture and remaining salt.

YIELD: 4–6 servings
PREPARATION TIME: 10–15 minutes
BAKING TIME: 50–60 minutes

## CEDAR-PLANKED SALMON

*The wood gives the salmon such a heady flavor.*

2 CEDAR OR ALDER PLANKS (CAN BE PURCHASED AT ANY
    GOURMET STORE)
6 SALMON FILLETS (ABOUT 6 OUNCES EACH)
2 TABLESPOONS EXTRA VIRGIN OLIVE OIL
1 TEASPOON SALT
¼ TEASPOON FRESHLY GROUND BLACK PEPPER

1. Soak the planks in water for 2 to 4 hours.
2. Start the grill.
3. When the coals are red-hot, position the rack 4 inches from heat. The coals are the right temperature if you can only hold your hand above the rack for a count of 3.

*If you prefer to use your oven, follow these steps. It works great, but you'll lose the unique flavor.*

*1. Preheat the oven to 350°F.*
*2. Season the fillets with salt, pepper, and oil.*
*3. Arrange the fillets on the planks and bake for 12 to 15 minutes, depending on the thickness of the fillets.*

4. Arrange the fillets on the planks, drizzle with oil and season with salt and pepper. Place planks on the grill, and cover. Cook for 15 to 20 minutes, depending on the thickness of the fillets.

YIELD: 6 servings
PREPARATION TIME: 2–4 hours for planks, and 2-3 minutes for salmon
GRILLING TIME: 15–20 minutes

## APPLE TART

*This dish uses local Golden Delicious apples. It is even better with Vanilla Ice Cream.*

1 SHEET FROZEN PUFF PASTRY, THAWED
2 GOLDEN DELICIOUS APPLES
2 CUPS WATER
1 TABLESPOON LEMON JUICE
4 TABLESPOONS BUTTER, MELTED
¼ TEASPOON CINNAMON
4 TABLESPOONS MAPLE SYRUP
VANILLA ICE CREAM, FOR SERVING (SEE RECIPE ON PAGE 240)

1. Preheat the oven to 400°F.
2. Remove the puff pastry from the box, cover with a towel, and allow to thaw completely.
3. Peel, core and thinly slice apples. Place in water with lemon juice.
4. Unfold the pastry until it is flat. Smooth the seams. With a fork, poke holes all over the pastry up to ½ inch from the edge. This will allow the edges to rise more than the center.
5. Place the pastry on a parchment-lined baking sheet.
6. Remove apples from water, quickly pat dry and arrange the slices on the pastry, staying within the area with the holes.
7. In a separate bowl, combine the butter, cinnamon, and maple syrup, and brush apples with the mixture.
8. Bake in the oven for 15 minutes, or until edges are golden brown. Serve with Vanilla Ice Cream.

YIELD: 4 servings
PREPARATION TIME: 10–15 minutes
BAKING TIME: 15 minutes

# Cape Flattery Lighthouse
TATOOSH ISLAND, WASHINGTON

THIS LIGHTHOUSE IS LOCATED ON TATOOSH ISLAND, WHICH LIES OFF THE northwestern corner of Washington State's Olympic Peninsula—where the Makah Indians had lived and hunted and fished for centuries. When the Americans decided to build a lighthouse here in 1857, it was one more item in an ongoing conflict between the two nations, neither of which understood or respected the other. Today, the Makah are still struggling to maintain their own cultural heritage.

Cape Flattery Light was built with a stone tower in the center of the main building on a point on the island about one hundred feet above sea level, with a separate keepers' dwelling. This is considered one of the most remote and desolate areas for keepers, but it's a critical one: the entrance of the Strait of Juan de Fuca divides Canada and the United States and leads into substantial inland waterways for both countries.

# EARLY FALL DINNER

Northern Washington is known for its geoduck clams, which are prepared here in a fun, new way. Other dishes use Washington's artisanal cheese and sweet Walla Walla onions, with the state's own Cameo apples for dessert.

FRISÉE SALAD
WALLA WALLA ONION PIE
CHICKEN-FRIED GEODUCK
APPLES BAKED WITH HUCKLEBERRY JAM


## FRISÉE SALAD

*One more classic combination of flavors.*

2 CUPS APPLE CIDER
1 BUNCH FRISÉE (ABOUT ½ POUND)
1 BARTLETT PEAR, CORED AND SLICED THIN
¼ CUP ROUGHLY CHOPPED, TOASTED FILBERTS
4 OUNCES MILD BLUE CHEESE

1. Place the cider in a pot and boil until reduced to ¼ cup, about 10 to 15 minutes.
2. Wash and dry the frisée. Divide between 4 plates, and top with the pear slices, filberts, and blue cheese.
3. Pour 1 tablespoon of the cider reduction over each salad and serve.

YIELD: 4 servings
PREPARATION TIME: 5–10 minutes
COOKING TIME: About 10–15 minutes


## WALLA WALLA ONION PIE

*Walla Walla onions are grown in Washington, You can also use sweet onions from other parts of the country.*

1 SLEEVE RITZ CRACKERS (ABOUT 3½ OUNCES)
4 TABLESPOONS BUTTER, MELTED
4 TABLESPOONS VEGETABLE OIL
4 LARGE WALLA WALLA ONIONS, SLICED (ABOUT 6 CUPS)
4 OUNCES GRUYERE CHEESE, GRATED
3 EGGS, BEATEN
1 CUP SOUR CREAM
1 TEASPOON SALT, DIVIDED
⅛ TEASPOON FRESHLY GROUND BLACK PEPPER

1. Crush the crackers in a large plastic bag and slowly pour in the butter. Mix thoroughly. Press into a 9-inch pie plate and refrigerate for 30 minutes.

2. Heat a large skillet over medium heat. Add the oil, heat, then add onions. Season with ½ teaspoon salt. Cook for 15 minutes, or until the onions are tender.
3. Preheat the oven to 350°F.
4. Mix together the onions, cheese, eggs, sour cream, remaining salt, and pepper. Pour into the pie crust. Bake for 35 to 40 minutes. Watch carefully during the last 10 minutes so as not to burn the crust. Cover with foil, if necessary.

YIELD: 6–8 servings
REFRIGERATION TIME: 30 minutes
PREPARATION TIME: 20 minutes
COOKING TIME: 15 minutes for the onions, and 35–40 minutes for baking

## CHICKEN-FRIED GEODUCK

*A different way to cook this clam.*

4 GEODUCK CLAMS (ABOUT 1½ POUNDS EACH)
½ TEASPOON GARLIC POWDER
2 TEASPOONS SALT, DIVIDED
1 TEASPOON FRESHLY GROUND BLACK PEPPER, DIVIDED
1 CUP ALL-PURPOSE FLOUR
4 EGGS, BEATEN
1 CUP PANKO BREAD CRUMBS
2 TABLESPOONS VEGETABLE OIL

1. Bring a large pot of water to a boil. Blanch the geoduck clams for 10 seconds, remove from water, and submerge in ice water.
2. Remove the clams from their shells, being careful of the sharp edges. Cut away the viscera (the internal organs), but leave the siphon and mantle. Peel off the skin.
3. Wash the mantle and siphon, removing any grit. Separate the mantle from the siphon. Insert the tip of a pair of scissors in the opening of the siphon and cut it in half. Wash the insides. Depending on size, cut into serving-sized pieces, about 2 inches. Gently pound the pieces to tenderize.
4. Remove the softer tissue from the mantle. Cut into serving-sized pieces and set aside. The mantle is more tender than the siphon and should not need to be pounded. Cut into pieces.
5. Season the pieces with the garlic powder, ½ teaspoon salt, and ¼ teaspoon pepper.
6. Put the flour, eggs, and panko bread crumbs into 3 separate shallow dishes, dividing remaining salt and pepper between the dishes.
7. To bread the geoduck clams, dredge first in the flour, then in the eggs and, finally, in the panko bread crumbs. Each time, shake off any excess flour, egg, or breadcrumbs. Place on a rack and refrigerate for at least 20 minutes.
8. Heat a pan on medium-high heat; add the oil to the pan.

9. Preheat the oven to 200°F. Geoduck clams may need to be cooked in batches, and they can be kept warm.
10. After oil is hot, place the geoduck clam pieces in the pan. Cook for 2 to 3 minutes. Turn over and cook for 2 additional minutes, or until golden brown.
11. Place in a warm oven while remaining clams are being cooked.

YIELD: 4 servings
PREPARATION TIME: 20–25 minutes
REFRIGERATION TIME: 20 minutes
COOKING TIME: 5–6 minutes per batch

## APPLES BAKED WITH HUCKLEBERRY JAM

*Baked apples are a great simple dish for any time of the year and any occasion.*

6 CAMEO (OR OTHER BAKING) APPLES
¼ CUP HUCKLEBERRY OR BLACKBERRY JAM
¼ CUP CHOPPED TOASTED FILBERTS
¼ CUP CHOPPED DRIED APRICOTS, PEARS, OR PLUMS
JUICE AND ZEST OF 1 LEMON
½ CUP APPLE CIDER

1. Preheat the oven to 350°F.
2. Prepare the apples by first removing a circular strip of peel from the top, around the stem. This will keep the apple from splitting during baking. Scoop out the core using a melon baller, but do not go all the way through the apple.
3. Mix the jam, filberts, chopped fruit, and lemon juice and zest together.
4. Place the apples in an ovenproof dish. Spoon the mixture into the apples' cavities and add the cider to the bottom of dish. Cover with aluminum foil.
5. Bake the apples for 30 minutes. Remove foil and discard. Baste the apples, and bake for 10 to 15 more minutes.

YIELD: 6 servings
PREPARATION TIME: 15–20 minutes
BAKING TIME: 40–45 minutes

# Eldred Rock Lighthouse
ELDRED ROCK, ALASKA

THE GOLD RUSH CAME LATE TO ALASKA—1896—THOUGH GOLD HAD BEEN DISCOVERED near Juneau some twenty-five years earlier. At the height of this wild time, disaster struck several ships bringing hopeful gold miners to and from the boomtown of Skagway. In 1905, a lighthouse was finally built on Eldred Rock, an island in the Lynn Canal located north of Juneau. The oldest original lighthouse in Alaska, it is an octagonal building with the tower rising from the center of the roof. There are several outbuildings on this small island that were used for the keeper's supplies and generator.

Backed by a dramatic snow-covered mountain across the channel, Eldred Rock Lighthouse has withstood howling storms with gales of nearly one hundred miles an hour, winter's constant darkness, and summer's endless daylight, for over a century. Today, only birds and otters live here, and whales, sea lions, and seals are the island's most frequent visitors.

Local lighthouse aficionados raised funds for the lighthouse's 2005 renovation by producing a play based on one of the most famous shipwrecks in the area, the *Clara Nevada*, which went down under mysterious circumstances with many passengers and a large cargo of gold. No trace of the ship was ever found.

# Weekday Lighthouse Dinner

We found a photograph of the keepers of Eldred Rock Light eating dinner together in the 1970s. Because the lighthouse was so remote, they also had movies and ping pong and pool tables for their amusement. They also had good comfort food, apparently: the menu that night was deviled eggs, salad, meatloaf, mashed potatoes, and sliced carrots. We added the Baked Alaska for dessert.

Deviled Eggs

Iceberg Lettuce Salad with Ranch Dressing

Mashed Yukon Gold Potatoes

Glazed Carrots

Elk Meatloaf

Baked Alaska

## DEVILED EGGS

*As basic as you can get, and Ed can eat a dozen, himself!*

6 EGGS
2 TABLESPOONS MAYONNAISE
1 TEASPOON BROWN MUSTARD
1½ TEASPOONS MINCED ONION
⅛ TEASPOON SALT
⅛ TEASPOON FRESHLY GROUND BLACK PEPPER
⅛ TEASPOON PAPRIKA, SMOKED OR PLAIN

1. Bring a large pot of water to a boil. Gently add the eggs to the water, return to a boil, and reduce to a simmer.
2. Cook for 12 minutes. Remove from heat, drain, and run under cold water.
3. Drain all the water from the pot, and swirl the pot so the eggs strike each other and their shells crack. Peel the eggs under cold running water.
4. Cut the eggs in half lengthwise. Carefully remove the yolks, and put the yolks into a bowl. Set the whites aside.
5. Blend the yolks, mayonnaise, mustard, onion, salt, and pepper until smooth.
6. Spoon or pipe the yolk mixture into the egg whites. Sprinkle each deviled egg with paprika.

YIELD: 12 deviled eggs
PREPARATION TIME: 10–15 minutes
COOKING TIME: 12 minutes

## ICEBERG LETTUCE SALAD WITH RANCH DRESSING

*Believe it or not, the man who invented ranch dressing was from Alaska. This is an authentic version, not nearly as sweet as a bottled dressing.*

6 CUPS CHOPPED ICEBERG LETTUCE
1 BUNCH RADISHES
1 CUCUMBER
2 CELERY STALKS
RANCH DRESSING (RECIPE FOLLOWS), FOR SERVING

1. Wash the radishes, remove the leafy tops, and slice the bulbs into discs.
2. Peel the cucumber and slice in half lengthwise. Using a spoon, remove the seeds then slice crosswise.
3. Using a potato peeler, peel the celery and remove the fibrous strings. Slice crosswise.
4. Toss all the ingredients together and serve with Ranch Dressing.

YIELD: 6 servings
PREPARATION TIME: 10–15 minutes

*Ranch Dressing*

½ CUP MAYONNAISE
½ CUP BUTTERMILK
½ CUP SOUR CREAM
1 TABLESPOON FRESH, OR 1 TEASPOON
   DRIED, PARSLEY
1 TABLESPOON FRESH, OR 1 TEASPOON
   DRIED, THYME
1 TEASPOON ONION POWDER
½ TEASPOON GARLIC POWDER
¼ TEASPOON SALT
⅛ TEASPOON FRESHLY GROUND BLACK
   PEPPER
⅛ TEASPOON SUGAR

1. Blend all the ingredients.

YIELD: 1¾ cups
PREPARATION TIME: 5–10 minutes

## MASHED YUKON GOLD POTATOES

*What other variety of potato would you use? Yukon Gold is so delicious, with its natural buttery flavor.*

2 POUNDS YUKON GOLD POTATOES
1 TABLESPOON PLUS 1 TEASPOON SALT, DIVIDED
4 TABLESPOONS BUTTER, MELTED
¾ CUP MILK, WARMED

1. Peel the potatoes and cut into equal-sized pieces.
2. Put the potatoes in a pot with 1 tablespoon salt and cover with cold water. Bring to a boil and cook potatoes for 20 to 25 minutes, or until they can easily be pierced with a fork. Preheat the oven to 300°F.
3. Drain the potatoes, place on a baking sheet, and place in the oven for 5 to 10 minutes. This will dry out the potatoes and make them fluffy.
4. Put the potatoes through a food mill or potato ricer. Fold in the butter, milk, and remaining salt.

YIELD: 4–6 servings
PREPARATION TIME: 5–10 minutes
COOKING TIME: 20–25 minutes on the stovetop, and 5–10 minutes in the oven

## GLAZED CARROTS

*This is Ed's foolproof way to make glazed carrots.*

1½ POUNDS CARROTS
1 CUP WATER
2 TABLESPOONS BUTTER
½ TEASPOON SALT
⅛ TEASPOON FRESHLY GROUND BLACK PEPPER

1. Peel the carrots and cut into ½-inch discs. Put in a pot and add water. Bring to a boil, and reduce to a simmer. Cook for 10 to 15 minutes, stirring every few minutes.
2. Add the butter, and continue stirring until carrots are tender and glazed. Season with salt and pepper.

YIELD: 4 servings
PREPARATION TIME: 5–10 minutes
COOKING TIME: 10–15 minutes

## ELK MEATLOAF

*You can also make this with venison. Both are very lean meats.*

2 TABLESPOONS VEGETABLE OIL
1 ONION, DICED
1 CARROT, DICED
1 CELERY STALK, DICED
2 POUNDS GROUND ELK
¼ POUND FATBACK, GROUND
1½ CUPS FRESH SOURDOUGH BREAD CRUMBS, CRUST REMOVED
2 EGGS, BEATEN
1 CUP TOMATO SAUCE

1 TABLESPOON CHOPPED FRESH, OR 1 TEASPOON DRIED, ROSEMARY
1 TABLESPOON CHOPPED FRESH, OR 1 TEASPOON DRIED, PARSLEY
1 TABLESPOON CHOPPED FRESH, OR 1 TEASPOON DRIED, THYME
1 TABLESPOON CHOPPED FRESH, OR 1 TEASPOON DRIED, SAGE
2½ TEASPOONS SALT
½ TEASPOON FRESHLY GROUND BLACK PEPPER

1. Heat a pan over medium heat and add the oil. Cook the onions, carrots, and celery for 10 to 15 minutes, or until vegetables are tender.
2. Preheat the oven to 350°F.
3. Mix together the elk, fatback, bread crumbs, eggs, tomato sauce, cooked vegetables, rosemary, parsley, thyme, sage, salt, and pepper.
4. Place the elk mixture in a loaf pan and bake for 50–55 minutes.

YIELD: 6–8 servings
PREPARATION TIME: 15–20 minutes
COOKING TIME: 10–15 minutes for the vegetables, and 50–55 minutes in the oven, or to 145 °F

## BAKED ALASKA

*This dessert was created decades before Alaska became a state. It is periodically revived in restaurants and for dinner parties, because it's such a fun concept—eating baked ice cream.*

*There are three components to this recipe: cake, ice cream and meringue. Prepare cake and ice cream at least 4 hours or the day before serving.*

*Cake*

1 TABLESPOON BUTTER, SOFTENED
1 CUP PLUS 1 TABLESPOON CAKE FLOUR, DIVIDED
2 EGGS, SEPARATED
1 CUP SUGAR, DIVIDED
3 OUNCES HOT WATER
½ TEASPOON VANILLA EXTRACT
1 TEASPOON BAKING POWDER
¼ TEASPOON SALT

1. Preheat the oven to 325°F. Using 1 tablespoon of each, butter and flour 2 (8 x 8-inch) square cake pans.
2. Using an electric mixer, beat the yolks until thick and light yellow. Add ½ cup sugar and beat until thickened. Pour in the water and vanilla.
3. Using a separate bowl, beat the egg whites until just stiffened, then slowly beat in ½ cup sugar. Fold the egg whites into the yolks. Blend in the flour, baking powder, and salt, and mix into the eggs until just incorporated.
4. Spread in the pans and bake 20 to 30 minutes, or until golden brown and springy; an inserted cake tester will come out clean.
5. Remove the cakes from the pans and cool on a rack to room temperature.

YIELD: 2 (8x8-inch) square cakes
PREPARATION TIME: 15–20 minutes
BAKING TIME: 20–30 minutes

*Vanilla Ice Cream*

1 CUP SUGAR, DIVIDED
2 TEASPOONS VANILLA EXTRACT
2 CUPS WHOLE MILK
2 CUPS HEAVY CREAM
8 EGG YOLKS

1. Heat ¾ cup of the sugar, and the vanilla, the milk, and the cream over medium heat in a heavy saucepan. Cook until the sugar is dissolved, bubbles begin to form on the edge, and steam begins to come off the surface. Remove from heat.
2. Whisk the egg yolks and remaining sugar together in a bowl. Continue to whisk and slowly add ½ cup of the milk mixture to the egg yolks. When blended, add back to the saucepan, whisking constantly. Turn heat to medium-low and whisk until the mixture thickens and coats the back of a spoon, about 5 to 7 minutes. Do not allow to boil.
3. Cool, then refrigerate for 2 hours or until chilled. Put into an ice cream maker and follow the manufacturer's instructions.

YIELD: About 1½ quarts
PREPARATION TIME: 5 minutes
COOKING TIME: 15–20 minutes
CHURNING TIME: See the manufacturer's instructions

*Meringue*

8 EXTRA-LARGE EGG WHITES
1 CUP SUGAR

1. Beat the egg whites to soft peaks. Beat in the sugar, a few tablespoons at a time, until glossy with stiff peaks.

YIELD: About 8 cups
PREPARATION TIME: Less than 5 minutes

*Assembly*

1. Preheat the broiler and put serving plates in the freezer.
2. Place the cakes on a broiler-proof surface. Scoop and spread the ice cream onto the cakes, not quite to the edge.
3. Spread the meringue on top of the ice cream, completely covering the ice cream and cakes.
4. Place under the broiler, until meringue starts to brown and peaks are dark brown; this will only take a few minutes.
5. Remove from broiler. Slice and serve immediately on chilled plates.

YIELD: 8–10 servings
PREPARATION TIME: 5–10 minutes
BROILER TIME: 5 minutes

# Cape Hinchinbrook Light
HINCHINBROOK ISLAND, ALASKA

THE UNITED STATES PURCHASED THE ALASKAN TERRITORY FROM RUSSIA IN
1867 for $7 million, but ships from the U.S. and other nations had also been trav-
eling to and from Alaska for centuries before then. Those seeking to enter Prince
William Sound have been guided by the Cape Hinchinbrook Lighthouse since 1910.
It took a year and half to complete the lighthouse due to the severe climate here,
and construction had to be completely abandoned during the winter. Then, earth-
quakes in 1927 and 1928 compromised the structural integrity of the lighthouse. So
the next tower was built on rock, with a reinforced concrete, Moderne-style, and
earthquake-resilient design in 1933–1935.

In Alaska, fish and meat are the mainstays of every meal, mostly because of this
state's long coastline and short growing season for fresh vegetables. The harsh climate also precludes raising cattle and chickens, two dietary staples of those who live
in the Lower 48. Here in the north, fresh fish and seafood are abundant, and meat
comes only from wild game that lives in the nearby mountains—making a wonderful
meal to be enjoyed with relatives and friends whenever possible. In each season, it's

also important to smoke enough meat and fish to preserve it for the rest of the year. And in the summer, everyone gathers native salmonberries; eat some, freeze some, and make the rest into jam right away.

# LATE SUMMER BRUNCH

Nowadays, catching salmon, crab, and other fish and seafood is strictly regulated, and as a result, Alaskan seafood has very specific seasons. Nature decrees a short season for fruits and vegetables. For example, berry-picking season lasts only a few days. Alaskans know to enjoy them during those brief days, or later as preserves or jam.

KING CRAB LEGS WITH MELTED BUTTER
DUNGENESS CRAB AND SMOKED SALMON QUICHE
SOURDOUGH TOAST
FRESH BERRIES IN SEASON

## KING CRAB LEGS WITH MELTED BUTTER
*This seafood has too delicate a flavor for anything but butter.*

**Note:** in most of the United States, we get our King Crab Legs precooked and frozen.

3 KING CRAB LEGS (ABOUT 1 POUND EACH, PRECOOKED AND FROZEN),
   THAWED
8 TABLESPOONS BUTTER, MELTED

1. Crack the legs and separate at the joints.
2. Place in a steamer and cook for 6 to 8 minutes.
3. Remove from the steamer, place on a platter and serve with the butter.
4. Kitchen shears work well for removing the shell.

YIELD: 6 servings
PREPARATION TIME: 5 minutes
COOKING TIME: 6–8 minutes

## DUNGENESS CRAB AND SMOKED SALMON QUICHE
*Crab and salmon are both caught during the same season in Alaska, so it makes sense that they should be eaten together.*

2 WHOLE EGGS
3 EGG YOLKS
3 CUPS HALF-AND-HALF OR LIGHT CREAM
1 CUP DUNGENESS CRABMEAT, DRAINED
½ CUP SMOKED SALMON

¼ CUP CHOPPED FRESH CHIVES
½ TEASPOON SALT
¼ TEASPOON FRESHLY GROUND BLACK PEPPER
¼ CUP CRUMBLED SALTINES
1 (9-INCH) RICH PIE CRUST (RECIPE FOLLOWS), PREBAKED

1. Preheat the oven to 375°F.
2. Beat together the whole eggs, egg yolks, and half-and-half.
3. Fold in the crabmeat, salmon, chives, salt, and pepper.
4. Sprinkle saltines on the bottom of the pie crust. This will absorb any liquid from the crab mixture. Pour the crab mixture into the pie crust and bake for 45 to 50 minutes.

YIELD: 4–6 servings
PREPARATION TIME: 10–15 minutes
COOKING TIME: 45–50 minutes

*Rich Pie Crust*

1½ CUPS ALL-PURPOSE FLOUR
⅛ TEASPOON SALT
¾ CUP VEGETABLE SHORTENING, COLD
3 TABLESPOONS COLD WATER
2 EGG YOLKS, LIGHTLY BEATEN

1. Mix the flour and salt in a bowl and cut the shortening into the flour with 2 knives or a pastry blender, until the mixture is in clumps the size of peas. Gradually add the water and the egg yolks, and blend together.
2. Form the pie dough into a ball, cover with plastic wrap, and refrigerate for at least 30 minutes.
3. Lightly flour work surface. Roll out the pie dough to be 1 inch larger than the pie plate. Fold the dough over rolling pin and place in the pie plate. Unfold to cover the entire plate. Fold the extra dough under, and crimp the edges.
4. With a fork, poke holes in the bottom of the crust, and place in the refrigerator for at least 10 minutes.
5. Preheat the oven to 450°F. Take the pie crust from the refrigerator, line the bottom with foil, and fill it with dried beans or rice. Bake for 15 to 20 minutes, or until lightly browned. Remove the pie crust from the oven, remove the foil and beans, and let cool on a rack.

YIELD: 1 (9-inch) pie crust
PREPARATION TIME: 15–20 minutes
REFRIGERATION TIME: 40 minutes
COOKING TIME: 15–20 minutes

## SOURDOUGH TOAST

*Don't skimp on the sourdough. Buy good-quality butter, too.*

1 LOAF SOURDOUGH BREAD
8 TABLESPOONS BUTTER, MELTED

1. Preheat broiler on high.
2. Cut the bread into ½-inch slices.
3. Place on a rack under the broiler, and broil for 2 to 3 minutes.
4. Turn the slices over, brush with the butter, and cook until golden brown.

YIELD: 6–8 servings
PREPARATION TIME: Less than 5 minutes
COOKING TIME: 4–6 minutes


## FRESH BERRIES IN SEASON

*In Alaska in August, it's salmonberries.*

1 QUART FRESH BERRIES
½ PINT SOUR CREAM
2 TABLESPOONS BROWN SUGAR

1. Carefully wash and drain berries.
2. Mix the sour cream and sugar.
3. Serve the berries in small bowls, with a dollop of the sour cream mixture on top.

YIELD: 4 servings
PREPARATION TIME: Less than 5 minutes

# THE GREAT LAKES
# REGION

The Great Lakes hold almost a fifth of the fresh water on Earth; only the polar ice caps hold more. They are a vital resource for North America.

Glaciers carved the Great Lakes out of the center of North America thousands of years ago. Native Americans followed the glaciers' retreat, settling in what is now the Midwestern region of the United States. French explorers and then fur trappers started to arrive here in the 1620s, about the same time the Pilgrims first set foot on Cape Cod in New England. By 1787, this region was called the Northwest Territory; territorial battles between the Native Americans and European settlers continued into the 1800s.

In the early 1800s, the lakes were connected by manmade canals to the St. Lawrence River and also to the Hudson River, both of which lead to the Atlantic Ocean. The Great Lakes became connected to the Mississippi River in 1900, when the Chicago River's flow was altered to move water out of, instead of into, Lake Michigan to reduce its levels of pollution. (Currently, there is talk of reversing the river's flow and returning it to its natural state.)

Immigration picked up throughout the nineteenth century and into the mid-twentieth century, with many Scandinavians, Germans, and Poles arriving by water routes. Hundreds of lighthouses were built here to safeguard passenger and freight shipping. But storms on the Great Lakes are ferocious, and legendary tragedies on the water have occurred as recently as the 1970s.

The Great Lakes are: Lakes Superior, Michigan, Huron, Erie, and Ontario.

Eight states border one or more of the Great Lakes: Wisconsin, Minnesota, Illinois, Indiana, Michigan, Ohio, Pennsylvania, and New York.

Michigan now has more lighthouses than any other state in the country: 124.

Today, the wild rice, quail, duck, venison, and other game native to these shores are mainly farmed, not wild, as are the berries, cherries, and other fruits that once were scavenged. Cherries and cranberries—both dried and fresh—are exported all over the country to feed Americans newly conscious of their antioxidant properties. Midwestern Friday-night fish fries and classic summer fish boils take full advantage of the wide variety of freshwater catches like bluegill, lake perch, salmon, trout, walleyed pike and whitefish.

# Split Rock Lighthouse

TWO HARBORS, MINNESOTA—LAKE SUPERIOR

EVERY YEAR ON NOVEMBER 10, THIS LIGHT'S BEACON IS RELIT TO HONOR the dead of a tragically famous 1975 shipwreck. Folk singer Gordon Lightfoot wrote his well-known ballad about this event, "The Wreck of the *Edmund Fitzgerald*." When the *Edmund Fitzgerald*, a Great Lakes freighter, went down, the entire boat and its crew disappeared into the cold, dark waters.

As early as 1905, thirty ships had been lost in these waters, yet this lighthouse was not completed until 1910. The harsh winters and the lighthouse's distance from schools allowed the keepers' families to live here only during the summer months. In the early years, Split Rock was decommissioned annually in December, when the Great Lakes' shipping season ended.

From out on Lake Superior, this rock formation looks like it is cut in two, hence the name Split Rock. The lighthouse sits on a sheer, 120-foot cliff. But this isn't the only danger. Underground iron ore all around wreaks havoc with compasses. The lake is extremely deep here—at least five hundred feet—but no one knows exactly how deep, because measurements have not been consistent. Adding one more interesting element to its story, the lighthouse may be haunted by an older man in a uniform and also by a

This northern state has been a leader in developing new varieties of apples and other fruits since a large tract of land was set aside for this purpose by the University of Minnesota in 1908. The research group has introduced nearly one hundred cold-hardy versions of apricots, blueberries, cherries, wine and table grapes, plums, raspberries and strawberries.

According to the university's Barbara DeGroot, "Star performers among the University of Minnesota apple introductions are Haralson (introduced in 1922; tart and firm), Beacon (1936; sweet/tart firm), Prairie Spy (1940; tart firm), Regent (1964; sweet/tart firm), Honeycrisp (1991; sweet/tart), and Zestar (1998; sweet/tart tender)."

The Horticultural Research Center also opens its beautiful and important gardens to the public:

Contd....

woman wearing perfume. Perhaps it's all these thrills that made Split Rock one of the most visited lighthouses by the mid-twentieth century; it also sits in a state park with a lighthouse museum.

## FALL DINNER

Minnesota's Native Americans found abundant wild rice, quail, duck, and venison, as well as walleyed pike and other lake fish. Settlers brought hardy Northern European vegetables like parsnips, Brussels sprouts, and turnips. Over the past 100 years, the University of Minnesota has developed special varieties of apples, grapes, and other fruits to grow in this challenging climate.

LEEK AND PARSNIP SOUP
SAUTÉED QUAIL ON A BED OF FRISÉE
BRAISED BRUSSELS SPROUTS
WILD RICE WITH MUSHROOMS AND WALNUTS
BROILED WALLEYED PIKE WITH PARSLEY BUTTER
APPLE PUDDING CAKE

### LEEK AND PARSNIP SOUP

*Leeks and parsnips are complimentary flavors in this soup. No additional seasoning is needed.*

1 POUND PARSNIPS
1½ POUNDS LEEKS
4 TABLESPOONS BUTTER
1 TEASPOON SALT
6 CUPS VEGETABLE STOCK
1 CUP HEAVY CREAM
¼ TEASPOON FRESHLY GROUND BLACK PEPPER

1. Peel the parsnips and cut into ½-inch pieces.
2. Remove the dark green parts of the leeks. Cut off the root ends, and cut the leeks in half lengthwise. Chop crosswise to make half moons. Submerge the cut leeks in water and agitate. Lift the leeks out of the water, set in a strainer and rinse.
3. Melt the butter in a large pot. Add the leeks, parsnips, and salt. Sauté for 15 to 20 minutes, or until vegetables are tender.
4. Pour in the stock. Cover, bring to a boil, and reduce to a simmer. Simmer for 20 to 25 minutes. Add the heavy cream and pepper and heat but do not boil.

YIELD: 4–6 servings
PREPARATION TIME: 10–15 minutes
COOKING TIME: 40–45 minutes

## SAUTÉED QUAIL ON A BED OF FRISÉE

*This is fine dining—and worth it. The quail is delectable on a bed of piquant greens.*

4 SEMI-BONELESS QUAIL
1 TEASPOON FINELY CHOPPED FRESH ROSEMARY
4 TABLESPOONS EXTRA VIRGIN OLIVE OIL, DIVIDED
2 TABLESPOONS RENDERED DUCK FAT OR 2 TABLESPOONS
    VEGETABLE OIL
1 SHALLOT, SLICED
½ CUP RED WINE
½ CUP BEEF STOCK
3 TABLESPOONS BUTTER
1¼ TEASPOONS SALT, DIVIDED
¼ TEASPOON FRESHLY GROUND BLACK PEPPER, DIVIDED
1 SMALL BUNCH FRISÉE (ABOUT 4 OUNCES)
2 TEASPOONS BALSAMIC VINEGAR

1. Marinate the quail in the rosemary and 2 tablespoons olive oil for at least 1 hour (no more than 4 hours).
2. Heat a pan on medium-high. Season the quail with 1 teaspoon salt. Add the duck fat and the quail to the pan.
3. Sauté 3 to 4 minutes. Turn the quail over, add the shallot, and sauté for 4 more minutes.
4. Remove the quail from the pan. Put the wine and stock in the pan, stirring to make sauce, and being careful when adding the wine.
5. Reduce the sauce by half. Add the butter and mix in. Return the quail to the pan, and turn to coat with the sauce.
6. Dress the frisée with the balsamic vinegar and remaining olive oil. Season with remaining salt and pepper.
7. Place the frisée on individual plates. Top with the quail and spoon the sauce over top.

YIELD: 4 servings
PREPARATION TIME: 5–10 minutes
MARINATING TIME: 1hour
COOKING TIME: 10–12 minutes

## BRAISED BRUSSELS SPROUTS

*Even if you think you don't like Brussels sprouts, you'll like these. The flavorings are perfect.*

1 POUND BRUSSELS SPROUTS
2 TABLESPOONS VEGETABLE OIL

4 SLICES BACON, CHOPPED
2 SHALLOTS, THINLY SLICED
1 CUP CHICKEN STOCK
½ TEASPOON SALT
⅛ TEASPOON FRESHLY GROUND BLACK PEPPER

1. Trim the bases of the sprouts and cut them in half, through the stem.
2. Heat oil in a large, heavy pan over medium heat. Sauté bacon for 2 minutes. Place the sprouts in the pan, cut side down, and allow to cook for 5 minutes, or until they begin to brown. The color will add to the flavor.
3. Add the shallots, toss the vegetables, and continue to cook for 5 to 10 minutes.
4. Pour in the stock and simmer for 5 minutes, or until most of the stock has evaporated.
5. Season with the salt and pepper before serving.

YIELD: 4 servings
PREPARATION TIME: 10–15 minutes
COOKING TIME: 20 minutes

## WILD RICE WITH MUSHROOMS AND WALNUTS

*Use this for your holiday meals as well. The nuttiness of the wild rice—not technically rice, but a grass—pairs well with the walnuts.*

1 CUP FRESH OR RECONSTITUTED WILD MUSHROOMS
3 TABLESPOONS BUTTER
1 SMALL ONION, DICED
1 CELERY STALK, DICED
1 TABLESPOON FRESH, OR 1 TEASPOON DRIED, THYME
2 CUPS COOKED WILD RICE
1 CUP CHICKEN STOCK
¾ CUP CHOPPED WALNUTS, TOASTED
1 TEASPOON SALT
¼ TEASPOON FRESHLY GROUND BLACK PEPPER

1. Reconstitute the dry mushrooms by covering with boiling water or stock. Allow to sit for 10 minutes. Remove, drain and dice
2. Melt the butter in a pan over medium to low heat. Sauté the onion, celery, mushrooms, and thyme for 10 minutes, or until the vegetables are tender
3. Mix in the cooked rice and stock. Simmer until the mixture is almost dry. Add the walnuts and season with the salt and pepper.

YIELD: 6 servings
PREPARATION TIME: 15 minutes with reconstituting mushrooms
COOKING TIME: 20–25 minutes (not including the wild rice, which usually takes 45–60 minutes)

## BROILED WALLEYED PIKE WITH PARSLEY BUTTER

*"Walleye" as it's known, is a very mild fish. The butter and parsley really wake up its flavors.*

2 TABLESPOONS VEGETABLE OIL
1½–1¾ POUNDS WALLEYED PIKE FILLETS
1 TEASPOON SALT
¼ TEASPOON FRESHLY GROUND BLACK PEPPER
4 TABLESPOONS BUTTER
¼ CUP FINELY CHOPPED FRESH PARSLEY
½ LEMON

1. Preheat broiler on high.
2. Line a baking sheet with aluminum foil. Brush foil with oil.
3. Lay fillets, skin side down, on foil and season with the salt and pepper.
4. Place the fillets under the broiler and broil 4–5 minutes. Remove the fillets and place on a serving platter. Cover with foil.
5. Melt the butter in a pan. When it begins to foam, add the parsley and cook for 2 minutes.
6. Squeeze the lemon and pour the parsley butter over the fillets. Serve.

YIELD: 4–6 servings
PREPARATION TIME: Less than 5 minutes
COOKING TIME: 4–5 minutes

## APPLE PUDDING CAKE

*This recipe is from Apple Jack Orchards in Delano, MN. It's made with Honeycrisp apples, which were developed by the University of Minnesota especially for growing in this climate. Great with whipped cream.*

1 CUP CHOPPED BLACK WALNUTS
⅔ CUP VEGETABLE SHORTENING
1⅓ CUPS SUGAR
2 EGGS
2 TEASPOONS BAKING SODA
2 TEASPOONS CINNAMON
1 TEASPOON NUTMEG
2 CUPS ALL-PURPOSE FLOUR
6 CUPS HONEY CRISP APPLES, PEELED, CORED AND CHOPPED
APPLE PUDDING CAKE SAUCE (RECIPE FOLLOWS)
1 CUP HEAVY WHIPPING CREAM, FOR SERVING (OPTIONAL)

1. Preheat the oven to 325°F. Grease a 13×9-inch pan.
2. Heat a frying pan over medium-low heat. Toast the walnuts until they begin to change color and become fragrant, about 7 minutes. Pour into a dish and set aside.
3. In the large bowl of a mixer, cream together the shortening and sugar. Add the eggs, 1 at a time, and beat well after each addition.

4. Sift together the baking soda, cinnamon, nutmeg, and flour. Beat into the sugar mixture.
5. Fold in the apples and nuts. The mixture will be stiff. Spread into the prepared pan. Do not bake it yet!
6. Pour the Apple Pudding Cake Sauce evenly over batter. Do not stir.
7. Bake for 1 hour. Serve warm with whipped cream, if desired.

YIELD: 10–12 servings
PREPARATION TIME: 10–15 minutes
BAKING TIME: 1 hour

*Apple Pudding Cake Sauce*

1½ CUPS PACKED BROWN SUGAR
2 TABLESPOONS ALL-PURPOSE FLOUR
4 TABLESPOONS BUTTER
1 TEASPOON VANILLA EXTRACT
1 CUP WATER

1. In a medium saucepan, stir together the brown sugar and flour. Stir in the butter, vanilla, and water.
2. Bring to a boil while stirring occasionally. Boil gently for 3 minutes, stirring often. Remove from heat.

YIELD: About 3 cups
PREPARATION TIME: Less than 5 minutes
COOKING TIME: 5 minutes

# Sand Hills Lighthouse Inn
AHMEEK, MICHIGAN—LAKE SUPERIOR

NATIVE AMERICANS HAD LIVED ALONG LAKE SUPERIOR FOR NEARLY TEN THOUSAND YEARS WHEN the first Europeans arrived in 1622. Over the next century and a half the region was visited and inhabited by French explorers, Jesuits, fur traders, and the English—until it became part of the United States after the American Revolutionary War. Scandinavian farmers began to move here in the nineteenth century, attracted by inexpensive land to farm, and then by the logging industry which offered plentiful employment.

Furs and lumber were the impetus for shipping in Lake Superior from the beginning, but it would take centuries of water disasters until lighthouses were built. Sand Hills was the final manned lighthouse on the Great Lakes and it was completed less than one hundred years ago, in 1919. The tower is attached to dwelling space for three keepers, making this an impressive monument. During World War II, it housed two hundred Coast Guard men in training.

Sold at auction first in 1958, a few years later it was bought and used as a summer house by current owners Mary Mathews and Bill Frabotta. For years, they dreamed of restoring the lighthouse—and they finally did in the 1990s, after they "retired." It's now an oasis on the lake: a charming inn filled with modern conveniences and historic style, open year-round.

# DANISH BREAKFAST

Mary Mathews' heritage is Danish, and she prepares her own Danish coffee cake every day. She makes it from scratch, as she does her scones, pecan rolls, and all other baked goods here. She grinds her own specially blended coffee, too: what's great pastry without the right coffee? In case you were wondering, the breakfast also includes egg dishes, and Bill's famous potatoes, which feature the Italian seasonings of his heritage.

DANISH COFFEE CAKE
BILL'S FAMOUS POTATOES
BRUNCH OVEN OMELET

## DANISH COFFEE CAKE

1 CUP WATER
8 TABLESPOONS BUTTER
1 CUP ALL-PURPOSE FLOUR
4 EGGS
1 TEASPOON ALMOND EXTRACT
DANISH COFFEE CAKE CRUST (RECIPE FOLLOWS)
DANISH COFFEE CAKE FROSTING (RECIPE FOLLOWS)

1. Preheat the oven to 350°F.
2. Heat a saucepan over medium heat. Add the water and butter, and melt the butter in the water.
3. Bring to a low boil and add the flour. Stir vigorously until it forms a ball and leaves the sides of the pan, about 2 minutes.
4. Remove from heat and add the eggs and almond extract. Beat vigorously again until very thick dough forms. Spread evenly over the prepared Danish Coffee Cake Crust.
5. Bake for 35 to 40 minutes
6. Cool completely. Spread with Danish Coffee Cake Frosting.

YIELD: 6–8 servings
PREPARATION TIME: Less than 5 minutes
COOKING TIME: 35–40 minutes

*Danish Coffee Cake Crust*

1 CUP ALL-PURPOSE FLOUR
8 TABLESPOONS BUTTER, COLD
2 TABLESPOONS COLD WATER

1. With a pastry blender, combine the flour and butter until a fine, crumbly mixture forms. Add the water. Using a fork, work in the water until a dough forms.

2. Divide this mixture in half and, on an ungreased cookie sheet, press out into 2 (4×11-inch) strips of dough. The dough can be refrigerated if it becomes difficult to work with.

YIELD: 2 (4×11-inch) crusts
PREPARATION TIME: Less than 5 minutes

*Danish Coffee Cake Frosting*

1½ CUPS POWDERED SUGAR
2 TABLESPOONS BUTTER, SOFTENED
1½ TEASPOONS VANILLA EXTRACT
1½ TABLESPOONS WATER

1. Combine all the ingredients and blend thoroughly.

YIELD: About 2 cups
PREPARATION TIME: Less than 5 minutes

## BILL'S FAMOUS POTATOES

**Note:** A nonstick skillet is best for this potato dish.

2 POUNDS RUSSET POTATOES
4 TABLESPOONS VEGETABLE OIL, DIVIDED
2 TEASPOONS ITALIAN SEASONING
½ TEASPOON ONION POWDER
½ TEASPOON CURRY POWDER
1 TEASPOON SALT
⅛ TEASPOON SUGAR

1. Peel and thinly slice the potatoes. Place in a bowl of cold water for 5 minutes. Drain and pat dry with a paper towel.
2. Transfer the potatoes to a large bowl. Add the Italian seasoning, onion powder, curry powder, salt, and sugar. Toss until the potatoes are evenly coated. Add 2 tablespoons vegetable oil and continue to toss.
3. Heat a nonstick frying pan with rounded bottom edges on medium-high heat; add remaining vegetable oil to the pan.
4. After the oil is hot, about 2 minutes, layer the potatoes in the pan and cook for 2 minutes. Carefully turn the potatoes over. Continue turning until all of the potatoes are evenly cooked, about 10 minutes.
5. Press down on the potatoes and allow to brown. Carefully slide the potatoes onto a plate. Place the pan on top of the plate and flip so the browned side of the potatoes are on the top. Slide potatoes back into the pan and continue to cook until the bottom has browned. Slide onto a serving plate.

YIELD: 6–8 serving
PREPARATION TIME: 5–10 minutes
COOKING TIME: 15–20 minutes

## BRUNCH OVEN OMELET

4 TABLESPOONS BUTTER
18 EXTRA LARGE OR JUMBO EGGS
1 CUP MILK
1 CUP SOUR CREAM
1½ TEASPOONS SALT
¼ TEASPOON FRESHLY GROUND BLACK PEPPER
2 GREEN ONIONS, FINELY CHOPPED
3 OUNCES AMERICAN CHEESE, CUBED

1. Preheat the oven to 325°F.
2. Place the butter in a 13×9 inch ovenproof dish and melt in the oven.
3. Beat the eggs, milk, sour cream, salt, and pepper using an electric mixer on medium-high speed for 2 minutes.
4. Pour into the prepared dish. Sprinkle the green onions and cheese over the egg mixture as evenly as possible.
5. Bake until eggs have set.

YIELD: 8–10 servings
PREPARATION TIME: 10–15 minutes
BAKING TIME: About 1 hour

# Eagle Bluff Lighthouse

DOOR COUNTY, WISCONSIN—LAKE MICHIGAN

PASSENGERS AND CARGO FLOODED INTO THE MIDWEST AFTER THE ERIE CANAL WAS completed in 1825, and by the turn of the century, there were nearly 350 lighthouses on the Great Lakes. Door County had thirteen of those; ten remain today. But just inland from the shore, the land remained wild much longer. Bricks had to be brought by boat from Milwaukee and Detroit to build this lighthouse in 1868, when it was deemed necessary to guide ships in and out of the great port of Green Bay.

Eagle Bluff Lighthouse was automated in 1925, and the buildings were not well maintained after that. However, in 1960, the Door County Historical Society decided to research Eagle Bluff's history. They were intrigued by the lighthouse, and soon Eagle Bluff became the first lighthouse in the United States to be restored to its original condition and decor. Luckily, Walter Duclon, the youngest member of a lighthouse keeper's family who had arrived in 1883, was still living in the area and helped ensure the restoration was authentic. Many of the original fixtures were found to have remained in the community and they were refurbished to complete the lighthouse's interior.

Early on, keepers here received government deliveries of food staples and fuel. In addition, they had their own gardens, and as a matter of course, they hunted as well. Keepers noted the abundance of fish as one of the most pleasurable aspects of life at this lighthouse. It is located at the tip of what is now Peninsula State Park, and it has become a valued part of the community.

## WISCONSIN FESTIVAL

Door County has many summer festivals, and the Fish Boil is a highlight here, with its setting at the edge of a lake full of a variety of fish. Traditionally, the table was first set with several relishes. But in Wisconsin, which is famous for cheese as well as beer, what could be better than starting the meal by serving the relishes alongside a lovely, rich soup? Wisconsin dairy gives it a big finish, too, in the form of homemade frozen custard.

CORN RELISH
ONION RELISH
CORN FRITTERS
WISCONSIN CHEDDAR CHEESE AND BEER SOUP
DOOR COUNTY FISH BOIL
STRAWBERRY FROZEN CUSTARD

### CORN RELISH

*This is the Midwestern favorite that Ed's mom used to make.*

3 CUPS CORN KERNELS (ABOUT 6 EARS)
4 SCALLIONS, SLICED
1 RED BELL PEPPER, SEEDED AND DICED
2 CHERRY PEPPERS, SEEDED AND DICED
½ CUP BROWN SUGAR
½ CUP CIDER VINEGAR
1 TEASPOON CELERY SEED
1½ TEASPOONS POWDERED MUSTARD
1 TEASPOON SALT
½ TEASPOON FRESHLY GROUND BLACK PEPPER

1. Put all the ingredients in a pot, bring to a boil, then reduce to a simmer. Cook for 10 minutes, stirring occasionally.
2. Remove from heat and allow to cool.

YIELD: 4 cups
PREPARATION TIME: 10–15 minutes
COOKING TIME: 10 minutes

## ONION RELISH

*When you set the table, you have to put out the relishes. It's a given.*

6 CUPS SLICED ONIONS
1 CUP SUGAR
2 CUPS CIDER VINEGAR
1 TEASPOON DRIED OREGANO
2 TABLESPOONS MUSTARD SEEDS
¼ TEASPOON SALT
⅛ TEASPOON FRESHLY GROUND BLACK PEPPER

1. Combine all the ingredients in a pot and simmer for 30 minutes. Cool before serving.

YIELD: About 3 cups
PREPARATION TIME: 10-15 minutes
COOKING TIME: 30 minutes

## CORN FRITTERS

*Omitting the basil and pepper—and adding 2 tablespoons sugar—makes these fritters a great breakfast snack, too, if served with honey or maple syrup.*

2½ CUPS ALL-PURPOSE FLOUR
3 TEASPOONS BAKING POWDER
1 TEASPOON SALT
½ TEASPOON FRESHLY GROUND BLACK PEPPER
3 EGGS, BEATEN
¼ CUP CHOPPED FRESH, OR 2 TEASPOONS
    DRIED, BASIL
2 CUPS CORN KERNELS, (ABOUT 4 EARS)
VEGETABLE SHORTENING, FOR FRYING

1. Combine the flour, baking powder, salt, and pepper in a medium bowl. In a separate bowl, combine the eggs, basil and corn.
2. Add the wet ingredients to the dry ingredients and mix, just until you can't see the flour. Do not overmix.
3. Refrigerate for 10 minutes.
4. Heat ½ inch vegetable shortening in a heavy pot over medium-high heat to 375°F.
5. Preheat the oven to 200°F. Fritters may need to be cooked in batches, and they can be kept warm in the oven.
6. Spoon walnut-sized portions of batter into the hot oil, being careful not to overcrowd them in the pot. Cook for 2 to 3 minutes per side, turning over occasionally, until browned.
7. Drain on a rack. Place in a warm oven while the balance of the batter is being cooked. Serve hot.

YIELD: 20–25 pieces
PREPARATION TIME: 5–10 minutes
REFRIGERATION TIME: 10 minutes
COOKING TIME: 4–6 minutes per batch

## WISCONSIN CHEDDAR CHEESE AND BEER SOUP

*Why put beer in soup? Why not just have a bowl of soup with a beer on the side? You'll find out when you make this.*

4 TABLESPOONS BUTTER
4 SHALLOTS, MINCED (ABOUT ½ CUP)
4 TABLESPOONS ALL-PURPOSE FLOUR
4 CUPS MILK, WARMED, DIVIDED
1 ½ POUNDS CHEDDAR CHEESE, GRATED
1 CUP BEER
1 TEASPOON CURRY POWDER
1 TEASPOON SALT
¼ TEASPOON FRESHLY GROUND BLACK PEPPER

1. Heat butter in large pot. Add shallots and sauté over medium heat for 10 minutes, or until tender. Stir in the flour and cook for 3 to 4 minutes. Whisk in 1 cup of warm milk, stirring constantly until thickened.
2. Slowly add the cheese, ¼ cup at a time, stirring constantly.
3. Whisk in remaining milk and beer. Bring to a boil, whisking until thick.
4. Blend in the curry powder, salt, and pepper.

YIELD: 6 servings
PREPARATION TIME: 15–20 minutes
COOKING TIME: 25–30 minutes


## DOOR COUNTY FISH BOIL

*It's traditionally served with garden fresh coleslaw and homemade breads.*

½ CUP SALT
18 SMALL RED POTATOES (IF LARGE, CUT IN HALF OR QUARTERS)
6 WHITEFISH FILLETS (ABOUT 6 OUNCES EACH) OR OTHER MILD, WHITE FISH
8 TABLESPOONS BUTTER, MELTED
2 LEMONS, CUT INTO WEDGES

1. Bring a large pot of water to a rolling boil. Add the salt and potatoes.
2. Cook for 10 minutes or until partially done.
3. Add the fillets and cook for 8 to 10 minutes, or until the fish is firm and begins to flake. Skim any film that forms on top of the water.
4. Remove the potatoes and fish from the water. Place on a platter and serve with the lemon wedges and individual dishes of butter.

YIELD: 6 servings
PREPARATION TIME: 5–10 minutes
COOKING TIME: About 25 minutes (not including boiling the water)

## STRAWBERRY FROZEN CUSTARD

*You can't go to Wisconsin without indulging in frozen custard—maybe it's the fresh cream from the Dairy State. The rest of the world thinks it's ice cream, but Wisconsinites know better.*

1 CUP STRAWBERRIES, HULLED AND CHOPPED
1 TABLESPOON CRÈME DE CASSIS
½ CUP SUGAR, DIVIDED
1 CUP WHOLE MILK
1 CUP HEAVY CREAM
4 EGG YOLKS

1. Mix together the strawberries, crème de cassis, and 2 tablespoons sugar. Refrigerate at least 4 hours or overnight.
2. Heat ¼ cup sugar, the milk, and the cream over medium heat in a heavy saucepan. Cook until the sugar has dissolved, bubbles begin to form on the edge, and steam begins to come off the surface. Remove from heat.
3. Whisk together the egg yolks and remaining sugar in a bowl. Continue to whisk and slowly add ½ cup of the milk mixture to the egg yolks. When blended, add back to the saucepan, whisking constantly. Turn heat to medium-low, and whisk until the mixture thickens and coats the back of a spoon, about 5 to 7 minutes. Do not allow to boil.
4. Mix the strawberries into the custard mixture and cool, then refrigerate for 2 hours or until chilled. Put into an ice cream maker. Follow the manufacturer's instructions.

YIELD: About 4 cups
PREPARATION TIME: 5 minutes
REFRIGERATION TIME: 6 hours
COOKING TIME: 15–20 minutes
CHURNING TIME: See manufacturer's instructions

# Grosse Point Lighthouse
EVANSTON, ILLINOIS—LAKE MICHIGAN

GROSSE POINT LIGHT WAS BUILT EXACTLY TWO HUNDRED YEARS AFTER THIS POINT NEAR THE Chicago River was first charted by French explorers. By the time the lighthouse was built in 1873, Chicago had become a major hub along the main Great Lakes shipping routes. First, furs from traders, and then farm goods and lumber, were shipped out from the Midwest. Cargo numbers increased dramatically, until eventually more ships were docking here than in New York and San Francisco toward the end of the nineteenth century. Grosse Point's beacon was first lit on March 1, 1874, the day that traditionally marked the beginning of the shipping season on the Great Lakes each year.

Sixty years later, in 1934, Grosse Point was the first U.S. lighthouse to be automated using a photoelectric cell to turn the light on and off. It was also the first of the Great Lakes lighthouses to be designated a National Historic Landmark (in 1999).

Built in a beautiful, Italianate style, both the tower and keeper's dwelling have been restored and are maintained as the focal points of the lovely Lighthouse Park District in Evanston, Illinois. The Evanston Garden Club has also created surrounding gardens dedicated to native wildflowers and butterflies.

# HEARTY NORTHERN EUROPEAN SUPPER

In Chicago, Illinois, citizens could dine simply or elegantly at any given meal: a picnic of plain and hearty Midwestern food, or a European-style dinner of many courses at a downtown hotel. This meal is a cross between the two—a satisfying, multicourse supper with local ingredients made into familiar German-style dishes.

BARLEY SOUP
KLOESE (POTATO DUMPLINGS)
BOILED BEETS WITH BUTTER
ROASTED PORK LOIN WITH GRAVY
CHOCOLATE FUDGE CAKE

## BARLEY SOUP

*This is a light version of barley soup and a great start for a hearty meal.*

4 TABLESPOONS VEGETABLE OIL
1 ONION, DICED
1 CELERY STALK, DICED
1 CARROT, DICED
6 CUPS BEEF STOCK
¼ CUP PEARL BARLEY, RINSED
½ TEASPOON SALT
¼ TEASPOON FRESHLY GROUND BLACK PEPPER
¼ CUP CHOPPED FRESH PARSLEY

1. Heat a large pot over medium heat. Add the oil and allow to heat up for 1 to 2 minutes. Sauté onions, celery and carrots for 10 to 15 minutes, or until vegetables are tender.
2. Pour in the stock and barley, add salt and pepper, and simmer for 1 hour.
3. Add the parsley just before serving.

YIELD: 4–6 servings
PREPARATION TIME: 5–10 minutes
COOKING TIME: 10–15 minutes for the vegetables, and 1 hour for simmering the soup

## KLOESE (POTATO DUMPLINGS)

*You have to serve these dumplings with the Roasted Pork Loin with Gravy.*

2 POUNDS POTATOES
1½ CUPS ALL-PURPOSE FLOUR
2 EGGS, BEATEN
5 TEASPOONS SALT, DIVIDED
⅛ TEASPOON FRESHLY GROUND BLACK PEPPER

1 GALLON WATER
UNSEASONED CROUTONS
4 TABLESPOONS BUTTER, MELTED

1. Place the potatoes in the microwave and cook for 15 to 20 minutes, or until they can be pierced with a fork. Turn potatoes over halfway through the cooking time.
2. Remove the potatoes from the microwave, split open, and cool until they can be handled. Remove the skins and run the potatoes through a food mill or potato ricer.
3. Place the potatoes in a bowl, and mix in the flour, eggs, 1 teaspoon of salt, and the pepper. Remove to work surface, and knead 10 to 15 times, until you no longer see any flour.
4. Bring the water to a boil. Add remaining salt.
5. Form the potato mixture into 1½-inch balls, each with a crouton in the center. Place the dumplings in the water, and simmer for 15 minutes.
6. Remove from the water, drain, and pour the butter over the top.

YIELD: About 16 dumplings
PREPARATION TIME: 10–15 minutes
COOKING TIME: 15–20 minutes in the microwave, and 15 minutes to cook the dumplings

*In a microwave, the side of the potato that is in contact with the plate has a tendency to get tough. So turn potatoes over halfway through cooking.*

## BOILED BEETS WITH BUTTER

*A great color counterpoint for this meal; simple and tasty, too.*

2 POUNDS RED BEETS
2 TEASPOONS SALT
⅛ TEASPOON WHITE PEPPER
3 TABLESPOONS BUTTER, MELTED

1 Trim the beets, leaving 1 inch of stem attached.
2. Put the beets in a pot, cover with water, and add the salt. Bring to a boil, and cook for 30–60 minutes, or until easily pierced with a fork. Timing will depend on the size of the beets.
3. Remove the beets from the water and allow to cool enough to handle. Put on latex gloves, so your hands don't change color. Remove remaining stems, then slip the skins off the beets.
4. Slice the beets into discs, season with pepper, and toss with butter.

YIELD: 4–6 servings
PREPARATION TIME: Less than 5 minutes
COOKING TIME: 30–60 minutes

## ROASTED PORK LOIN WITH GRAVY

*Use pork loin (not tenderloin) and make sure you get the sirloin cut. Even your local supermarket should be able to provide this. It's incredibly flavorful.*

**Note:** If you use a center-cut loin, be more aware of the internal temperature. This cut has less marbling than the sirloin, and it is more likely to dry out.

1 PORK LOIN, BONELESS SIRLOIN CUT (ABOUT 3 POUNDS)
1 TEASPOON SALT
¼ TEASPOON FRESHLY GROUND BLACK PEPPER
¼ CUP ALL-PURPOSE FLOUR
3 CUPS BEEF STOCK

1. Preheat the oven to 450°F.
2. Rub the loin with the salt and pepper. Place the loin, fat side up, on a rack in a roasting pan.
3. Roast at 450°F for 15 minutes. Reduce the temperature to 300°F and continue to cook for 1¼ hours. Check the internal temperature after 50 minutes of roasting. Remove the loin when it reaches an internal temperature of 150°F to 155°F.
4. After removing the loin from the oven, place the loin on a carving board, cover loosely with foil, and let rest for 15 minutes.
5. Drain all but ¼ cup of fat from the pan. Place the roasting pan on the stovetop, blend in the flour, and cook for 1 to 2 minutes. Whisk in the beef stock, and reduce until thickened. If your roasting pan is not compatible with the stovetop, transfer the drippings and fat to a pot, and follow the above steps to make the gravy.
6. Carve the loin and serve with the gravy.

YIELD: 6–8 servings
PREPARATION TIME: Less than 5 minutes
COOKING TIME: About 1½ hours, and 10 minutes for the gravy

## CHOCOLATE FUDGE CAKE

*This is a brownie–like cake that's great for anyone with a sweet tooth.*

2 CUPS CAKE FLOUR
1 TEASPOON BAKING SODA
1 TEASPOON BAKING POWDER
½ TEASPOON SALT
2 OUNCES SWEET BAKING CHOCOLATE
2 OUNCES UNSWEETENED BAKING CHOCOLATE
9 TABLESPOONS BUTTER, SOFTENED, DIVIDED
1⅛ CUP SUGAR
2 EXTRA-LARGE EGGS
2½ TABLESPOONS APPLE CIDER VINEGAR
COCOA FROSTING (RECIPE FOLLOWS)

1. Preheat the oven to 325°F. Butter 2 (9-inch round) cake pans with 1 tablespoon of butter.
2. Mix the dry ingredients in a bowl.

3. Melt the chocolate in the microwave on medium heat.
4. In electric mixer, cream together 8 tablespoons of butter and sugar until fluffy. Add the eggs, 1 at a time, beating well after each addition. Pour in the vinegar and melted chocolate, and mix well.
5. Slowly add the flour mixture, mixing until fully incorporated.
6. Spread the batter into the prepared cake pans.
7. Bake 30 minutes, or until an inserted toothpick comes out clean. Do not overbake.
8. Unmold the cakes. Place 1 layer so the bottom is facing up on a platter. Spread ¼ cup of the Cocoa Frosting on top of this layer. Place the second layer on top so the bottoms of the layers are together, and frost the entire cake with remaining Cocoa Frosting.

YIELD: 2 (9-inch) cake layers
PREPARATION TIME: 15–20 minutes
BAKING TIME: 30 minutes

*Cocoa Frosting*

3 CUPS POWDERED SUGAR
2 TABLESPOONS BUTTER, SOFTENED
1 TEASPOON VANILLA EXTRACT
¼ CUP UNSWEETENED COCOA
2–4 TABLESPOONS MILK

1. In an electric mixer, stir together the sugar, butter, vanilla, and cocoa. Add the milk, a little at a time, until the desired consistency is achieved for the frosting.

YIELD: About 3 cups
PREPARATION TIME: 5 minutes

# Pointe Aux Barques Light

PORT AUSTIN, MICHIGAN—LAKE HURON

POINT AUX BARQUES LIGHTHOUSE IS THE OLDEST CONTINUOUSLY OPERATING lighthouse on the Great Lakes. The brick beacon and housing were built in 1857 after an earlier tower and dwelling from 1848 cracked and then burned.

French fur trappers originally named this spit of land that marked the entry into Saginaw Bay for their small boats (barques). Later, the lighthouse was needed to guide larger ships over the shallows at this critical turn. The light is located at the tip of Michigan's "thumb," and the keeper's house is now a museum at the edge of the Thumb Underwater Bottomland Preserve.

# LATE SUMMER MEAL

The people who settled this area were a hardy breed, and they didn't expect much in the way of comfort. French fur trappers looked to the lakes and shoreline for their food, catching trout and other fish along the water. Later, when ore and minerals were found in Michigan, miners arrived, bringing Cornish-style pasties to Michigan: hearty, hand-held "pies" stuffed with vegetables and a bit of meat, if there was any. Cherries, both sour and sweet, are a feature of Michigan life—and a major industry now: they're one of the few fruits that grows beautifully red and juicy in this northern climate.

STEWED TOMATOES WITH BREAD
VEGETABLE PASTIES
PAN-FRIED TROUT WITH BROWN BUTTER AND SAGE
CHERRY PIE

## STEWED TOMATOES WITH BREAD

*Ed's mom used to make this side dish for Thanksgiving; here is a refinement of that recipe.*

2 TABLESPOONS VEGETABLE OIL
1 MEDIUM ONION, DICED
1 CLOVE GARLIC, DICED
1 (14-OUNCE) CAN DICED TOMATOES
1 TEASPOON DRIED OREGANO
2 CUPS CUBED BREAD (USE A HEARTY BREAD, LIKE CRUSTY ITALIAN OR FRENCH)
2 TABLESPOONS BUTTER
1 TEASPOON SALT
¼ TEASPOON FRESHLY GROUND BLACK PEPPER

1. Heat a pan over medium heat. Measure in the oil and sauté the onion and garlic for 10 minutes, or until vegetables are tender.
2. Stir the tomatoes and oregano into the onions. Simmer for 10 minutes.
3. Stir in the bread and butter, reduce heat to low, and cook for 5 minutes, stirring occasionally. Season with the salt and pepper.

YIELD: 4 servings
PREPARATION TIME: 5 minutes
COOKING TIME: 25 minutes

## VEGETABLE PASTIES

*The miners used to warm these up for lunch on their shovels over an open fire, but you can use your oven (not your microwave). Rutabaga is the traditional filling here, and we've seasoned and mashed it for a simple update.*

*Pastie Dough*

3 CUPS ALL-PURPOSE FLOUR
1 TEASPOON SALT
1 CUP VEGETABLE SHORTENING, COLD
½ CUP COLD WATER

1. Combine the flour and salt. Blend together the flour and shortening until the mixture resembles coarse meal.
2. Make a well, pour in the water, and mix. If the dough is crumbly, add an additional tablespoon of water. Remove to a floured work surface and knead 15 to 20 times. Form into 6 discs, cover, and refrigerate for at least 30 minutes.

YIELD: 6 discs
PREPARATION TIME: 10-15 minutes
REFRIGERATION TIME: at least 30 minutes

*Pastie Filling*

1 RUTABAGA, PEELED AND CUBED (1½–2 POUNDS)
1 ONION, QUARTERED
1 GARLIC CLOVE
1¼ TEASPOONS SALT, DIVIDED
5 TABLESPOONS BUTTER, SOFTENED
1 TABLESPOON CHOPPED FRESH SAGE
2 TABLESPOONS CHOPPED FRESH PARSLEY
⅛ TEASPOON FRESHLY GROUND BLACK PEPPER
1 EGG, BEATEN
1 TABLESPOON WATER

1. Put the rutabaga, onion, and garlic in a pot, cover with water, and add 1 teaspoon salt. Cover, bring to a boil, and simmer for 20 to 25 minutes, until the rutabaga can be easily pierced with a fork.
2. Preheat the oven to 375°F.
3. Drain the vegetables and put in a bowl. Add the butter, sage, parsley, remaining salt, and pepper. Mash using a hand masher.
4. Roll out the dough into 6 discs, ⅛ inch to ¼ inch thick. Place about ½ cup of the rutabaga in the center of the dough. Wet 1 edge of the dough using a brush or your fingertips. Fold so the sides meet, forming a half moon. Crimp the edges. Cut a slit in the top as a steam vent. Mix together the egg and water, and brush tops with the egg wash.
5. Place on a baking sheet and bake for 30 to 35 minutes.

YIELD: 6 servings
PREPARATION TIME: 10 minutes
BAKING TIME: 30–35 minutes

## PAN-FRIED TROUT WITH BROWN BUTTER AND SAGE

*The brown butter goes well over the vegetable pasty in this menu, too.*

6 TROUT FILLETS (ABOUT 6 OUNCES EACH)
¼ CUP CORNMEAL
¼ CUP ALL-PURPOSE FLOUR
1 TEASPOON SALT
¼ TEASPOON FRESHLY GROUND BLACK PEPPER
2 TABLESPOONS VEGETABLE OIL
3 TABLESPOONS BUTTER
8–10 FRESH SAGE LEAVES

1. Rinse the fillets under cold water and pat dry with a paper towel.
2. Combine the cornmeal and flour. Season each fillet with salt and pepper, and dredge in cornmeal mixture.
3. Preheat the oven to 200°F. Fillets may need to be cooked in batches, and they can be kept warm.
4. Heat a pan on medium-high heat; add the oil to the pan. When the oil is hot, after 2 minutes, add the fillets, skin side down. Cook for 2 to 3 minutes, turn over, and cook for an additional 2 minutes. The skin should be golden brown.
5. Remove the fillets from the pan and place in a warm oven. Add the butter and cook until it begins to brown. Stir in the sage leaves and pour over the fillets.

YIELD: 6 servings
PREPARATION TIME: 5–10 minutes
COOKING TIME: 5–6 minutes per batch

## CHERRY PIE

*Michigan is famous for its cherries.*

1 (9-INCH) DOUBLE PIE CRUST (RECIPE FOLLOWS), UNBAKED
5 CUPS PITTED FRESH, OR 3 (14.5-OUNCE) DRAINED CANS, SOUR CHERRIES
¼ CUP QUICK-COOKING TAPIOCA
1½ CUPS SUGAR
¼ TEASPOON ALMOND EXTRACT
3 TABLESPOONS BUTTER, CUT INTO PIECES

1. Preheat the oven to 450°F. Position a rack in the bottom third of the oven.
2. Place the bottom half of the double pie crust into a pie plate.
3. Mix together the cherries, tapioca, sugar, and almond extract.
4. Pour the cherries into the pie crust and dot with the butter. Lay second pie crust on top. Roll edges under and crimp. Use your fingers or a fork to seal the edges. Cut 4 slashes in top crust to vent.
5. Place on a cookie sheet and place in oven and bake at 450°F for 20 minutes. Reduce temperature to 350°F, cover with aluminum foil and continue to bake for 35 minutes, until the juice begins to bubble.

YIELD: 6–8 servings
PREPARATION TIME: 10–15 minutes (without pitting cherries)
BAKING TIME: 55–60 minutes

*Double Pie Crust*

3 CUPS ALL-PURPOSE FLOUR
¼ TEASPOON SALT
1½ CUPS SHORTENING, COLD
⅔ CUP COLD WATER

1. Mix the flour and salt in a bowl and cut the shortening into the flour with 2 knives or a pastry blender, until the mixture is in clumps the size of peas. Gradually add the water and blend together.
2. Form the dough into a ball, cover with plastic wrap, and refrigerate for at least 30 minutes.
3. Lightly flour work surface, divide the dough in half, and roll out pie dough to be 1 inch larger than the pie plate. Fold the dough over rolling pin and place in pie plate. Unfold to cover the entire plate.. Repeat the rolling process with the other half of the pie dough. Use this half to top the pie.

YIELD: 2 (9-inch) pie crusts
PREPARATION TIME: 20–25 minutes
REFRIGERATION TIME: 30 minutes

# Fairport Harbor Lighthouse
FAIRPORT HARBOR, OHIO—LAKE ERIE

IN THE EARLY 1800S, FAIRPORT HARBOR WAS CONSIDERED THE ENTRY TO the Midwest, which was then known as the Western Reserve, a land grant from the state of Connecticut. The first lighthouse was constructed here very early in United States history—in 1825, the same year the Erie Canal was finished. This version of the lighthouse dates from 1871. It was set in a fine-looking, busy harbor, which is how the town—and then the lighthouse—got their names.

Over time, the harbor and its entry to the mouth of the Grand River were improved, and a breakwater was built to the west. By 1925, it became apparent that there was more need for a lighthouse on the breakwater than in the harbor. Fairport Harbor Light was slated for destruction, but the townspeople rallied and saved it, turning the buildings into a maritime museum and thus preserving the heyday of the town's history.

Many immigrants from Germany and Poland came through this area, and some stayed here in Ohio. They were thrifty, and soon learned which river and lake fish were the best and most plentiful. They grew potatoes, corn, and beans, and kept cows for the butter, milk, and cream that was so vital to their diet.

# GRILLED GREAT LAKES FOURTH OF JULY PICNIC

Beginning with kielbasa, which was once an exotic Polish import, this menu uses the outdoor grill, the stove, and the oven to feed a hungry gathering. After the sausage, there are beans, potatoes, and corn; greens from the garden; and perch and bluegill from the lake. To finish, enjoy a heap of fresh strawberries on top of sweet biscuits with cream.

GRILLED KIELBASA WITH SPICY MUSTARD

POTATO AND THREE CHEESES GRATIN

GREAT LAKES BAKED BEANS

GRILLED CORN

BRAISED GREENS

FRIED BLUEGILL AND LAKE PERCH

STRAWBERRIES AND SWEET BUTTERMILK BISCUITS WITH
    WHIPPED CREAM

## GRILLED KIELBASA WITH SPICY MUSTARD

*A great appetizer or a snack on its own.*

VEGETABLE OIL, TO COAT GRILL RACK
2 POUNDS KIELBASA SAUSAGE
SPICY MUSTARD (RECIPE FOLLOWS), FOR SERVING

1. Start the grill.
2. When the coals are red hot, clean and oil the grill rack, and position the rack 4 inches from heat. The coals are the right temperature if you can only hold your hand above the rack for a count of 2.
3. Put the kielbasa on the grill. Cook for 10 minutes, turning over frequently.
4. Remove from the grill and cut into bite-sized pieces.
5. Serve with the Spicy Mustard.

YIELD: 6–8 servings
PREPARATION TIME: Less than 5 minutes
GRILLING TIME: 10 minutes

*Spicy Mustard*
*If you have a chance, make this 2 or 3 days ahead for the flavors to meld, and keep in a glass jar in the refrigerator. You can store it for 2 or 3 weeks under refrigeration.*

¼ CUP YELLOW MUSTARD SEED
¼ CUP BROWN MUSTARD SEED

¼ CUP CIDER VINEGAR
½ CUP APPLE CIDER
1 TEASPOON PREPARED HORSERADISH
¼ TEASPOON GARLIC POWDER
¼ TEASPOON ONION POWDER
¼ TEASPOON SALT

1. Grind the mustard seeds to a medium texture.
2. Mix with remaining ingredients.

YIELD: 1 cup
PREPARATION TIME: Less than 5 minutes, not counting 2–3 days to allow flavors to blend

## POTATO AND THREE CHEESES GRATIN

*The mustard is very important—it amplifies the cheese and potato flavors.*

2 POUNDS RUSSET POTATOES
¼ POUND CHEDDAR CHEESE, GRATED
¼ POUND SWISS CHEESE, GRATED
¼ POUND GOUDA CHEESE, GRATED
1 TEASPOON YELLOW MUSTARD
1½ CUPS MILK
1½ CUPS HALF-AND-HALF OR LIGHT CREAM
1 TEASPOON SALT
¾ TEASPOON FRESHLY GROUND BLACK PEPPER

1. Preheat the oven to 375°F.
2. Peel and slice the potatoes as thinly as possible. Place the potatoes in a bowl, and mix in the cheeses, mustard, milk, half-and-half, salt, and pepper.
3. Layer the potato mixture into a baking dish, cover, and bake for 45 minutes. Remove the cover and continue to bake for 45 minutes, or until the top is golden brown.

YIELD: 6–8 servings
PREPARATION TIME: 20–25 minutes
BAKING TIME: 1½ hours

## GREAT LAKES BAKED BEANS

*Bacon, one of our favorites, makes a great cameo appearance here.*

8 SLICES BACON, DICED
1 CUP CHOPPED ONIONS
1 POUND DRIED GREAT NORTHERN BEANS SOAKED OVERNIGHT IN WATER,
    UNDER REFRIGERATION
3 CUPS CHICKEN STOCK
1 CUP KETCHUP

¼ CUP BROWN SUGAR

¼ CUP MOLASSES

2 TEASPOONS POWDERED MUSTARD

2 CUPS DICED TOMATOES

2 TEASPOONS SALT

½ TEASPOON FRESHLY GROUND BLACK PEPPER

1. Preheat the oven to 300°F.
2. Sauté the bacon and onions in a large pot, over medium heat, for 10 minutes, or until onions are tender.
3. Drain the beans. Add the beans, stock, ketchup, brown sugar, molasses, mustard, tomatoes, salt, and pepper to the onions. Bring to a boil.
4. Transfer to a 2-quart casserole dish and bake, covered, for 3½ to 4 hours. Add more water or stock if the beans begin to look dry. Remove the cover for the last 15 minutes of baking time so top layer of beans is slightly browned.

YIELD: 8–10 servings
SOAKING TIME: Overnight
PREPARATION TIME: 20–25 minutes
BAKING TIME: 3½–4 hours

## GRILLED CORN

*When you go to the state fair, grilled corn is what you eat—as long as it's dipped into a vat of melted butter.*

6 EARS FRESH CORN

8 TABLESPOONS BUTTER, MELTED

1. Pull back the husks on the ears of corn. Remove the silks and reposition the husks to cover the ears. Cover with water and soak for 1 hour.
2. Start the grill.
3. When the coals are red hot, position the rack 4 inches from heat. The coals are the right temperature if you can only hold your hand above the rack for a count of 3.
4. Lay the corn on the grill and cook for 15 to 20 minutes. Turn over several times during the cooking process, until the husks are charred. Serve with melted butter.

YIELD: 6 servings
PREPARATION TIME: Less than 5 minutes
SOAKING TIME: 1 hour
GRILLING TIME: 15–20 minutes

## BRAISED GREENS

*Ham hocks give the greens a nice smoky flavor. You can also use a smoked turkey leg.*

2 POUNDS COLLARD, KALE, OR TURNIP GREENS, WASHED

4 TABLESPOONS VEGETABLE OIL

2 ONIONS, SLICED

2 CLOVES GARLIC, SLICED

2 SMOKED HAM HOCKS (ABOUT 1¼ POUNDS)
1 CUP CHICKEN STOCK
¼ TEASPOON CAYENNE PEPPER
2 TEASPOONS SALT
¼ TEASPOON FRESHLY GROUND BLACK PEPPER

1. Remove tough stem bases from the greens, then chop the leaves and thin stems into 2-inch pieces.
2. Heat the oil in a pot over medium heat. Sauté the onions and garlic for 10 minutes, or until vegetables are tender.
3. Stir in the greens and ham hocks, and cook for 4 minutes.
4. Pour in the stock, and season with the cayenne, salt, and black pepper. Simmer for 60 minutes. Test the thickest stem for doneness. The stem should give under pressure.

YIELD: 6 servings
PREPARATION TIME: 15 minutes
COOKING TIME: 10–15 minutes to sauté the onions and garlic, and 1 hour to braise the greens

## FRIED BLUEGILL AND LAKE PERCH

*Don't let their small size fool you. Cook up a mess o' them.*

1½–1¾ POUNDS OF FILLETS
VEGETABLE OIL, FOR FRYING
½ CUP ALL-PURPOSE FLOUR
½ CUP CORNMEAL
1 TEASPOON SALT
¼ TEASPOON FRESHLY GROUND BLACK PEPPER
SLICED LEMONS, FOR SERVING

1. Rinse the fillets and pat dry with paper towels.
2. Heat a large cast iron pan over medium-high heat. Cover the bottom of the pan with ⅛ to ¼ inch of oil. Allow to heat up until it begins to shimmer.
3. Put the flour, cornmeal, salt, and pepper in a plastic sealable bag. Put 6 ounces of fillets at a time in the bag, and shake. Remove the fillets, and shake off excess flour.
4. Preheat the oven to 200°F. Fillets may need to be cooked in batches, and they can be kept warm.
5. Touch a tip of one fillet to the oil. It should bubble wildly. Gently place the fillets in the oil. The fillets will arch; flatten them with a spatula. Do not overcrowd the pan.
6. Fry until done, turning over once, about 2 minutes per side.
7. Remove the fillets and drain on a rack, and place in warm oven.
8. Serve with sliced lemons.

YIELD: 4–6 servings
PREPARATION TIME: Less than 5 minutes
COOKING TIME: 4 to 6 minutes

## STRAWBERRIES AND SWEET BUTTERMILK BISCUITS WITH WHIPPED CREAM

*This is our version of strawberry shortcake. The biscuits lend a richness to the dish that's echoed in the cream, with strawberries as a sweet and tart counterpoint.*

2 QUARTS FRESH STRAWBERRIES
½ CUP SUGAR
1½ CUPS HEAVY CREAM
16 SWEET BUTTERMILK BISCUITS (RECIPE FOLLOWS)

1. Wash and hull the strawberries. Combine with the sugar and allow to rest for 30 minutes.
2. Whip the heavy cream into stiff peaks.
3. Cut the Sweet Buttermilk Biscuits in half, and top with strawberries and whipped cream.

YIELD: 8 servings
PREPARATION TIME: 10–15 minutes
RESTING TIME: 30 minutes

*Sweet Buttermilk Biscuits*

2 CUPS ALL-PURPOSE FLOUR
4 TABLESPOONS SUGAR
1½ TEASPOONS BAKING POWDER
½ TEASPOON BAKING SODA
¼ TEASPOON SALT
8 TABLESPOONS BUTTER, COLD
2 EGGS, BEATEN
½ CUP BUTTERMILK

1. Preheat the oven to 425°F.
2. Mix together the flour, sugar, baking powder, baking soda, and salt. Cut in the butter until the mixture resembles a coarse meal.
3. Pour in the eggs and milk all at once. Mix and turn out onto a floured surface. Knead for 15 seconds.
4. Roll out the dough to ½-inch thickness, and cut into 2-inch squares. Cut the squares into triangles. Place on a baking sheet so each biscuit is snug against the next. Bake for 10–12 minutes.

YIELD: 16 biscuits
PREPARATION TIME: 15 minutes
BAKING TIME: 10–12 minutes

# Fort Niagara Lighthouse
YOUNGSTOWN, NEW YORK—LAKE ONTARIO

ORIGINALLY, THIS LIGHTHOUSE WAS SIMPLY A FORT, AND NOT A SHIPPING beacon. It had been established in the late 1700s for the protection of French fur traders who met here to start their long portage over land to Lake Erie. It was captured by the British in 1759 during the French and Indian War.

To aid the many ships traversing the Niagara River's entrance to Lake Ontario, a small wooden light was erected in 1823. A new fifty-foot stone tower replaced the original light in 1872, and a keeper's house and other outbuildings were added. In 1900, the tower was built up by an additional eleven feet for increased visibility. However, after there was an issue about preserving the trees surrounding the tower, the lighthouse was decommissioned, and a new beacon was set up nearby in 1993.

At the end of Lake Erie, Niagara Falls has always drawn sightseers to the grandeur and romance of this natural phenomenon—so much so that thousands of newlyweds have chosen to honeymoon at Niagara Falls. This tourist ritual was considered déclassé for a few decades, but now the pendulum has swung back: more people than ever before are going out to appreciate the Great Lakes, their shores, and these impressive Falls.

# Honeymoon Breakfast

For the modern honeymooner, a mixture of new and classic foods—Great Lakes caviar on blinis with crème fraîche, followed by farm-style ham steaks and shirred eggs baked in potato cups. For the finish, there's a sweet variation of broiled grapefruit to refresh the palate.

WHITEFISH CAVIAR WITH CORNMEAL BLINIS AND CRÈME FRAÎCHE
SHIRRED EGGS IN CRISPY POTATO CUPS WITH MORNAY SAUCE
FRIED HAM STEAK
BROILED GRAPEFRUIT

## WHITEFISH CAVIAR WITH CORNMEAL BLINIS AND CRÈME FRAÎCHE

*American caviar is really coming into its own. We started eating these. We ate more. And then we wanted more the next day.*

1 PACKET ACTIVE DRY YEAST
2 CUPS MILK, SCALDED
¾ CUP ALL-PURPOSE FLOUR
¾ CUP CORNMEAL, FINE GROUND
1 TABLESPOON SUGAR
1 TEASPOON SALT
3 EGGS, SEPARATED
4 TABLESPOONS BUTTER, MELTED
1 (½-PINT) CONTAINER CRÈME FRAÎCHE, FOR SERVING
1 (1-OUNCE) JAR WHITEFISH CAVIAR

1. Stir the yeast into scalded milk that has cooled to between 105°F and 115°F. Let it stand for a few minutes, so the yeast can become active.
2. Put the flour, cornmeal, sugar, and salt into a bowl. Stir in the milk–yeast mixture, cover and let rise for 1 hour.
3. Stir the egg yolks into batter. Whip the egg whites into stiff peaks, and fold into the batter.
4. Preheat the oven to 200°F. Blinis may need to be cooked in batches, and they can be kept warm.
5. Heat the griddle on medium heat, and brush with the butter.
6. Pour ¼ cup of batter for each blini. Cook for 2 to 3 minutes per side. Place in the oven to keep warm.
7. Place 1 teaspoon of crème fraîche on each blini, and top with caviar.

**Note:** The recipe for blinis yields 18 to 20 portions, so save what is not eaten to warm up the next day in the toaster.

YIELD: 2 servings
PREPARATION TIME: 10–15 minutes
RISING TIME: 1 hour
COOKING TIME: 4–6 minutes per batch

## SHIRRED EGGS IN CRISPY POTATO CUPS WITH MORNAY SAUCE

*This is a professional-looking dish. You can easily make it for any number of people you want to impress.*

2 MEDIUM RUSSET POTATOES
2 TEASPOONS SALT, DIVIDED
4 TABLESPOONS BUTTER, MELTED
¼ TEASPOON FRESHLY GROUND BLACK PEPPER
4 EGGS
MORNAY SAUCE (RECIPE FOLLOWS), FOR SERVING

1. Preheat the oven to 450°F.
2. Cut the potatoes in half crosswise and scoop out the centers using a melon baller. Leave the sides about ¼ inch thick. Slice a bit off each bottom so they will not roll.
3. Put the potato cups in a pot, cover with water, add 1 teaspoon of salt, and bring to a boil. Cook for 5 minutes.
4. Remove the potatoes from the water and let them rest for 5 minutes. Brush with the butter, inside and out. Place each potato individually, or as pairs, in custard cups or ramekins, scooped side up.
5. Season them with ½ teaspoon salt and ⅛ teaspoon pepper.
6. Bake in the oven for 20 minutes, or until golden brown.
7. Reduce temperature to 350°F. Carefully break 1 egg into each potato cup and bake for 5 to 6 minutes.
8. Remove from the oven, and season with remaining salt and pepper. Spoon the Mornay Sauce over the top.

YIELD: 2–4 servings
PREPARATION TIME: 5–10 minutes
COOKING TIME: 5 minutes
BAKING TIME: 25 minutes

*Mornay Sauce*

2 TABLESPOONS BUTTER
2 TABLESPOONS ALL-PURPOSE FLOUR
1 CUP MILK
1 BAY LEAF
2 TABLESPOONS SWISS CHEESE, GRATED
2 TABLESPOONS PARMESAN CHEESE, GRATED

1. Melt the butter in a pan. Stir in the flour and cook for 1 to 2 minutes.
2. Whisk in the milk. Add the bay leaf. Cook for 10 to 15 minutes.
3. Remove the bay leaf and whisk in the cheeses. Cook until melted.

YIELD: About 1½ cups
PREPARATION TIME: 5–10 minutes
COOKING TIME: 10–15 minutes

## FRIED HAM STEAK

*This is a breakfast classic from the old days.*

1 TABLESPOON VEGETABLE OIL
2 TABLESPOONS BUTTER
1 POUND ½-INCH-THICK HAM STEAKS, FULLY COOKED

1. Heat a pan over medium heat. Add the oil and butter.
2. When the butter has melted, add the ham and cook for 3 to 5 minutes per side.

YIELD: 2–4 servings
PREPARATION TIME: Less than 5 minutes
COOKING TIME: 6–10 minutes

## BROILED GRAPEFRUIT

*Sweet and tart all in one bite.*

1 GRAPEFRUIT
¼ CUP BROWN SUGAR

1. Preheat the broiler.
2. Cut the grapefruit in half. Use a paring or grapefruit knife to separate the segments, leaving them in the skin.
3. Sprinkle with the brown sugar and place under the broiler for 3 minutes, until the sugar begins to bubble.

YIELD: 2 servings
PREPARATION TIME: Less than 5 minutes
COOKING TIME: 3 minutes

# Bibliography

http://adventure.howstuffworks.com/cape-flattery-lighthouse.htm

http://www.arecibolighthouse.com/page.html

http://www.apva.org/capehenry/

http://www.beavertaillight.org/

http://www.caborojopr.com/cabo-rojo-puerto-rico-attractions.html

http://capemeareslighthouse.org/

http://www.crescentcity.org/

Crompton, Samuel Willard and Michael J. Rhein. *The Ultimate Book of Lighthouses*. San Diego, CA: Advantage Publishing Group/Thunder Bay Press, 2000.

D'Entremont, Jeremy. *The Lighthouses of Massachusetts*. Beverly, MA: Commonwealth Editions, 2007.

De Wire, Elinor, photos by Daniel E. Dempster. *Lighthouses of the South*. Stillwater, MN: Voyageur Press, 2004.

http://www.delnortehistory.org/lighthouse/

http://dhr.dos.state.fl.us/archaeology/underwater/maritime/lighthouses/light.cfm?name=St_JohnsLight_Station

www.eaglebluﬄighthouse.org

www.ebls.org

Elizabeth, Norma and Bruce Roberts. *Lighthouse Ghosts*. Birmingham, AL: Crane Hill Publishers, 1998.

Elovaara, Arnold K. *Lighthouse Keepers Cookbook of Maine*. Caribbean Press, 2001.

http://www.fbi.gov/libref/historic/famcases/nazi/nazi.htm

http://www.fws.gov/caribbean/Buckisland/

http://www.fws.gov/caribbean/caborojo/default.htm

http://gocalifornia.about.com/cs/calighthouse/a/lh_batpt.htm

www.greatlakesforever.org

http://www.grossepointlighthouse.net/

Grant, John and Ray Jones. *Legendary Lighthouses.* Old Saybrook, CT: The Globe Pequot Press, 1998.

Grant, John and Ray Jones. *Legendary Lighthouses, Vol. II.* Old Saybrook, CT: The Globe Pequot Press, 2002.

http://www.hawaiiag.org/history.htm

http://www.hecetalighthouse.com/

http://home.comcast.net/~debee2/NNNS/FortNiagara.html

http://www.co.honolulu.hi.us/cchnl.htm#history

http://www.jaxbeach.com/mayport.htm

Lanigan-Schmidt, Therese. *Ghostly Beacons: Haunted Lighthouses of North America.* Atglen, PA: Whitford Press/Schiffer Publishing, 2000.

http://www.law.umkc.edu/faculty/projects/ftrials/superior/timeline.html

http://www.lighthouse.cc/boston/

http://lighthouse.cc/sheffield/

http://www.lighthousedepot.com

http://www.lighthousefriends.com/light.asp?ID=344

http://www.lighthousefoundation.org/alf_lights/portsmouthharbor/fphl_maint_05032006.htm

http://www.lighthousefriends.com/

http://www.lighthouseinn.com/

http://lighthouse.cc/matinicusrock/

http://www.makah.com/history.html

Marcus, Jon (text) and Susan Cole Kelly (photos). *Lighthouses of New England.* St. Paul, MN: Voyageur Press/MBI Publishing, Inc., 2001.

http://www.menorcansociety.net/

http://midatlantic.rootsweb.ancestry.com

http://www.mnhs.org/places/sites/srl/

http://www.ncweb.com/org/fhlh/

http://www.nps.gov/history/maritime/nhl/grossept.htm

http://www.nps.gov/history/nR/travel/prvi/pr22.htm

www.ohiohistorycentral.org

http://www.outerbanks.com/corollalight/

http://www.palosverdes.com/pvlight/

http://pointnopointlighthouse.com/default.aspx

http://www.pointeauxbarqueslighthouse.org/

www.ponceinlet.org

www.pontchartrain.net

http://www.portisabellighthouse.com/

http://rinconpr.net/municipio/

Roberts, Bruce and Ray Jones. *California Lighthouses: Point St. George to the Gulf of Santa Catalina.* Philadelphia: Chelsea House Publishers, 2000.

Roberts, Bruce and Ray Jones. *Eastern Great Lakes Lighthouses: Ontario, Erie, and Huron.* Philadelphia: Chelsea House Publishers, 2000.

Roberts, Bruce and Ray Jones. *Gulf Coast Lighthouses: Florida Keys to the Rio Grande.* Philadelphia: Chelsea House Publishers, 2000.

Roberts, Bruce and Ray Jones. *Pacific Northwest Lighthouses: Oregon, Washington, Alaska, and British Columbia.* Philadelphia: Chelsea House Publishers, 2000.

Roberts, Bruce and Ray Jones. *Southeastern Lighthouses: Outer Banks for Cape Florida.* Philadelphia: Chelsea House Publishers, 2000.

Roberts, Bruce and Ray Jones. *Western Great Lakes Lighthouses: Michigan and Superior.* Philadelphia: Chelsea House Publishers, 2000.

http://www.rudyalicelighthouse.net/OntLts/FtNiagra/FtNiagra.htm

http://www.sandhillslighthouseinn.com/

http://www.savemayportvillage.net/id5.html

http://www.sheldonmuseum.org/eldredrock.htm

Shelton-Roberts, Cheryl and Bruce Roberts. *Lighthouse Families.* Birmingham, AL: Crane Hill Publishers, 1997.

Snow, Edward Rowe. *The Lighthouses of New England.* Updated by Jeremy D'Entremont. Beverly, MA: Commonwealth Editions, 2002.

http://www.surfrider.org/rincon/

www.terrypepper.com

http://www.tillamookcheese.com/

Trumbauer, Lisa. *Lighthouses of North America*. Nashville, TN: Williamson Books, 2007.

http://www.unc.edu/~rowlett/lighthouse/doomsday.html

http://www.unc.edu/~rowlett/lighthouse/vi.htm

United States Coast Guard. *Historically Famous Lighthouses*, CG-232, 1972.

United States Coast Guard. *Historically Famous Lighthouses*. Pub. CG-232, 1999.

http://www.vinow.com/stthomas/History/#

http://www.visitmaui.com/agents/history.html

Wood, Ted. *Ghosts of the West Coast*. New York: Walker and Company, 1999.

# Index

# About the Authors

ONE OF BECKY SUE EPSTEIN'S FAVORITE AFTER-DINNER WALKS takes her around Cape Cod's Nobska Point Lighthouse at sunset.

Pat Rabby

Epstein is a lifestyle writer specializing in food, wine, and travel. Currently based in New England, Epstein is a senior editor for the national lifestyle publication *Intermezzo* magazine. She is also a contributor to *The Tasting Panel*, *Santé Magazine*, *Beverage Business*, *iwineradio*, and other trade and consumer publications, both print and online. Spending time on nearby Cape Cod led to her writing the "Tastes of the Cape" column for the *Cape Cod Times'* monthly *Prime Time*, exploring seacoast foods and restaurants' signature recipes.

Formerly in California, Epstein began her food career as a restaurant reviewer for the *Los Angeles Times* while working in film and television. She has written for many publications, from *Art & Antiques* and *Food & Wine* to *Wine Spectator* and *Yankee* magazine. Her first book, *Substituting Ingredients*, is a classic food reference.

BROUGHT UP IN THE MIDWEST, ED JACKSON HAS BEEN INTRIGUED BY LIGHTHOUSES SINCE HE took regular evening walks past North Point Lighthouse in Milwaukee, Wisconsin, and toured many Door County lighthouses. He was originally drawn to the concept of lighthouse food many years ago while watching a television show in which a lighthouse keeper went out to catch his dinner, fresh from the sea.

While living in Chicago, Jackson owned a graphic arts company for over a decade before moving east to pursue his love of food. He graduated from the prestigious Culinary Institute of America in Hyde Park, New York, in 2000 with the President's Scholarship Award. His stages included Charlie Trotter's in Chicago, Bradley Ogden at Caesar's Palace in Las Vegas, and Clio Restaurant in Boston. Since relocating to the Boston area with his family, he has worked at several prominent restaurants, including Maison Robert, Tremont 647, and The Tuscan Grill.

Currently, Jackson is in production on a video cooking series called *Chef Ed Cooks*. He also does private catering, offers cooking demonstrations at Williams

Sonoma and other establishments, and teaches classes. Though trained in classic French culinary techniques, Jackson is best known for food that's unpretentious, that people can recognize and feel comfortable eating.

You can contact Becky and Ed at Becky@AmericanLighthouseCookbook.com and Ed@AmericanLighthouseCookbook.com.